Six Paths to Leadership

"Students and professors interested in developing leadership competencies, through bringing the 'real world' of leadership into the classroom, will benefit greatly from the challenges, opportunities, and strategies outlined in the book. Leadership researchers will benefit from examining the distinctions that leaders face across contexts. Every chapter provides insights that merit additional study."
—Leanne E. Atwater, *C.T. Bauer Professor of Leadership and Management, University of Houston*

"*Six Paths to Leadership* provides a grounded and actionable roadmap to identifying and leveraging the unique aspects of the leadership journey you're taking."
—Scott Eblin, *Top 30 Coaches in the World, Global Gurus and author*, The Next Level: What Insiders Know About Executive Success

"This is one of those rare books to keep on hand and return to frequently. Leadership is about making smart decisions and these trusted advisors provide just the right balance of theory and practice to guide you on your journey."
—Amanda Renteria, *CEO, Code for America; former COO California Department of Justice; former Senate Chief of Staff*

"By demonstrating, with robust and fascinating data, that there are multiple paths (at least six archetypes) with distinctive qualities and considerations, this book puts an end to the fallacy of a single approach to leadership development—and, in the process, makes the path to leadership much more accessible to a wider set of emerging leaders."
—Ethan Bernstein, *Professor of Leadership and Organizational Behavior, Harvard Business School*

"Mark and Meredith make the case that the journey more than anything else influences leadership success. Being cognizant of others' journeys as well as your own can shape better leaders. This is an overdue perspective and changes how we construct leadership development training."
—Russell M. Klosk, *Managing Director, Accenture Strategy, Talent & Organization/Human Potential*

"As an experienced HR professional, this book gives insight to those aspiring to become leaders and those who are leaders to have a clearer expectation of themselves and the what the organizations are asking of them. It is a compass and guidepost to help our leaders function at their highest levels no matter how they are acquiring the title of leader."
—Darlene Slaughter, *Chief Diversity and Engagement Officer, March of Dimes*

"Finally, a leadership book that brings an understanding of context to the forefront so that the strategies and tools shared are specific, relevant, and spot on. Whether you are planning for your career or onboarding into a new position, *Six Paths to Leadership* is a must read for any leader, coach, or HR professional supporting others on their path to success."

—Amy Jen Su, *Executive Coach & Author*, The Leader You Want to Be

"Too often, aspiring leaders focus on what they must develop; this book reminds us that the how is just as important. As someone who has traveled several pathways (insider, outsider, legacy), this book caused me to reflect on how important it was to adjust my style, and my expectations, based on the way I entered the role. I'd especially recommend this to leaders embarking on a transition so they may be intentional about how they leverage the strengths of the pathway to maximize success."

—Andrew Schmidt, *Director, Enterprise Talent Acquisition at Lockheed Martin*

"As young people chart their careers and aim to hold leadership positions, it's worth thinking about the paths people take to get there. *Six Paths to Leadership* describes the way leaders in both the public and private sector achieved their positions as well as the unique leadership challenges of different paths up. The stories, examples and analysis will help leaders from different sectors on their way up or transitioning to something new."

—Austan Goolsbee, *Ph.D., Robert P. Gwinn Professor of Economics, University of Chicago; former Chair of the White House Council of Economic Advisers*

"This book includes two important paths to leadership that are often ignored but are predominant: the family (Legacy) leader and the founder (Creator). In all, the authors identify the many paths of leadership. The book is worth reading and I highly recommend it!"

—Dianne H. B. Welsh, *Hayes Distinguished Professor of Entrepreneurship, University of North Carolina at Greensboro*

"Contrary to popular belief, one size does not fit all for advancement to leadership positions. This book is a clear and compelling examination of the leadership paths across any organization. Mark and Meredith provide a useful and practical guide to understanding how to have success, and still be oneself. Refreshing!"

—Patrick Malone, *Ph.D., Director, Key Executive Leadership, American University*

"Fascinating, rich, rigorous, and applied. What really sets Six Paths apart from other leadership books is the authors masterful use executives' own words to illustrate practical and valuable lessons for a wide array of leaders from the boardroom to the classroom."

—Mel Fugate, *Ph.D., Professor of Management, Mississippi State University*

Mark A. Clark · Meredith Persily Lamel

Six Paths to Leadership

Lessons from Successful Executives, Politicians, Entrepreneurs, and More

Mark A. Clark
Kogod School of Business
American University
Washington, DC, USA

Meredith Persily Lamel
Aspire@Work
Bethesda, MD, USA

ISBN 978-3-030-69016-8   ISBN 978-3-030-69017-5   (eBook)
https://doi.org/10.1007/978-3-030-69017-5

Cover illustration: Lauren Koch
Cover design by eStudioCalamar

This Palgrave Macmillan imprint is published by the registered company Springer Nature Switzerland AG
The registered company address is: Gewerbestrasse 11, 6330 Cham, Switzerland

Preface: To Our Readers

You are in the right place! Whether you are just starting a new position, thinking about your next move on your own leadership path, or reflecting on the long road you have traveled, we believe that you can benefit from the ideas and experiences related in *Six Paths to Leadership*. Every leader has a story, and you can follow along with their narratives, drawing on their experiences as you blaze your own leadership path. Whatever steps you are taking, we hope to offer you valuable insights on your journey. Although we expect that our readers will come from many backgrounds, we believe that each will benefit through:

- explanations of **six distinct paths to leadership** positions and influence, including how they are differentiated and where they carry similarities
- reviewing important **opportunities** and **challenges** associated with each of the six leadership paths
- learning **strategies** to leverage these opportunities and to mitigate the challenges
- personal insights from **successful leaders** who have walked each of these paths
- professional tools to support steps along your leadership path, developing approaches to achieve success for your organization and your career.

Six Paths to Leadership

This book asserts that a leader's effectiveness can be enhanced by, and may even depend on, understanding the distinct opportunities and challenges of the leader's particular path. Many books discuss the characteristics that a leader should have, skills that should be developed, and actions that may increase the leader's likelihood of success across broad situations. While there is considerable value in such guidance, our approach takes this further by demonstrating the variations that leaders face as they walk divergent paths, and how they must alter their assumptions and behaviors in order to succeed. The paths to leadership include the context in which the leader operates and the manner in which they enter the leadership position, representing a broad view of how leaders operate. Developed through our fieldwork with leaders—managerial training, executive coaching, strategic planning, classroom teaching, and other engagements—and illustrated through interviews with a diverse set of leaders, our six paths include perspectives from:

1. the "**Insider**" who has been *promoted from within*,
2. the "**Outsider**" who is an *external hire*,
3. the "**Representative**" who is *elected* to the position,
4. the "**Proxy**" who has been *appointed* by a principal authority,
5. the "**Creator**" who is the *founder* of the organization, and
6. the "**Legacy**" who leads on the *family* path.

In our experience working with and researching leadership, leader success is strongly related to the ability to recognize and meet the opportunities and challenges inherent in each path. We investigated these ideas through interviewing a large set of leaders across paths (as described more fully in the next chapter), including executives, politicians, and many other. We asked about challenges, opportunities, and related strategies related to leadership paths, which are outlined in the chapters of this book. We also included stories to help illustrate their points, and a set of reflection questions for each path, and a set of process tools collected in the book's Appendix and online at www.six pathstoleadership.com.

Leading Across Paths

As anticipated, we also found that many of the leaders we interviewed have walked multiple paths throughout their careers, at various times gaining positions through at least two different roles as an **insider, outsider, representative, proxy, founder, or legacy**. This helped us to gain insight into how these paths differentiate. For instance, the planned time of the leader in a new position varied across paths, such that while most leadership positions continue until they are disrupted, appointed leaders generally have a set limit to their time in position. We also found many themes woven across paths, with similarities in basis but varying in expression. One example of this is that although it is typically deemed necessary for leaders on all paths to espouse a vision, they may do so in different ways. **Elected** leaders are more likely to reflect the vision of key blocks of voters, while founding leaders are more likely to espouse a personal vision. More of these themes are listed in Table 1.1 and discussed below.

Leadership Paths and Your Role

We expect that the insights and lessons of this book will be a valuable resource in realizing leadership potential and career goals. Whether you are a leader, aspire to leadership, support the development of leaders, make decisions on hiring leaders, or are a student of leadership, greater understanding of the six leadership paths will increase your ability to meet your professional goals.

For Leaders and Aspiring Leaders

As a leader, you are in a fishbowl that exposes both your actions and your results. Your colleagues are evaluating your abilities and deciding whether to accept your leadership. Effective leaders often spend some time learning from the experiences of others, reading, observing, and studying, as a way of broadening beyond the range of your own eyes. Regardless of your leadership experience, it may be helpful to consider the opportunities and challenges of each leadership path, increasing intentionality of priorities, how you approach your role, and how you fit the specific organizational context.

Aspiring leaders, whether near the beginning of their careers or simply considering a change to a new role, may benefit from comparing lessons from the various leadership paths with their own leaders, gaining a deeper appreciation for the specific factors which influence leader perspective, behavior, and performance. This will inform their choice of positions to pursue in their own career, and which paths may best suit their ambition. Like other leaders we interviewed, Peace Corps Director Dr. **Jody Olsen** cautioned that her path (Appointed) "*is definitely not for everyone!*" Aspirants should ask themselves:

- Which elements of the different paths best play to my strengths? Which of my skills need development in order to attain success on each leadership path?
- How can I leverage my understanding of a given leadership path into a new job or position of influence? For instance, do I have a sense of what my value and perspective would be as an **external hire**? Do I have the ability and determination to manage former peers, if **promoted**?

Leaders beginning a new position, ideally, will take time to understand themselves and their contexts—how they fit the path they are on, and how it might differ from their past experiences. This transition stage is an ideal time to investigate factors associated with the path that the leader is entering, identifying critical opportunities and challenges that may buoy or break the experience. Next, leaders should turn their lens inward, being honest about their own capabilities, preferences, and limitations. This is not self-examination in a vacuum, but instead a challenge to use knowledge and tools developed by others to accomplish an authentic self-portrait. Finally, leaders should look to their environment—their place, time, and culture—to determine what that particular context needs and what it supplies, including how the leader might fit in as their best selves. Once hired, leaders can quickly become overwhelmed by unfamiliar roles and situations. By showing what others have faced on particular paths, and reporting what they learned along the way, we provide shortcuts for some of the most difficult moments in those first 6–12 months in a new leadership position, such as,

- For most positions, we recommend that leaders embark on some type of "listening tour" soon after beginning their position. But who are the priority stakeholders to target? For **appointed** leaders may want to include career staff, inter-agency leaders, and predecessors, while **promoted** path leaders should target their direct reports and engage with a new set of peers across the organization.

While more *established leaders* may follow a similar process to their junior counterparts, they have the advantage of more experience, perhaps even across multiple paths. This increases the likelihood that the leader can compare factors and strategies, with a deeper understanding of their nuances, in some cases enabling the leader to import ideas from other paths into his or her own. As leaders grow in experience, they may find increased agency in determining their own path, and perhaps their next move across paths. However, these leaders also have a potential handicap from their experience. What worked for them in the past, on one path, will not necessarily serve them well in a new path. This may require changing or adapting some of their practices and habits from the previous path, and more intentionally thinking about their leadership in the context of a new path.

- Transitioning among paths posed challenges, as a few of our interviewees discussed when **hired externally** for corporate roles after serving in **appointed** government positions, and vice versa. For instance, government appointees often have very specific goals and limited scope of authority, while external hires are often brought in to disrupt the status quo and bring in a perspective that does not exist internally.

For Executive Coaches and Mentors

Investments in leader development, whether through relatively focused efforts of certified executive coaches or broader mentoring relationships, are critical to orienting leaders in the desired direction as well as targeting their long-term trajectory. Those who support leaders in this way will benefit from the clear sets of factors identified in each path's chapter and the theme variations across paths identified in Table 1.1. Further, the words and stories of the leaders we interviewed identify scenarios that can serve as discussion starters with the new leader.

We believe that executive coaches are particularly important for new leaders early in their tenure, when their positions may be most precarious not only for the leaders but also for those who depend on their effectiveness. Coaches may play a critical role, launching the new leaders off on the right foot and accelerating their onboarding. Coaches can share the insights of our interviewees to illuminate blind spots for the new leaders, identifying the opportunities and challenges of each path to incite the leaders' self-and system-awareness. It may also be helpful to employ the reflection questions, placed at the end of each path's chapter, as exercises or discussion guides for coaching sessions. We find that **founders** and **family** business leaders, for example, are faced with unique questions where coaches and mentors can add value.

- How can founder values, goals, and work practices be effectively shared with upcoming leaders as the organization grows? How should governance and leadership positions be determined for the second generation and beyond? How can a family business leader effectively serve the family as well as other stakeholders? Where is the line between the family and the business?
- With the support of factors, strategies, and tools offered in this book, leader supporters can help to accelerate their transition to high-performing leaders.

We would love to hear feedback on how well these conversations work to support the coach's role and to increase leader success!

For Human Resource Partners

Human resource (HR) professionals are tasked with the complexities of supporting leaders as they move into new positions, although there are often too few resources available to support them effectively. We believe that the clear sets of factors identified for each path, along with the words and stories of the leaders interviewed will be especially helpful for HR support through processes of recruitment, selection, orientation, and early socialization. For example,

- In many cases, we find that very little attention is paid to onboarding of executive leaders who are **promoted** from within. As a result, these leaders often fail to leave their previous role behind or do not approach the new role with the same intentionality of an outside hire. We provide tools that target such challenges, structuring a process for conversations about how to leverage the insider point of view while also managing challenges such as prior reputations.
- The failure rate of **external hire**s at the executive level ranges from 40 to 60% in the first 18 months, according to *Harvard Business Review*. These failures come at significant cost to companies, often calculated at 1.5 to 3 times annual salary of the position being replaced, according to the *Society of Human Resource Management*.[1]

---

[1] Cappelli, P. (2019, May–June). Your approach to hiring is all wrong. *Harvard Business Review*.

- Leaders who are crossing paths and industry sectors, as with our government-to-corporate example above, may greatly benefit from HR professionals who can provide the essential information of how the new leader's position fits into the organization and its work practices.

For Hiring Managers and Organizational Decision-Makers

There are many important stakeholders involved in shaping and developing an organization's workforce, including investors, executives, and hiring managers. Collectively, these decision-makers have oversight of broad personnel policies and practices as well as specific choices of how to bring in new leaders, such as to **promote** from within or **hire externally**, and in how build a system that will incentivize the high-potential leaders while encouraging others to leave the organization if they are not a good fit. By capturing the opportunities and challenges of the six paths, we offer a rich picture of how the organization should be structured and resourced to support its success. These insights will help in situations such as:

- Becoming enamored by the promise of **externally hired leaders**, yet failing to recognize (or share) the internal challenges they may face, or the likelihood of a longer timeline needed to achieve productivity.
- Believing in the low risk of **promoting** leaders from within, without accounting for the challenges of managing former peers, or in being perceived by colleagues as an underqualified leader.
- For investors, having the tough conversations with founder leaders about their shortcomings and how to better surround themselves with complementary leadership styles.

For Students and Academic Research

For those who study leadership, including students and scholars at all levels, we hope this book will be interesting due to the novel identification and exploration of the six paths to leadership, as well as our associated findings. Those studying leadership in contexts, particularly in applied settings, may wish to further explore and expand these paths and related processes and factors. We fully expect that further distinctions and additions, as well as insights that are helpful to working leaders, lie beyond our initial exploration into this topic. For instance,

- There are many studies about leader traits, behaviors, and beliefs which could be tested for application to particular paths. It might not be surprising to find some differences among paths, such as a higher risk tolerance for leaders on the **founder** path or perhaps a collectivist orientation for successful **family** leaders.
- There may be important lanes within specific paths that are associated with specific differentiated strategies or behaviors, such as with elected leaders who vary in their length of term, previous positions held, and constituencies they represent.

For All of Our Readers

Whether for your own career and development goals, or to understand and support leaders across a variety of contexts, the structure and findings of *Six Paths to Leadership* are a valuable addition to the leadership literature. We outline each leadership path's opportunities and challenges, illustrated with quotes and stories from our interviewees, and augmented with reflection questions and process tools. Together these can help leaders and their supporters to think through the factors and issues which will influence leadership effectiveness, and to provide support for the critical conversations associated with leader development. For those aspiring to leadership positions or concerned with augmenting their current success, understanding the leadership path means being intentional about direction, diagnosing contextual opportunities, exploring personal deficiencies, and leveraging strengths. There have been many leaders, walking many paths. Some of their ideas are presented here. The next step on your path is up to you.

Washington, USA   Mark A. Clark
Bethesda, USA   Meredith Persily Lamel

Acknowledgments

The authors would like to express sincere thanks to the many people who were involved in this book and our overall leadership paths project. This includes our families, who didn't complain (much!), the leaders who we interviewed, our team of American University student research assistants over the past three years—Mukadaisi Wumaier, Linda Smith, transcriptionists Hermon Beryehun and Eric Neugeboren, and others who helped us to cross the finish line. Thanks also to our book coach, Cathy Fyock, and our panel of reviewers Mel Fugate, Brigid Schulte, Amy Jen Su, Claire Thomas, and Juliet Eilperin. Finally, we would like to thank our many students and clients over the years who inspired the purpose of the book and whose collective stories helped drive our research and framework.

We also owe a debt of gratitude to Marcus Ballenger, our commissioning editor from Palgrave Macmillan, for believing in our book and supporting us along the way.

Contents

About the Authors

Mark A. Clark, Ph.D. is Management Department Chair and Associate Professor at the Kogod School of Business, American University in Washington, DC, where he teaches leadership-related courses. He has over 30 years of experience in organizational research and action consulting, including leadership development, team facilitation, strategic planning, workforce analysis, training design, and program development. Dr. Clark's research centers on high performance contexts, investigating the effects of leadership, strategic human capital, teams, knowledge networks, and diversity on organizational outcomes. He has published and presented over 100 scholarly papers in top academic outlets and at conferences internationally. Dr. Clark's ability to translate research into practice has led him to consult with a wide range of private and public sector clients, including Fortune 500 companies, healthcare institutions, entrepreneurial ventures, public sector institutions, and professional sports teams. He has held visiting scholar appointments at multiple European universities including *Instituto de Empresa SEK* in Spain, *ISCTE University of Lisbon* in Portugal, *Erasmus University* in The Netherlands. He earned his master's degree in Policy & Leadership from Ohio State University and his doctorate in Business Administration from Arizona State University.

Meredith Persily Lamel is CEO of Aspire@Work and provides executive and team coaching for C-suite corporate and nonprofit leaders. Her background also includes leadership training, coaching, and facilitation for over eighty Members of Congress and Senators as well as their senior staff. Based in Washington D.C., she is an expert in industries that intersect the public and private sectors, regularly supporting leaders who transition between government and corporate organizations into highly influential roles. Persily Lamel has delivered leadership programs in 17 countries across five continents and in 38 states and the District of Columbia. Meredith served on the full-time faculty of American University's Kogod School of Business and now teaches public sector leaders in American University's School of Public Administration Key Leadership Programs. She earned her B.A. from Brown University and M.B.A. from the University of Chicago Booth School of Business. She holds a certificate in leadership coaching from Georgetown University and Professional Coach Certification from the International Coaching Federation.

List of Tables

1

The Six Paths and their Influence on Leaders

To determine how leaders can be most effective, we must understand how they come to their positions of influence. Leadership is a product of the varied contexts in which leaders travel, how they come into their influential positions, and their strategies for addressing the opportunities and challenges of their particular path. While leadership approaches, styles, and techniques have been subjected to considerable analysis—variously characterizing leadership as charisma, vision, bundles of traits, or sets of behaviors and competencies—the high failure rate of executive leaders makes it apparent that these aspects alone do not indicate whether a leader will succeed. Understanding the contextual factors that leaders encounter and strategies to address their opportunities and challenges, particularly early in their transition, can smooth the early bumps along the path and ultimately increase leader effectiveness, benefiting organizations, leaders, and those who are influenced by their actions.

In this book, we explore these contexts as a set of six paths to be navigated by leaders, with particular attention to the **opportunities** and **challenges** that affect their early steps. As part of this approach, we also compare public and private sector leaders to better understand the range of factors influencing success in their contexts, such as in the relatively uncommon contrast of elected officials and corporate executives. In the sections below, we first briefly describe each of the six paths with a label for the associated leader—*promoted from within (Insider), hired externally (Outsider), elected (Representative), appointed (Proxy), founder (Creator)*, and *family (Legacy)*—along

© The Author(s), under exclusive license to Springer Nature
Switzerland AG 2021
M. A. Clark and M. Persily Lamel, *Six Paths to Leadership*,
https://doi.org/10.1007/978-3-030-69017-5_1

with our inspiration and investigative research methods. We then outline a set of important themes that, while present across all paths, vary in the way they manifest for leaders within each path (summarized in Table 1.1). In the chapters that follow, we discuss each path in depth, offering **strategies** to leverage each path's opportunities and manage its challenges. We conclude by summarizing the factors of all paths together and offering thoughts on how they may apply to leaders as they continue on their own journeys. Finally, we add an appendix of professional tools and templates designed to enhance leader effectiveness within and across paths, which are mentioned in their respective chapters.

Importantly, we invoke words and stories of successful leaders to illustrate the factors and strategies associated with each path. Gained through over 65 interviews with leaders across all six paths, these perspectives augment our own understanding developed over decades of working with leaders. The interviewees come from both the public and private sectors, working in a variety of industries, organizations, and roles. Through this approach, we seek not only to add to the understanding of leadership in context, but also to improve the practice of socializing and onboarding leaders into their new positions and organizations across sectors that are not often directly compared.

While leaders may be the greatest beneficiaries of what we share in this book, coaches and other support professionals will also gain from the approach outlined here, as will the organizations housing the successful leaders. The clear-eyed vision earned through understanding specifics of a leadership path will jumpstart leader effectiveness, whether in the first critical months of a new position or in a reexamination of a leadership approach. We believe that all leaders, whether emerging or experienced, will learn not only from those who have walked the same path, but also from the experiences of those who have come to leadership through another route. Our findings are represented by these six distinct paths to leadership:

1. Promoted from Within (the **Insider**): filling a leadership position from the inside as a result of a change in responsibilities within an organization,
2. Hired Externally (the **Outsider**): individuals plucked from the organization's external market to assume a leadership position,
3. Elected (the **Representative**): constituents vote (whether at the ballot box, among a membership, or in some other representative form) these leaders into their position,
4. Appointed (the **Proxy**): individuals are appointed into position by a political principal, board of directors or owners,

5. Founder (the **Creator**): entrepreneurs who start organizations and rise into leadership positions as the company grows,
6. Family (the **Legacy**): individuals who assume a leadership position in the second generation or beyond of a family business or legacy.

1.1   Inspiration for the Six Paths

Our research impetus springs from our own fieldwork with leaders, primarily through managerial training and executive coaching engagements. As a business professor at American University in Washington DC, Mark invests considerable energy into teaching through live consulting projects, noting the commonalities and differences in those leading these organizations. In his research and consulting roles, Mark primarily works through leaders of private for-profit, not-for-profit, and public sector organizations to test academic findings and approaches in applied settings. Meredith's consulting background includes training, coaching, and facilitation for Members of Congress, Senators, and their senior staff, as well as private sector leaders and executives. Her perspective on federal government and corporate leaders is enhanced through her faculty positions in American University's Kogod School of Business and School of Public Affairs Key Leadership programs.

We find that the leaders we work with have been shaped by their paths, while varying in their strategies for influencing their specific situations. Meredith was struck by the importance of these path distinctions, for example, while working with a second-generation Representative to US Congress—a person who represented two paths; **elected** and **family**. Despite the advantage of the family name, which the member of Congress had fully leveraged to land the elected position, the lawmaker spent tremendous energy to differentiate from the parent, to create an individual identity but potentially missing out on a critical opportunity of the family leadership path. At around the same time, Mark was working with a former corporate executive who had been **promoted** up through one organization and **hired externally** into others, before transitioning to the role of **appointed** board member for multiple Fortune 500 companies and other not-for-profit organizations. This seasoned leader commented on the surprises inherent in his new roles, including the source of his influence, and the need to use different strategies to achieve his goals.

Experiences such as these convinced us that a new framework might be necessary to categorize and explain differences relating to how leaders entered their positions and addressed their divergent contexts. Such an examination could increase understanding of path distinctions and related factors that are underexplored in the leadership field. It could help explain why, for instance, that Meredith found that the types of strategic coaching conversations she was having with elected leaders and government executives varied so dramatically from the conversations she was having with her corporate clients. It was not simply a matter of public versus private sector; it seemed to relate more directly to the paths that the leaders had traveled to their positions. For example, the career leaders in the public sector, who often mark multiple promotions in the same agency, had more in common with their equivalents in the private sector when it comes to strategies they should pursue upon obtaining their leadership position. Yet, to be successful, other public sector leaders, such as those in elected and appointed paths, would need to approach their first 100 days in an entirely different way.

1.2   Methods Used to Explore Path Commonality and Distinctions

It was apparent that identifying multiple leadership paths and distinguishing their effects would be interesting and worthy of exploration. Because our ideas emerged from practice without knowing much about the boundaries or factors associated with the paths, we formulated research questions and planned an interview-based qualitative study. Our method primarily included interviewing leaders about early experiences and their entry to leadership positions, then checking these preliminary findings against other interviews and brief surveys to determine the validity of the six paths and their attributes. In this way, we were able to employ an orderly process to develop and explore our nascent framework, testing its efficacy in the marketplace with working leaders in organizational settings.

Alternative paths. We also explored the idea of paths beyond the six discussed in this book. For instance, we spoke with several financiers who were often titular leaders of organizations by virtue of their investment. However, we could not make the case that they exercised leadership as a separate path; they were more likely to simply structure the broad resources for the venture, while delegating the leadership influence and operational management to others. We also listened to the emerging interview data for whether we should split the Proxy (appointed) path in two, with separate lanes for government versus corporate, but did not find sufficient support for such division in terms of clear differences in opportunities, challenges, and strategies.

Research questions. Based on the preliminary ideas drawn from our work with leaders, our basic research questions were:

- What are the different paths to leadership positions?
- What are the differences within and commonalities across the distinct leader paths?
- What are the challenges and opportunities of each leadership path?

Interview Sample. Our sampling rationale was first targeted toward a variety of executive-level leaders across public and private sector organizations, increasingly based on our preliminary identification of six paths to leadership described above. Although we initially set parameters for qualifying targeted subjects, such as executives of mid-to-large cap businesses that have over 1000 employees, we found that it was difficult to maintain these standards across dissimilar paths and industries. For instance, federal **elected** officials did not generally have direct control over large budgets, nor did they tend to employ a large staff.

To identify interviewees, we used our professional networks, in some cases cold-calling leaders in organizations that added diversity to the sample, and at times used a modified snowball sampling process where familiar referrals led us to previously unknown leaders. More than 65 leaders were interviewed, including over 40 C-suite executives and board members, seven members of US Congress, 12 founders, and 10 family leaders, several top appointees at federal agencies, and a variety of other leaders, experts, and key informants. Many of these leaders had experiences that yielded insights within and across multiple paths, as their careers had taken them from one leadership path to another.

Although we include many successful and impressive leaders in our interview sample, as intimated above our goal was not to select the "best" leader within each path but instead to achieve a broad range of accessible leaders. Indeed, even to identify such leaders would require a very different methodology. Rather, we sought to explore both distinctive and shared experiences of leaders across paths, including leaders with varying levels of accomplishment and a broad range of personal strengths and characteristics. We believe that this will help our findings to apply to a more extensive set of leaders who are taking their first steps onto a given path.

Finally, while our sample was comprised of a diverse set of leaders, including 16 women and at least 8 identifying with historically underrepresented groups, there was a larger representation of Caucasian males than would mirror the US population, if leaders were equally distributed. The skew may have been a function of the availability of leaders in the networks we sampled, but highlights a point that we believe is worthy of further study in terms of its influence on leadership paths. Some of our interviewees did discuss aspects of diversity issues in leadership that may be relevant, as related in Chapter 2.

Interview structure. We conducted semi-structured interviews, asking various planned questions as well as queries that emerged organically as each interview unfolded and over time as our insights grew. Typically both authors together interviewed each leader, and each interview lasted about one hour. Our interview guide was based on our research questions, emphasizing factors and strategies reflecting the challenges and opportunities of the various paths, as well as stories to illustrate interviewee points.

Analysis. Using statements derived from early interviews, we validated the six paths with multiple audiences through a Q-sort. A Q-sort is a procedure where participants are given brief statements and descriptors (e.g., characteristics of a leadership path) and categories (i.e., potential paths) and asked to match them. All interviews were audio-recorded and professionally transcribed verbatim. Our findings are based on a preliminary hand-coded analysis of the interviews by the authors, complemented with a separate software-assisted (NVivo) in-depth analysis by the authors with the assistance of a research assistant. Finally, the authors discussed the resulting themes and factors, and compiled illustrative quotes and stories to support the path factors and themes.

1.3   Findings

The results of our investigation offer critical insights and strategies, currently missing from the repertoire of leaders and their supporters, for managing across six distinct paths into leadership positions. We organize our findings in two categories: (1) themes that are held in common across all paths, varying in how they manifest; and (2) the set of opportunities, challenges, and strategies that are relatively unique within each path. In the chapters that follow, we illustrate many findings through the words and stories of our interviewees. In most cases, we identify those interviewed with their full consent, while in a few cases identities are kept confidential at the request of those quoted.

Table 1.1 Leadership paths: Variations on commonly held themes

Themes and variations	Insider: promoted	Outsider: externally hired	Representative: elected	Proxy: appointed	Creator: founder	Legacy: family
Vision	Has track record of supporting the organization's vision	Connects with a vision distinct from the former organization	Must connect vision to constituents, may defer to party leaders	Vision reflects the principal (appointer) and guides expectations	Vision and ability set direction, attracts investors, employees, and customers	Goes beyond business needs to encompass family across generations
Passion	Previously aligned with team, product, or organization	Industry experience demonstrates passion; may spur loyalty concerns	Represent key constituencies and issues	Connect to principal's agenda or values	The product, idea, or process of building a venture	Family brand, history, future, and values
Personal brand	Blends with organization brand; difficult to re-brand in new position	Valued outside perspective from prior companies; may reflect competitor brand	Established through assignments and campaigns	Reflects the principal; challenge to fit in	Significant draw for potential investors, employees, customers	Assumes and sometimes extends the family brand
Credibility	Existing relationships and track record within organization	Expertise; need to prove loyalty and trust	Judged by differing stakeholder standards and interests, which may conflict	Reflects the principal; must be proven to staff	Gained through ability to attract investors and customers as well as comprehensive knowledge of the business	Reflects the family brand, track record, and relationships
Culture	Accepts and fits organizational culture; may not see deficiencies	Assessed for cultural fit, differences weighed against value added	Sets office culture; may straddle constituent and government cultures	Ability to fit principal's values with idiosyncratic agency culture	Source of the culture; can realize own vision that reflects personal values	"Family DNA" infuses the organization

(continued)

Table 1.1 (continued)

Themes and variations	Insider: promoted	Outsider: externally hired	Representative: elected	Proxy: appointed	Creator: founder	Legacy: family
Power and authority	Clear source and connections but may struggle leading former peers	Reflects the talent and knowledge brought into the organization	From committee assignments and leadership positions; clearly outlined by position or jurisdiction	Appointment roles and responsibilities specify areas of authority	Clear perceptions of rights to design and administer; tempered with need for buy-in	Inherent in the family role (ownership, management, leadership); need governance structure
Perspective	Insider view; may be perceived as less willing to embrace change	Understands alternate perspectives; may be viewed as a disruptor	Each is unique; expected to reflect perspective of constituents and stakeholders	Understands and represents the principal's perspective	"Founder's syndrome" wields disproportionate influence on company goals and operation	Can be insular if not encouraged to seek outside experiences
Resources/access	Insider status may provide access otherwise not available to position holder	Beneficial outside connections; limited organizational access until proven trustworthy	Positional power enables access to most audiences; may be beholden to influencers	Access to the principal and conduit of this access for others and resources	Tremendous pressure to manage and build financial resources and operations	Access to family owners to solicit feedback and support; difficulty in managing privileged stakeholders
Expertise/skills/markets	Organizational know-how and know-who; challenged to develop new capabilities	Brings scarce and valued skill to the organization	Connection with the community and interests they represent	Often less qualified and knowledgeable than career direct reports; brings knowledge of, and access to, the principal	Early years build capabilities across the business; later need to develop leadership capabilities and delegate to others	Intimate historical knowledge; often need outside experience to develop and test skills

1.3.1 Variations on Commonly Held Themes

Table 1.1 outlines nine common themes that cut across all paths, depicted with their variations within each path. This list of themes, while not necessarily exhaustive in terms of all that the paths have in common, represents factors that were reported as relevant for leaders on all paths. We believe this to be an important point; many of our results reported otherwise in this book focus on distinctions among the six paths, but these commonalities hint at the potential for leaders to import ideas and strategies across paths. We detail a few of these themes and variations below as examples from Table 1.1.

Vision. Perhaps unsurprisingly, leaders on all six paths were associated with having a vision for the organization. However, this vision was likely to manifest and operationalize differentially.

- A founding leader is likely to have a personal vision that sets the origin and early direction for the organization, designed to attract particular stakeholders such as investors and fellow entrepreneurs.
- Appointed leaders, on the other hand, would generally borrow some of their vision from the principal who appointed them, at least in terms of guiding the direction for which they were appointed.
- Differing from both of these are family leaders, whose vision often goes beyond business concerns to include familial relationships, often spanning generations.

Passion. Similarly, interviewees across all six paths reported that passion was important to their leadership experience. However, the focus of this passion varied greatly.

- Promoted leaders often expressed attachment and loyalty passion for the people, teams, and sometimes projects they had worked with over their time with the organization.
- Elected leaders were likely to express passion for issues, sometimes because they resonated with constituents, at times because the issue was more of personal interest.
- Appointed leaders tended to frame their passion within the purpose of their principal appointing authority. Given the nature of high-level appointees on corporate boards and government agencies, typically appointees are able to choose the principals with whom they align.
- Founders were more likely to be passionate about an idea, a product to be created, or even about the process of starting a new venture.

- Legacy leaders often expressed their passion in terms of family values, history, and brand.

Culture. Although the nature of culture means that it often flies under the radar, our interviewed leaders were generally well-aware of its presence and function.

- An interesting, if somewhat obvious variation exists between promoted leaders, who often carry the culture of the organization, sometimes to the point of difficulty of seeing its deficiencies, and externally hired leaders who may misunderstand or even chafe against the culture of their new organization, but at times have been hired to effect change.
- Founders are often the source of cultural values and practices within the organizations they create. As the venture grows into an organization, this personal embodiment of culture may wane, sometimes resulting in a fragmented or weakly held culture.
- Legacy leaders were likely to mention some form of "family DNA" (as termed by a few) which fuels the culture of the organization and helps them to make decisions.

Other themes listed in Table 1.1, which emerged from our interviews and work with leaders, included personal brand, credibility, power and authority, perspective, resource access, and expertise.

1.3.2   Outlining Opportunities, Challenges, Strategies: Six Paths Chapters

Our second category of findings, by far given the most attention in this book, is the set of opportunities, challenges, and strategies that emerged and were supported from our research process. For each path, we offer a chapter organized around these factors and tactics, illustrated through quotes and stories from our interviews. Finally, at the end of the book we summarize and compare these challenges, as well as offer an appendix of sample tools for leaders to use. Below, we give brief previews of the topics covered in our path chapters.

- *Insider: The Promoted Path (Chapter 2).* We start our path discussion with promotions, referring to those who move up within an organization, which is a path that may seem familiar to many of our readers. The opportunities abound for a leader who has grown up in the organization, and she can be a true ambassador of the cultures she has experienced. Such leaders can also use and build on the relationships and record of service that they have developed over time, as well as taking advantage of the organization's developmental opportunities. Challenges exist as well; promoted leaders must learn to manage their former peers, gear themselves for pushing needed change, and adapt to their new role. Some promoted leaders may find themselves breaking through ceilings that formerly limited people of historically disadvantaged categories, although this is not limited to this path.

- *Outsider: The External Hire Path (Chapter 3).* This category, new leaders brought in from outside the organization, may also be a relatively familiar path for our readers. These leaders bring with them a fresh perspective and professional network, and are often hired for their specific expertise and track record. The outsider status confers confidence, at times as a mandate, to make changes that insiders might find risky. Outsiders may be challenged by the need to assimilate or adapt to the different culture, people, and processes of a new organization, often without formal support to make this leap. In some cases outsiders continue to overidentify with their previous employers, which may exacerbate their lack of support from new rivals as the outsider's status as a newcomer makes him more visible to others.

- *Representative: The Elected Path (Chapter 4).* Contrasting elected leaders, those voted into position as representatives of others, with other paths may be novel for many of our readers. There are important differences for Representatives[1] largely emanating from their status as the "entity" who embodies the power of the position, allowing opportunity to leverage their vision and resources to connect with constituents according to the needs and interests of all parties. This comes with potential challenges that are in some ways akin to celebrity status, including public visibility, demanding expectations, and busy schedules. Other challenges vary by the particular administrative system, such as election cycle, term limits, and demands attached to party hierarchy.

- *Proxy: The Appointed Path (Chapter 5).* As another path that relatively few of our readers may have walked, the journey of a Proxy leader also provides lessons in its contrasts with other paths. Proxy leaders generally are appointed for a specific purpose and expertise, and are typically meant to faithfully represent the principal who appointed them. Their opportunities therefore often relate to the principal, using his or her reputation and

---

[1]We use the "Representative" label in the generic sense of the word, as it applies to many titles of elected leaders.

power to get things done, or to allow others to share access to the principal's power. Appointed leaders are often limited in their time and focus, which can be challenging for themselves and those they work with. In some cases, those working with appointed leaders may resent their focus, such as when the Proxy seems underqualified on their own merit, or seems more concerned with pleasing the principal than helping the organization more broadly.

- *Creator: The Founder Path (Chapter 6).* This path is populated by entrepreneurs who start ventures according to their vision, passion, and expertise, leveraging this into organizations which they can lead through growth and success. Those on the founder path typically must develop a number of skills as part of their journey, ranging from reading financial statements to empowering others to share in their goals. Along the way, they also must deal with resource scarcity, limitations of their own abilities and reach as the organization grows, and difficulty in determining which early employees may or may not be suitable for that growth. In highly successful ventures, founders may be challenged by decisions of whether to share ownership and how to manage their quasi-celebrity status.
- *Legacy: The Family Path (Chapter 7).* While the right family connections may be helpful on any path to leadership, this is the only one that specifically requires a family relationship. The path comes with a family brand and culture, which can be leveraged by clarifying a family narrative and sharing its values and operative methods with all stakeholders in the organization. Legacy leaders also may benefit from early family mentors who share their passion and commitment, while demonstrating how to balance the security of the position with the responsibility to live up to the brand. Leaders on the family path are often challenged by close relations, particularly those who may not have voice in the management of the family venture, and at times may lack the perspective of leaders on other paths who have experienced multiple organizations and a less secure place in the hierarchy.

In each of the above chapters, we discuss these opportunities and challenges of the paths, with strategies to address each, supported through the words and stories of our interviewees. We conclude with a chapter that brings together our ideas, comparing opportunities and challenges across the six paths, connecting path strategies to both new and more experienced leaders. Finally, we offer an appendix of process tools based on chapter strategies, most of which may be adapted to a leader's particular situation.

1.4   A Customized Journey

Our six paths framework, based on ideas from decades of professional work and supported with more recent conversations with dozens of leaders across sectors, geographies, and contexts, makes a strong case that leadership is not "one size fits all" for either the person or for the mode of entry into the role. There are important distinctions across the six leadership paths, and understanding them may provide value for both emerging and experienced leaders. Indeed, failure to understand the advantages and disadvantages inherent in each path can confound new leaders who otherwise may follow the footsteps of leaders on incompatible paths. By identifying the commonalities within each path, leaders can focus attention on what is working for and against them. We also believe that leaders should learn not only from those who have walked their particular path, but also from the experiences of those making tracks in other directions. Considering the lessons from these paths can help leaders to be more effective from the first steps on their own path.

There are many leadership approaches offered in the marketplace and a slew of career-oriented guides on the shelves. These books, while skillfully exploring leadership and onboarding tactics, do not significantly differentiate among the multiple paths which offer leadership opportunities, and the varied settings through which these paths travel. Our approach and this book are distinguished by our delineation of specific paths, describing their distinctive opportunities and challenges along with strategies to leverage, apply, and manage them, as well as by offering insights grounded in the experience of a broad sample of leaders. We believe that leaders who select paths that most resonate with their personal preferences, leverage their unique attributes, will increase their potential for effectiveness. It is our hope that this work will be helpful to various audiences who seek to understand and support leader emergence and operation across multiple paths.

2

Insider: The Promoted Path

Too often promotions give a notion of expanded power. Just like a newly elected politician who narrowly wins a close election may claim a mandate for change, the newly promoted may misread the organization, such as what their job is, or how fast they should be moving. They feel like they've got a mandate and that may not be the case; they may overplay their hand.
—Senior Vice President, Fortune 50 company

Most successful leaders have been promoted—advancing up the organizational hierarchy of authority and responsibility—at some point in their career. Sometimes promotions come at regular intervals, such as in a traditional management development program where the leader moves among organizational divisions to learn the business, or as highly productive employees are recognized for their contributions through advancement. Founders and leaders in growing businesses may advance, with or without title changes, as the organization grows under them. When a leader is promoted, their sphere of influence increases within the organization, often extending visibly to outside stakeholders (i.e., any outside entity with an interest in the company, such as investors, customers, and suppliers), especially as the leader reaches the C-suite or equivalent levels. As pointed out in the quote above, in any of those cases the promoted leader holds significant advantages but also faces potential pitfalls.

This chapter reviews factors that influence the success of leaders as they are promoted—exploring opportunities and challenges, advantages and disadvantages, that are inherent in the promoted path. We draw from our experience working with leaders through consulting, coaching, and teaching across

M. A. Clark and M. Persily Lamel, *Six Paths to Leadership*, https://doi.org/10.1007/978-3-030-69017-5_2

a wide variety of organizations, from small startups to Fortune 50 firms, not-for-profits, government agencies, and others. More directly, we use the stories and words of the top executives who we interviewed. Through them, we outline the varying processes and factors that influence leader success, including a set of strategies for maximizing opportunities and addressing challenges. Some of these will be familiar from our exploration of other paths, while others are more likely to be encountered by those leaders who have been promoted into their positions.

2.1   Insider: Opportunities and Strategies of the Promoted Path

As leaders on the rise, those promoted have several inherent advantages to their position in the organization. The opportunities for promoted leaders that our interviewees focused on most related to either the leaders themselves—their knowledge of organizational culture and processes, their existing relationships, their credibility, and their loyalty—or the preparedness of the organization in planning for the succession and role of the promoted leader. Our interviewees also discussed strategies for how to leverage these opportunities, summarized in Table 2.1.

Table 2.1   Promoted path: Insider opportunities and strategies

Promoted path opportunities	Strategies to leverage
1. Cultural awareness	• Be a culture carrier for the company. Promote the positive aspects and lead cultural enhancement • Challenge the culture to benefit the organization, as they are not questioned for fit and loyalty
2. Relationship network within the organization	• Target new relationships and stakeholders • Redefine and set new habits with existing network
3. Proven track record and commitment	• Identify new areas of focus • Set goals and metrics for success in the new position, with milestones to track progress
4. Organizational succession planning and leadership development programs	• Use the succession plan process to develop new critical relationships and gain the necessary knowledge prior to assuming the role • Own your plan to be the successor

2.1.1 Cultural Awareness

The culture of an organization—its values, norms, and practices—is rarely written out in boldface for leaders to understand and follow. Instead, culture is embedded in the organization, and may be enacted differently than it is officially espoused to outsiders. Those who have been promoted are likely to be able to understand and benefit from the culture within their organization, because they have successfully navigated it on their climb up the ladder. This is an important advantage, because those who fit well within a culture are more likely to find acceptance for themselves and their ideas. Promoted leaders will also be more able to translate existing cultural values to novel situations that they may encounter as their duties grow and change, realizing greater success than outsiders in applying organizational beliefs and practices in an acceptable manner.

Some organizations, especially large companies with more traditional management training programs, supplement the insider's know-how with formal cross-training. **Jay Hammer**, CEO of nutritional supplement company Theralogix, draws on his time as a rising executive with retail companies Macys, Gap, and Urban Outfitters.

> *In terms of behavior, interaction, how to get the job done and how to lead, there were norms and expectations for someone growing up from within. As I was getting promoted, there was always a bit of "here's what you need to do to get to the next step." There were also constant opportunities for promotion, which created feedback loops as you sought those positions, even if you didn't get promoted – "here's why you didn't get that job" or "here's why we're giving you this job instead". So that creates understanding as to what's permitted and what's expected.*

One important effect of such management development programs is to deepen the cultural know-how of those who are newly promoted, thus increasing the odds of a smooth transition to the new position. The leaders, in turn, leverage this training for their own success and for the development of their successors. Smaller and less traditional organizations may have other ways of developing cultural fit, such as through a compensation system that rewards risk-taking and innovation, or sponsorship of sporting events, participation in philanthropic efforts, or other markers of the organization's values and interests. Promoted leaders may use their positions to continue or expand existing cultural themes, increasing their own influence through alignment with what is important to their employees.

Promoted leaders who see a business need for making a change, or who wish to leave their own mark on the organization, can use their status as insiders to challenge existing practices. **Alastair Bor** draws on his experience with wealth management company Perpetual Limited and infrastructure agency Transport for New South Wales (TNSW) to illustrate this.

> *If you haven't adapted to the culture, you wouldn't be there. But what impact have you had in changing the culture as well? … So we brought in an agile delivery methodology, which was all very foreign to government. It may have started off as an old, slow, government environment. But the culture, it's been moving. I get invited to speak about futuristic topics such as driverless cars and whatnot. Now people also invite me to talk about "how did you bring agility to the government?"*

Bor, now Chief Technology Officer at the multinational biotech company Ecofibre, used his standing within the organizational culture to know where effective change would be possible. He makes this part of his professional duties—"*I measure myself on that, as accountable to drive and to change the culture of the place*"—and in doing so enhances his own brand, within and outside of the organization. He can do this effectively in part because, as an insider, he was able to put his plans for change within the context of the organization's culture and nudge toward change. As he notes, "*the vision can be a lot more comprehensive because I know more about the inner workings of the place.*"

2.1.2   Relationship Network Within the Organization

Because promoted leaders have been part of the organization, they are likely to have existing social relationships that they can draw on for informational, political, or emotional support. They may have formal or informal mentors who can help newly promoted leaders navigate the corridors of power in an organization. At the least, promoted leaders are more likely to know where to go for needed information, and how an organization actually gets things done. Promoted leaders with a strong base can spend time shoring up their blind spots by seeking out colleagues and stakeholders who may be able to help in the next steps along the path.

In his time at the US Post Office, **Jack Potter** found that relationships built as he rose through the hierarchy could be, if properly managed, leveraged to move in the direction that the organization needed to go. **Potter** started as a mail sorter, what could be termed the lowest rung of the organizational ladder, but from the beginning established relationships through which he could advocate his beliefs about how the Postal Service should be run. As Postmaster General, he was able to call on these relationships to support the direction of the Postal Service that he believed would best serve its stakeholders and its future.

Chuck Firlotte, former CEO of Aquarion, points out that the existing relationships of a promoted leader can be leveraged through strong mentoring bonds.

> *You know the organization to be sure, and you know the politics. You can align yourself with a good sponsor, someone who will help bring you along.*

These mentor connections are not automatic, however; they should start with aligned goals and must be nurtured. As **Firlotte** points out, even recognizing a lack of mentor fit can be beneficial, prompting a leader to go in the direction right for him or her. During his ascension up the corporate ladder in his career, he had tough choices to make after one mentor retired and he began working with another. Although **Firlotte**'s initial impression was that their pairing would not be effective, the relationship did add value for him.

> *There was not a lot of chemistry between us, not a lot of shared interest. He seemed more about "show" than "go." We could have overcome those differences, maybe, but I also think that if I had gone in another direction I wouldn't have become CEO later.*

Firlotte credits the strength of his previous mentoring relationships with enabling him to take the risks necessary to move his career forward.

> *There's often an element of risk involved, where you say, "I'm going to do it," but it's not necessarily a safe haven. But it can be a necessary risk in order to achieve significant accomplishments.*

Tami Majer, Chief Human Resource Officer at 24 Hours Fitness, reminds us that managing relationships effectively is not just leveraging others; it also involves some self-examination for the leader. She found that for her, relationship management requires a *"balance of humbleness as well as getting out of my own way. Believing in myself was important."* **Majer**, who was promoted through several levels during her time at Mars, Inc, found that encouraging honest feedback from those with whom she built relationships throughout her journey ultimately enhanced her ability and confidence as a leader.

Ideally, promoted leaders should assess the network related to their new position soon after promotion. In the Appendix we provide tool 2.1 Personal Network Analysis and Action Plan. This exercise is critical for promoted leaders to identify the strengths of their network and the target areas for development. It is essential to assess the internal organizational network to consider with whom they should be prioritizing their time and leveraging their network so as to accomplish their goals. For example, while peers who provided emotional support now become direct reports to manage, leveraging their trust can transition these individuals into key influencers of engagement for the leader's new team.

2.1.3   Proven Track Record and Commitment

Over 50 years ago, The Peter Principle[1] satirized workplace promotions with the maxim "people in a hierarchy tend to rise to their level of incompetence." There is lasting power in this observation, because in many cases promotions are given in recognition for past performance more than for suitability for the elevated position. This may be especially an issue for early forays in management, such as the leap from individual contributor to team leader, because it is less likely that the leader has had time to develop or demonstrate significant managerial skills. When new leaders encounter difficulties in their promoted positions, it is often because they rely more on their past methods and successes than revising their approach to meet the demands of their new situation.

This need to find new means and measures of success for promoted leaders could be considered both as a challenge and an opportunity. We choose to classify it first as an opportunity because it begins with a clear advantage—the promoted leader has had success, and the organization is giving the leader an opportunity to build on these accomplishments. Challenges for promoted leaders involve choosing their method of learning the new job, including how to approach their new colleagues and subordinates, how to generate information and ideas, and what focus they should choose. Further, they face challenges stepping out of their former role, whether from the success they achieved, habits they have formed or because others continue to rely on them.

Gaurdie Banister, retired energy sector CEO and member of multiple Fortune 500 boards, staked out an approach that would reestablish relationships as well as generate potential directions for his company.

---

[1]Peter, L. J., & Hull, R. (1969). *The Peter Principle: Why Things Always Go Wrong*. William Morrow & Co., Inc.

I committed myself to a few things personally just around transparency in terms of how I was going to be a leader. I wrote up a 100-day plan, published it online to everyone, then proceeded to execute it. When I finished, I reported out to people on it. I wanted to ensure that people looked to my leadership style as, number one, I was going to be transparent with them. Number two, I was going to set goals. Number three, I would read out how I did…. I wanted to set the tone that this is how I am. We're going to be transparent with each other, I want the truth from everybody.

Banister's 100-day plan included the ambitious goal of interviewing 100 people, asks coworkers about what worked and did not work within the previous system, what goals the employees had for themselves, and what ideas they had for the company. In doing this, he further built a base of support beyond the engineers with whom he spent the early part of his career, also increasing his understanding of the company's human assets and possibilities for the company's direction.

While seeking out information in this way can be very effective, it does not preclude the possibility that newly promoted leaders can also bring insights from their own experience within the organization. **Jack Potter** details an example from the US Postal Service where he offered suggestions to one of the largest facilities in the country for streamlining mail handling and improving service, ideas gained from his time at more entry-level positions.

Very early in my career I was asked to participate in a review of workroom floor design at one of the largest plants in the Postal Service. Using some pre-meeting analysis I had done, I suggested they abandon the design they had spent millions of dollars to develop and go with a much simpler and more logical layout that would be easier for the workforce to comprehend. The recommendation was met with much skepticism and anger. I thought the manager was going to throw me out of the conference room. Subsequent to the meeting, cooler heads prevailed, and members of his staff that I had worked with in the past saw the merit of my suggestions and the plan was adopted.

The bottom line is you can't be a yes-man. It takes courage to step outside the mainstream. It would have been much easier and more politically correct to stay silent. But my recommendation had credibility because of the value of the concept and because of my previous experiences and reputation in the organization. If I didn't have that that reputation and the relationships that came from my earlier work, my recommendation might have died in the room.

Potter was able to turn his ideas into action by keeping a focus on success of the organization, rather than "*being about the politics*," as he puts it. By focusing on the business, rather than themselves, leaders promoted into new positions are able to offer ideas for change without being seen as a threat, even if it is not always easy.

As he advanced through the Postal Service, **Potter** built on his relationships and track record to instill efficiency and effectiveness in the operational systems. His track record and insider awareness spanned generations as he explains,

> *My father also worked for the Postal Service, and he gave me very useful advice. First, you have to maintain your integrity at all times. Second, let performance define you, rather than trying to align yourself with others. His third lesson was that the people who advanced, in his observation, were the ones who embraced change. The world is always changing around you, and if you're not part of the change process, or in the advancement of the institution to a higher level, then you're just one of the masses holding it back.*

Potter pairs this notion of integrity with action:

> *You get people to follow you by being successful; getting the job done well. You have to take people into consideration. Let's take efficiency as an example; your efficiency is doing it right and doing it once, as opposed to multiple times. In effect, you're working smarter, not harder. It's very easy to get buy-in when that's your message, as opposed to "work faster" or "put in more effort." In effect, you're putting yourself in their position and with that comes credibility for you and a great collaborative working relationship with the group.*

In this way, **Potter** aligns his relationships with his operational focus, driving toward improved organizational outcomes.

As newly promoted leaders plan their new methods and measures of success, it is important to prioritize their own inputs, and have a sense of where they will find the most success. Having often followed in their previous manager's footsteps, leaders can easily fall into the trap of continuing the previous leader's priorities. As leaders transition into more senior roles, their time ought to reflect on their own vision and which priorities will effectively support it (as well as where they should not be spending their time and efforts). **Tami Majer** of 24HourFitness suggests that leaders should keep Pareto logic in mind, understanding which 20% of factors and efforts will generate 80% of returns, rather than believing that every task and goal has equal chance of investment realization.

I think it is about the things that are going to bite you if you don't resolve them. What goes into the "80" is what's going to be about extracting value for what you're doing that helps the organization most. Then you can worry about the things around the fringes. Although you are trying to move fast when you first start, it is important to listen and learn, because the more you listen and learn, the more you are able to succinctly say what should fit into the 80 and what should fit into the 20.

Majer also emphasizes the importance of polling your colleagues, keeping your eyes open to observe cause and effect within your organizational processes. She notes, "*if you're going in blind, you are going to pick the wrong things.*"

2.1.4 Organizational Succession Planning and Leadership Development Programs

While it may be true that opportunities for promotions from one hierarchical level to another have diminished over the past few decades as organizations shed layers of bureaucracy, there still exist many traditional leadership development and succession planning programs, often in large or relatively traditional companies. It is a clear advantage and opportunity for promoted leaders to be part of such a system which not only recognizes them for promotion, but further plans a path wherein they can benefit from training, networking, and other resources to help them prepare for and adjust to the promoted position. Where such programs exist, aspiring and newly promoted leaders can maximize their opportunity by working within the system, as through the strategies shown below. When organizations lack formal succession mechanisms, leaders can borrow where possible to bring the advantages to their own situation.

Formal leadership development programs grew in popularity throughout the twentieth century, modeled on successes at companies such as General Electric and Ford Motor Company, who used multiyear divisional rotations to allow managers to experience the many functional areas that contributed value to the company. For successful leaders, such programs ensured a steady rise to the higher echelons of the organization and broadened their understanding of how the organization operated. Even when such programs are not particularly strong, a high rate of organizational growth can propel leaders up the hierarchy.

Jay Hammer, who spent his formative career in retail before running several successful startups, contrasts the criteria and process for promotion in these organizations, which occurred even when "*those companies shared a lot of the same operational, organizational, and hierarchical structure.*" At Macy's, promotions came to those who put in their time in the trenches. **Hammer** knew that within Macy's, obtaining and succeeding in promotions was dependent on "*the importance of managing upward*" through a "*clearly defined set of expectations*" accrued through performing well in lower-rung positions.

Hammer's executive development journey took him next to Urban Outfitters, another trendy clothing chain. He contrasts the expectations for leaders in established corporate cultures versus in ventures closer to their early stages in entrepreneurial, founder-influenced organizations.

> *Urban still felt fairly entrepreneurial, even though it was a large organization with multiple locations; it's now hundreds across their corporate divisions, plus thousands who work in the stores. But I was able to see at Urban how entrepreneur founders have a different style, even more than [Gap founder] Don Fisher…. Dick at Urban Outfitters [founder Richard Hayne] didn't act dictatorial, but he was imbued with the ability to act that way. In other words, if he had some crazy idea of how we wanted to do things, people would be inclined to go along.*

This value placed on innovative ideas and risks cascaded through the company, at least to a greater extent than most retail clothing chains, which in turn changed the measures of success for leaders seeking further promotion. **Hammer** describes how this continued to inform his leadership style at smaller startups, including today as CEO of Theralogix.

> *I had grown up in big organizations, but now organizations are trying to stay nimble, trying to not be burdened with lots of unneeded policies and procedures. So, we don't create rules and regulations if we don't need them. My leadership style is more, "let's all talk about the right thing to do here," then "let's figure out how to execute that together."*

Tom Monahan, now President and CEO of DeVry University, capped off his term as CEO of consulting firm CEB (formerly Corporate Executive Board) with its sale—$3.3 billion in enterprise equity value—to Gartner in 2017. He notes that promotions may happen more because of organizational growth, than due to individual readiness. He describes his rise at CEB through multiple roles and titles:

Along that timeline, it looked like I got promoted a bunch, but it was really just the jet stream of the company. It was that more was getting stuffed under me, because more needed to be managed.

Although we may presume some modesty on **Monahan**'s part, his point is that not all succession happens intentionally, and that the individual must be ready to capitalize on opportunities when they are presented. More typically, however, large and successful organizations will carefully plan executive succession, particularly at the top levels. The mentoring relationships mentioned previously come into play, as top executives often choose and groom their preferred successors. There are often political machinations, and sometimes outright battles for power, but effective companies are very careful about signals they send both to internal candidates and the external market.

Even the most intricately planned promotion process can be fraught with risks and subject to changes, especially at the executive level. **Monahan** explains some of the factors and complications involved in his ascent to CEO.

It was beginning to look and feel like a two-person leadership structure – both to my peers and to my board colleagues. That's a pretty healthy leadership development experience, to be a full member of the board as a rising executive, and it's one that isn't available today. [due to the passage of the U.S. Congress Sarbanes-Oxley Act, which restricts some governance structures]. The flip side is that it felt like a bit of a tell around succession, perhaps before everyone was ready to anoint me as the next CEO.

Over the next two years, CEB had doubled in revenues and CEO James McGonigle was ready to retire. But the board of directors wanted to be sure that **Monahan** was appropriately seasoned to fill the position, and that he had the necessary CEO skills. **Monahan** addressed the question of whether he yet had the appropriate competencies as, he maintains, any good first time CEO should:

I said "I'm sure I don't, and I'd like to get a little coaching," because by the time I actually took the role it would be even bigger, and even more complicated. So I started a series of conversations with my fellow directors, with no ambiguity around my role as both a board member and a CEO candidate. I wanted to set their view of what I thought was going to happen in the next 5-10 years. We had done the work of getting it to be profitable enough to go public, we scaled it reasonably well, our valuation was better than projections, etc. We're going to have to do M&A, and that could go incredibly well or incredibly bad. So I wanted to walk them through what I was thinking, just to see if their heads were nodding or not. I didn't want to sip from the poison chalice of unreasonable expectations.

Monahan's experience demonstrates multiple factors to consider in an internal promotion process. It is important to get a clear view of the context of a newly promoted leader's position. **Monahan** notes that, at higher executive levels, the preference is for internal candidates when the company is meeting its targets. This means that candidates must consider factors beyond the current situation in order to understand changing conditions, including those related to possible or likely reductions in performance levels. Newly promoted leaders should identify their stakeholders, spend time getting to know them, and reach agreement on their expectations and goals for future performance.

> *Typically when the Board selects a CEO from within, it's because they want the direction of the company to continue on course. But in our case, both the retiring CEO and I knew that in order to continue growing, we needed to do things differently. I had to make two things very clear before taking the job: 1) I am going to be a different kind of leader than my predecessor; and 2) I will be taking the company in a new direction.*
>
> *In my opinion, any internal successor should be very afraid of being cast as another version of their predecessor.*

Own your plan to be the successor. It should be noted that regardless of whether an organization has a formal succession plan to help leaders to get promoted or to succeed in the position, the leaders themselves also have an important role to play. **Jeff Nally**, an executive coach who has held multiple corporate human resource positions, describes his success in gaining promotions through his own initiative.

> *At Commonwealth Aluminum, I started as a training and development manager at their largest plant, then got promoted to the corporate office in an HR manager role, then Interim Director of Benefits and Comp, then went to lead HR at one of the acquired companies on the West Coast.... I wanted to do more than what was just in the training and development space once I mastered that, so I actually called out that I wanted to be promoted to do something new and different. I wanted to create the intention and expectation, to be my own succession manager and influence myself into positions as they become open.*

Nally notes that as an internal candidate, he had specialized knowledge that an outsider would lack. His knowledge of the organization, its structure and its people helped him to discern what moves might be possible. He also explains that it was not quite enough to simply gain his desired position; he had to employ strategies to ensure success. Primarily, Nally leveraged his existing organizational relationships, along with his skill in connecting to groups with divergent interests and managing their reconciliation.

> *The first position I moved into in the corporate office was employee relations manager. Even though I had done training and development at their largest plant, this was a United Steel Workers Union plant, which is the toughest and roughest group you can work with. I had gotten along with them in my prior role as a trainer, which helped to make progress later on the employee relations side. So my ability to build relationships with employees, even during tough times, and through strikes, made me a good fit for employee relations manager.*

It is evident that leadership development programs and succession planning confer advantages and opportunities for those promoted. Beyond this, the visibility of these support programs may also have benefits for others within the organization, providing a signaling effect that performance and loyalty are valued and rewarded. As **Michael Waldron**, Managing Director and Chief Compliance Officer (CCO) at Bayview Loan Servicing, observes,

> *Even promotions from within will be well received because it shows people that individuals are being recognized. They see that there is upward mobility within our organization.*

The Insider path is filled with opportunities that leaders can leverage to achieve success:

1. Promoting, challenging, and telling the story of the organization's culture
2. Capitalizing on the leader's existing network and creating new relationships
3. Building on the leader's track record in new areas
4. Developing through the organization's leadership and succession plans

Next, we will discuss the challenges that the Insider may encounter along the Promoted path.

2.2   Insider: Challenges and Strategies of the Promoted Path

Table 2.2   Promoted path: Insider challenges and strategies

Promoted path challenges	Strategies for managing
1. Manage former peers	• Listening tour, bring others along • Redefine and redeploy relationships
2. Shift perception to become a change agent	• Intentionally seek ways to create value (and feel valuable) for the organization • Honor the work done by predecessor • Carefully frame change initiatives
3. Adapt habits and metrics to new role	• Invest in new relationships • Manage expectations, build new narrative • Introspection for growth • Prioritize hiring replacement or delegate former responsibilities. Do not commit to doing both jobs
4. Be a "First"	• Emphasize expertise in business-line functions • Focus on the work, do not forget the people • Find your kitchen cabinet

2.2.1   Manage Former Peers

One of the most salient challenges of being promoted from within, I think, is just managing the relationships of those who used to be peers, but now are direct reports, and working through some of those sensitivities.
—Senior Vice President, Fortune 50 company

The most commonly cited challenge of the promoted leader may be the necessity of managing coworkers who first knew the leader in another role. Some of these colleagues may consider themselves to be friends with the leader. Others may have been rivals, at least in the sense of vying for the position that the promoted leader ultimately won. Many may simply be aware of the newly promoted leader's foibles and follies, providing a challenge to his or her credibility (Table 2.2).

Several of our interviewees discussed using what is a fairly widespread approach for leaders in a new position, to make a plan for the first 90 or 100 days on the job. Most often this plan includes a "listening tour" or similar means of gathering input from new subordinates, peers, and others important to the leader's future success. In the Appendix, tool 2.2 Listening Tour Action Plan we present a way to capture the insights uncovered through a listening tour.

As one senior human resource executive describes,

I subscribe to the first 90 days transition plan. The idea is that you always have to identify and know who your key stakeholders are, and to be able to bring those people along with you in meaningful ways.

A key part of this process is to find out what is working, as well as what may need rethinking. As **Chuck Firlotte** of Aquarion puts it, "*Spend time interviewing, especially your senior people. Listen more than you talk and get input from informed sources*" even beyond fellow employees, to include clients, industry experts, and others.

The importance of this process is not just for the good of the promoted leader, but also for the people and divisions being managed, according to **Jeff Nally**:

So while relationships are important, that whole internal promotion means that you have to ask, "what's my relationship with these people, these departments, these business units?" The org chart tells the macro story. But the "how I manage one on one" is the secret sauce to success in the first 90 days.

Leaders should look at these conversations as a means of discovering what could help colleagues fulfill their own goals, rather than simply furthering the leader's ambition. In describing US President Abraham Lincoln, Robert Ingersoll wrote "if you want to test a man's character, give him power." Echoing that sentiment, one of our executive interviewees gave a challenge to promoted leaders:

I'd say that when you come up from within, true leadership has to emerge. In other words, can you rise above what you were, or what your peers think you were, to play a true leadership role?

Those who will be serving with the newly promoted are not always ready accept the leader, which often requires deft handling. One of our interviewees, who serves as President of a division of a multibillion dollar food sector company, invokes strategies for bringing others along from his earlier career at an industry competitor.

Those who I was leading were a mix of older people who had seen me grow up from being an apprentice to now being their boss, to peers who I had been alongside, and younger associates who held me in reverence. I had followers, as well as those who didn't believe in what I was doing. I think that some of them smelled my fear. Of those, some chose to help me with that, and others who chose to try to kill me. There was one peer in particular whose intelligence I both valued and feared; I had a bit of an inferiority complex to him. So I ended up bringing him into my inner circle rather than having a detractor in the system, and found that worked to good effect.

Monahan outlines a creative solution that one former peer proposed:

There are many ways to renegotiate relationships. One former peer let me know that it wouldn't work for our styles for him to report directly to me, in my new CEO role. He had a solution – to carve out a specialty area where the company needed to grow, and hire another executive who would be his boss, and who would report directly to me. So instead of leaving the company or rotating out of the job, he led the search for his boss, then helped to onboard her. It worked great!

In this case, the restructure both allowed the executive to focus on his own strengths within the organization, without having a direct reporting relationship to his former peer.

Firlotte points out that difficulty in seeing beyond past roles goes both ways; the promoted leader must gain a clear view of those they want to lead, with some independence from their prior conceptions.

I think as an insider you certainly know the organization, so you have home court advantage, if you will. But sometimes that may be also a weakness for you. You may have also formed opinions and judgments of people that may or may not be accurate as well.

This failure to see others as they truly are can hamper leaders as they transition to positions with increased latitude to act. Sometimes the temptation for a newly promoted leader may be to do what they think is best—that could be why they were hired, after all. This can be a precarious path, as one executive warns:

Too many people rely on power. The biggest failure is the power play, "Now I'm the boss." Most times it's inadvertent, not as means of retribution, but rather to enact what you believe you were promoted to do.

In reality, however, more effective and lasting power comes through influence; "*you get more respect when you give your team space.*"

2.2.2 Shift Perception to Become a Change Agent

When you are promoted from within, your strength is your reputation, and your weakness is your reputation. The people who you know and who know you can both help and hurt you.
—**Gaurdie Banister**

Earlier in this chapter we proposed that internally promoted leaders carry the advantage of having a track record in their organizations, noting that the challenge is often to set the tone for "now what?" Here we further discuss ideas about the whys and hows that leaders can leverage their promotion to blaze a new path in a needed organizational direction, and to become a disruptor when needed. The flip side of the reputational benefits of being the insider, is the difficulty that others may have seeing you differently and welcoming your new ideas. There are potentially significant obstacles to overcome. Subordinates who formerly were peers, and even those in higher levels of management, may define the newly promoted leader by previous roles and job performance. As **Chuck Firlotte** discusses, past behaviors and beliefs may come to the fore from the leader as well as from the subordinates:

The insider's challenge is that the people you're managing were your peers yesterday. That can be a challenge because you may be invoking new ways of doing things that maybe you didn't necessarily live yourself – say, "I want everybody here at 8am." A silly example, but you get my point. Now you are the boss of the tribe that you ran with – the same folks that you went to the pub crawl with. I dealt with this early on by stopping any socializing outside the office, other than perhaps to make a token appearance. I also think that you form opinions of people from your time as peers. That's not always good, because you have certain biases that might be hard to overcome.

Similarly, **Ed Ahn** of X-Factor Capital notes,

> *Probably the most difficult position to come into is promoting from within. Every time you get promoted, the relationships with people around you are changing, and the power dynamics just become a little bit more complicated. I think of leadership as trying to deal with the package of histories.... So much of leadership is around dealing with that and trying to sculpt something new out of it. You may not be able to sculpt what you really want; you can only sculpt what the organization allows you to sculpt.*

This sculpting process calls for promoted leaders to take action, at least in so far as their position allows, deciding on which activities to start and which they need to leave behind. As **Tom Monahan** recalls this included, at times, hard decisions about valued colleagues who were also sometimes friends.

> *Even in my situation, where I had been clearly designated as the likely successor, there were still people who found it difficult to see me in the CEO role. We needed to find new ways to work together, and the question arises of how much time that you give a former peer to adjust. Two weeks in, it may be OK not to be completely on board; 2 months later, it's a problem. The mission of the organization comes first, and as CEO I couldn't let old definitions of professional relationships stand in the way of our progress.*

Monahan found that these colleagues were not able to see past their beliefs about how the leader should act, particularly when there was a "*need to behave differently in a new role*".

For newly promoted leaders, there is a real need to understand how to do things differently—to get beyond the Peter Principle where their best performance was always behind them.

As former human resource executive **Nally** puts it,

> *I see this as a real challenge of being promoted internally, and you don't just get over the first 90 days or 100 days. This takes a year to finally kind of get under your belt and know what that feels like and stop doing all the behaviors that got you success. It's like Marshall Goldsmith's book* What Got You Here, Won't Get You There. *You can't just keep doing the same things over to get the same success.*

At the same time, fulfilling the role of a disruptor may be difficult. Unlike a leader brought in from outside the organization to lead a planned change, a promoted leader may need to negate their own previous work, or that of their team and their predecessor—who also may still be in the organization, and may even be the new boss. To effectively offer direction, it will often be important for newly promoted leaders to honor the work of those who have served before. The imperative for disruption at some level is clear, however, for many leaders and the organizations as they navigate through rapid changes in technology, markets, and competitors.

Monahan reinforces this—"*A really important role for the leader is preparing the organization for constant change*"—but he acknowledges that it is difficult to do correctly. In his well-regarded book,[2] William Bridges sketched out a "transitions" model for leaders to guide organizational change, that also accounts for the shift in the individuals involved. Leaders are charged with creating clarity and communication in each of the three transition stages: ending, neutral zone, and new beginnings. **Monahan** further offers three practical factors to consider when proposing or enacting such transitions of people and strategies in organizations.

1. Do your homework when bringing in new talent, acquiring new divisions, or buying into a change process: "*in this day and age it's amazing how much diligence I left on the table.*" There is plenty of information available from analysts, clients, and former peers, "*yet there are times I didn't do that, I liked the person in conversation so much.*"

2. Make change only where and when change is needed:

   A second mistake I made was erring on the side of someone who screamed "change agent." You get to a boiling point where it isn't moving fast enough and think "I'm going to bring in a real change agent who looks and walks and acts like a change agent." But in general, the most effective change agents don't wear sweatshirts that say, "I'm a change agent."

3. Change tactics as the organization changes:

   I tended to underestimate the difficulty translating lessons from size of the company. I was with the same company from $20 million to a billion. I didn't fail horribly at either but didn't pay attention to the different skills needed all the time in hiring.

Monahan found in hiring executives that having worked at a large company was not a good indicator of whether they could do the job for him. A primary difference was in how they came to their previous positions; for instance, did they grow in title as a small company scaled up, was

---

[2]Bridges, W. (2009). Managing Transitions: Making the Most of Change. Da Capo Press.

their previous company an acquisition target that gifted them an executive title with the merged entities, or did they get seasoning at other large companies? Some of these, **Monahan** found were not a good fit for his growing company, as he found that they "*could be incredibly talented people but they'd be looking around for the support structure we hadn't built yet.*"

2.2.3   Adapt Habits and Metrics to New Role

The more senior you go in the organization, the more of a spotlight you are in.... You really have to be role modeling the behavior you want to be known for, all the time. I think generally speaking there's just sort of less forgiveness. I don't mean there's less caring or less empathy, but you don't have as many chances [to succeed or fail].

—**Tami Majer**, Chief Human Resource Officer, 24 Hours Fitness

It is apparent that newly promoted leaders must transition not only in their job duties, but also in their skills, management approaches, and sometimes in their personal outlook and habits as **Majer**'s words make clear. The visibility of higher-level positions can also warp the feedback that leaders receive. As **Firlotte** puts it,

I found that my jokes were a lot funnier the day I became CEO. All of the sudden people who wouldn't give me the time of day before were hugging me in restaurants.

He notes that this increased attention is "*just part of human nature*" and that for the leader it is necessary to "*stay grounded and conscious.*" It also implies that leaders must make an effort to reach out beyond their employees and even their former peers "*perhaps not necessarily running with the same tribe*" according to **Firlotte**, because those people may not give the crucial, unvarnished feedback needed to make good executive decisions. We encourage leaders to seek out peer leaders from other organizations, including through associations such as those described in the Proxy (Appointed Path) chapter, find good mentors through directors on the organizational board, and engage with clients and customers who will give candid insights, even if with their own biases.

Importantly, the promoted leaders must understand themselves in order to know how to best fit their skillset to the new role. Relative to those hired from the outside, internally promoted leaders may have had fewer opportunities to measure themselves across a variety of organizational situations. As former CEO of Influence Health **Mike Nolte** describes, "*a challenge is that you don't* *know what you don't know.*" One senior executive speaks to his struggle to seek out formal understanding of leadership processes and approaches while taking his first steps up the corporate ladder.

> *I didn't do much going into the next role other than to continue to nurture the intuitive leadership style that served me well previously. While I certainly discovered a real sense of vulnerability in that I didn't know how to do the job, at that point in my career I didn't have either the self-confidence or the emotional intelligence to disclose that vulnerability to a core team. I didn't have the perspective of seeking out coaching about the stage of my career. So, what I got was self-taught and didn't really have any objective frame to it.*

One solution, enacted by this executive later in his career, was to be proactive in learning about leadership, becoming more introspective, and seeking outside feedback through executive coaching and peer leader groups.

Firlotte echoes the notion of the importance of finding a good coach as leaders progress up the organizational hierarchy, a truism that may apply across leadership paths:

> *I think it is really healthy for a CEO to have a coach. You know, a good coach. It's sort of like guitar players, right? Everybody can play a guitar, but few can play them well. But I think having a coach for perspective on life is helpful.*

Certainly, it can be lonely at the top, whatever leadership path a leader has traveled. Leaders may be very visible, interacting with many people who pursue conversations with the leader, currying favor and asking for resources. On the positive side, this allows leaders to be supportive and do good things for others. However, effective leaders must learn to say no when warranted, protecting assets, including their own time, thus disappointing other in many cases. To increase the likelihood of success for themselves and their organizations, leaders must find a way to extend their own personal and professional networks. **Firlotte** advocates multiple coping strategies, including meditation, and believes that the various areas of life should be considered to be buckets to keep filled and level, including

> *emotional, psychological, physical energy buckets. I think it's important to be well-rounded that way, and to take care of yourself in all areas of life. You can't really have pals and friends in the office.*

Prioritization. It is also important to strategize methods ensuring that priorities continually reflect the vision of the leader. For the promoted leader, this also includes and letting go of former responsibilities and metrics of success. This transition may be particularly difficult when moving upward within the same division, where leaders may be supervising those now filling their previous position. In some cases, the job the newly promoted leader previously held may not yet be filled, which is often referred to as "cascading role vacancy" as managers are promoted. This situation requires further thoughtfulness in determining what tasks are critical to continue, what can be delegated, and what may be jettisoned.

Finally, **Firlotte** also notes a pattern for CEOs that may apply also to other management levels, which offers a caution to promoted leaders as they move up the organizational hierarchy.

> *I think there's an arc on becoming a CEO. First, you get the job and you're grateful and you're worried; like, how you can do it? Second, you're into the groove, hitting the KPIs [*Key Performance Indicators*], doing everything well. The third piece of the arc, only some fall into; it is arrogance, where you think you can do no wrong.*

Leaders may be more likely to fall into the third part of the arc when they spend too much time listening to their admirers, rather than balancing their professional network and information sources, as described above.

2.2.4   Be a "First"

One factor is of critical importance for understanding the range of challenges that leaders may face across any of the leadership paths—that of being one of the first promoted members of a historically disadvantaged demographic category such as a female or a racial minority. Understanding this challenge as experienced by promoted leaders is important not only for those facing the challenge, but also for organizations that wish to increase their success in building and supporting a diverse, equitable, and inclusive workforce. Strategies for such support can aid in recruitment, retention, and performance for both the individual and for the broader workforce, which improves its capacity for effectiveness by being more inclusive of the range of talent available in an organization's internal market.

Emphasize expertise in business-line functions. As Regional President of PNC Bank for Washington and Virginia, **Jermaine Johnson** leads the diversity and inclusion efforts for over 1600 employees in greater Washington DC. He emphasizes the need to give traditionally underrepresented minorities opportunity for business-line positions, such as division managers accountable for fiscal and resources management, often termed "P&L" authority (for profit and loss income statements). This approach contrasts career ladders that run strictly through staff support positions, such as human resource analysts or other job categories that do not directly work with clients or bring in revenue. The rationale for this is dual; first, placement in P&L line jobs is valuable for developing insights and experience in making tough decisions that ensure that the company remains viable. Second, and relatedly, leaders coming from such positions are generally more valued by the rest of the organization than those who have not contributed to its growth or faced a balance sheet.

Many organizations have faced problems, even when the workforce as a whole may include people of traditionally underrepresented demographic categories, with placing these employees in key organizational roles such as in critical functions or positions of influence. For instance, at times companies have relegated women to particular job classes, or below executive levels, rather than allowing or encouraging their entry into more meaningful P&L positions. Johnson came up through a business line, but notes,

> We have over 52,000 employees and in my last job, out of 42 markets, I was the only person of color who ran a market for the last seven years, who had both P&L and balance sheet responsibility for that market.

PNC is working to create more opportunities for those underrepresented at the executive levels which, as Johnson explains, includes looking carefully at the data:

> We drill down on the percentages that truly represent the populations that we have within PNC. The information that you'll see, I think, in most corporate social responsibility score cards are, in my view, far too broad. They don't drill down nearly specifically enough to have an idea of how [hiring and promotion practices differentially] touch your men, women, and the various ethnic groups that fall within the company.

PNC also supports affinity and mentoring groups, such as a long-running "Women's Connect" for early career females, and a more recent initiative, a black leaders forum. These programs create bonds among managers and future leaders, expose them to corporate decision-makers, and generally help them to see possible promotion ladders within the company. Progress in this area is moving along well, as Johnson notes:

*For the first time, PNC appointed two black leaders to our Executive Committee – Richard Bynum [*as Chief Corporate Responsibility Officer*], who was formerly the regional president for greater Washington the seat that I'm now sitting in, and Carol Brown, Head of Asset Management. I think that this was meaningful.*

Focus on the work, but do not forget the people. **Gaurdie Banister** was identified early in his engineering career as a high potential employee with the demeanor of a leader. In keeping with advice above to stay close to a core area of the company's business, he credited his success to his work proficiency. Speaking in the context of one of his former employers, he notes that "*as a company, Shell values technical work. In order to be successful going up through the ranks, you had to prove your technical chops.*" As he was promoted, he found that he needed to be more cognizant of the human element:

Now I'm the CEO of the company, and some reactions were "Is he the same guy? Is he going to say hello, does he remember us?" I worked really hard to be personable and still be grounded. My wife helped me a lot in that space too. She makes sure that humility is a character trait for me, you know, in a good way. That was important.

Banister, working in a predominantly White industry, particularly at the top managerial levels, did not overlook the significance of his status as an African American executive. Although he typically focuses on the technical expertise and managerial skill that placed him in top positions, he also has made a point of bringing awareness to companies of diversity and inclusion workforce issues. He recently published a feature article for Corporate Board Member magazine titled "How Black Lives Matter in Corporations – This Time Can Be Different.[3]" **Banister** wrote in his essay,

Companies have the opportunity to drive change deeper to get at the root of the problems. Directors must first get past the naivete of believing that the systemic racism and injustice encountered by Black Americans does not exist in their companies.

---

[3]Banister, B. (n.d.). *How Black Lives Matter in Corporations—This Time Can Be Different*. Corporate Board Member. Retrieved from https://boardmember.com/how-black-lives-matter-in-corporations-this-time-can-be-different/.

<u>Find your kitchen cabinet</u>. As will be demonstrated throughout this book, many leaders emphasized the need to find people with whom the leader can share and explore ideas, vent or commiserate, or simply confide. These individual or groups of people, as resource or refuge, can take many forms, and they represent a useful strategy for those who are in positions of "being first" or are seen to be embodying a traditionally underrepresented category of people. **Banister** called this group his "kitchen cabinet" of informal advisors, which he developed over time and kept separate from his official organizational relationships. When asked whether he had shared, during his rise in the oil industry, experiences that seemed unique to his standing as an underrepresented minority, **Banister** responded,

> *I didn't discuss it with anyone in Shell, but I did discuss it with my kitchen cabinet. When you're the only one, and I mean I was the highest-level African American exec for a time at Shell.... I never had that discussion directly inside the company, just because I didn't think it was safe. I worked in other venues like the Executive Leadership Council and other groups with African American senior executives who had similar experiences. We could share what our strategies were, what we did that was successful for us, or what was not successful. ... I was struggling, though. That's why I think all senior executives should have coaches; they should have people outside the system who they can share things with, in a safe way, where they don't have the risk that people will misinterpret it.*

2.3   Navigating the Insider Path

The promoted path is a highly appealing path, mostly because there are so many more knowns than other paths and because it tends to be a natural progression for a job well done. That said, over-familiarity with the organization, its internal workings and existing relationships can become a burden. Every new position is an opportunity to reset, refocus, and build on past experiences. As leaders navigate the promoted path, it may be beneficial to consider the perspective of an external hire, and how an outsider would approach the position differently.

In the Appendix we include tool 2.3 <u>My Personal Onboarding Plan</u>. Few organizations onboard the internal promotion to the same degree as they would onboard an outside hire. Nevertheless, while some needs might not exist, many still do. Successful leaders on the promoted path will therefore own their own onboarding and adapt a traditional onboarding process to their own experience.

Reflection Questions

- What is your personal readiness to not only be promoted, but to be ready to tackle the leadership challenges of the next level?
- What is your post-promotion plan? What will you prioritize? Who will you speak to, inside and outside of your organization?
- What is the organizational story around your promotion? How will that support your leadership?
- How will your relationships change as a result of your promotion? How will you manage them differently than you did in the past?

3

Outsider: The Hired Path

Before I took the job at MWAA [Metropolitan Washington Airports Authority], I had limited knowledge of the aviation industry. As it turned out, that was an advantage because I wasn't constrained by preconceived assumptions. The more I dug in, the more obvious it was that it was simply running a business. There were a lot of commonalities to the challenges facing the U.S. Post Office in terms of modernizing while keeping the business running. I was able to apply my Postal experience to MWAA. For example, like all other airports and businesses in general, we were facing a challenge of moving into a digital world, which required modernizing the organization's IT infrastructure and providing the necessary IT security. As an outsider I could see that very quickly; the key was to connect it to the economic model that airports operate on and the perspective of the people making decisions. Most decision makers did not view the airports authority as being a business, but rather as a service. They viewed it as a government operation and didn't consider that their employment is contingent on delivering results—passenger growth, efficiency, customer service, and profits.
*—**Jack Potter**, President & Chief Executive Officer, MWAA*

Leaders coming into organizations as "outsiders" are often enticed by high-value compensation and the prospect of career progression, making this path highly pursued and traveled. There are both opportunities and challenges inherent in the path. On the plus side, they may be valued by those

© The Author(s), under exclusive license to Springer Nature Switzerland AG 2021
M. A. Clark and M. Persily Lamel, *Six Paths to Leadership*,
https://doi.org/10.1007/978-3-030-69017-5_3

within the organization who see the new leaders as talent needed to reach expanding goals, as experts who fill a specific need, or as connections to specific target markets. On the other hand, leaders may also run into resistant cultures, complex organizational systems, or inconsistent messages about what is important.

In this chapter, we discuss these opportunities and challenges for leaders hired from outside of the organization, in most cases after having significant professional experience or building important credentials. In addition to our familiarity with hiring processes and their impacts in the fields where we have worked, personally or with clients, we distill wisdom offered by those executives interviewed in the course of our research. Our interviewees include leaders with experiences at companies such as Mars, Danone, GlaxoSmithKline, Nike, and many others. Supported by their insights and stories, we outline factors that influence the success of hired leaders and strategies to maximize opportunities and address challenges.

3.1 The Outsider: Opportunities and Strategies of the Hired Path

Table 3.1 Hired path: Outsider opportunities and strategies

Hired path opportunities	Strategies for leveraging
1. New perspective	• Determine readiness for change • Provide objective insights without criticizing past work • Listening tour
2. Expertise from outside	• Show how expertise fits the organization • Give input with empathy, sensitivity, and caution
3. External networks	• Utilize and share network relationships
4. Perception of earned hire	• Explore reasons for hire and how they were communicated • Align new ideas with strategy • Leverage the surrounding talent
5. Been there, done that	• Understand the relevant factors in the new organization
6. Willingness to take risks and introduce changes	• Inquire about past change efforts at the new organization

3.1.1 New Perspective

Perhaps the most basic reason to hire talent from outside the organization is to acquire novel perspectives from the external labor market. To build or continue success in our rapidly changing world, organizations must continually incorporate understanding of evolving markets into their strategy, adjusting tactics and reshaping their workforce to meet current and future demands. Bringing in an outsider, as **Jack Potter** described above, can help an organization to rethink how they do business. In his own experience moving to MWAA, he describes how the perspective shift applied beyond the employees to include the governing board of the organization (Table 3.1).

When it comes to mindsets that drive success in an organization, everyone must be in sync with the board of the institution. As government appointees, some MWAA board members viewed the airports as a service and, therefore, were less sensitive to the needs of the airlines, who ultimately make decisions about which airports they use. Some board members strongly believed that our government-owned airports should be built as the equivalent of monuments, valuing form over function. But the airlines would have to bear the cost of any investment in the facilities, so we had to strike a balance. This brings me back to the point that bringing this outside perspective is very healthy for an organization. I had to promote a change in a culture that resisted change and needed to move more toward a business approach.

This raises an important question of how to introduce this perspective so that it will be successfully adopted in the new organization. The leaders we interviewed offer suggestions.

Determine readiness for change. Externally hired leaders should not assume that everyone in the new organization is ready or willing to value their perspective. This readiness to accept an outside point of view is needed, as **Potter** explains, to gain from the new hire's perspective.

Sometimes an outsider will be afforded greater credibility to present new ideas because those ideas are viewed as being based on actual experiences in other businesses. However, there is a limit to that acceptance, and it is built on the need to relate to the business at hand. I've had that experience, and I now counsel folks coming into organizations that they are being given an opportunity for a seat at the table. I encourage newcomers that it is very important for them to learn from and understand the folks they are working with, what had been considered previously by the institution, and what may not have gotten traction due to the inertia of the organization. There still is a need to overcome that inertia. The challenge is to put together a convincing argument and portray it as a consensus idea, rather than just something being imposed. As an outsider, you have a short-lived advantage to bring new perspective to the table before you become part of the fabric of the institution. But the best way to make an impact is to start by listening to people's ideas and understanding the historical approaches of the institution, then address those challenges using your unique, outside experience. The trick is to incorporate those ideas into the fabric of the institution, not just impose them.

Provide objective insights without criticizing past work. Sometimes the need for a new perspective is very specific, in response to an event or circumstance originating outside the organization, which provides an aura of objectively necessary change. **Stephanie Davis** was brought into Volkswagen Group of America as Chief Ethics & Compliance Officer in 2017, not long after the Volkswagen parent company had agreed to pay a $15 billion settlement in response to a very public automobile emissions controversy. **Davis** explained that as an external hire she based her input on the reason she was hired, rather than dwelling on past company missteps or the people who may have made mistakes. She needed to understand her own source of differing perspective, both in relation to her personal and professional characteristics, to hone her message so that it would be well-received.

At Volkswagen worldwide, 200000 people are in management positions, 20000 of them women. That's 10%, and fewer in top management where I am. So, we like to hire and promote people that are like us; in Volkswagen's case, I think that's doubly true. But bringing in a fresh perspective, it's not just a female thing. It's also that I haven't been here for 25 years; I didn't start together on the factory floor and work my way up. I have a different perspective and I have, because of my consulting background and my legal background, maybe a broader view from a compliance perspective than a lot of people have in this organization. So when I said, "OK, we need to do this many trainings, we need to focus on this, this, and this". People said, "Oh, I never thought to do it that way." Right? Because they hadn't been other places.

Listening tour. New leaders on most paths could benefit from launching a listening tour,[1] as described in the previous chapter of this book. Such an effort can help to effectively leverage the opportunity inherent in a fresh perspective, in support of assessing readiness and providing insights without criticizing past work. Outsider leaders can accomplish this process by prioritizing time to meet with their stakeholders, including direct reports, peers, and others to learn about their ideas, concerns, and goals. For outside hires,

---

[1]The post-hire listening tour may not as critical, for instance, in the elected and appointed paths, as they often have clearer directives and possibly prior knowledge of the stakeholder expectation.

this can be especially critical due to their lack of organizational connections and history which can help them to effectively do their job. Thus, the potentially unique angle for outside hires is that the leaders can emphasize both ideas and relationships, in that they want to use their expertise to help their stakeholders to be more effective, and that they are seeking to build ties with each particular stakeholder, without the burden of previous relationships in the organization. When possible, the content or questions of a listening tour for the external hire should be informed by insights from others. When leaders work with an HR partner or their manager to identify not only whom to speak with, but also what information and experiences they should inquire about with specific individuals, their listening tours will be even more informative.

One interviewee, a senior human resource executive at a $75 billion company, discussed his approach to the listening tour for leveraging new perspectives and expertise, both for himself and the senior managers who he advises. Getting in the door of others is buoyed by the outsider credibility, but must be supported by a careful process.

There's always a dance going on; you try to have as many conversations as you can to understand the context. You need to develop situational awareness of what you're walking into. There are different strategies, sometimes you may ask directly, other times there is a bit of reading the tea leaves so to speak, partially because others just don't even know what information you're after, or there are political considerations. Part of it is figuring out what you must do to advance your own agenda, but you also must build capital. So, help them with something to make them look good, in order to get the help that you need.

3.1.2 Expertise from Outside

Along with seeking a novel perspective, organizations drawing from external labor markets are typically hoping to gain new sets of skills through their hires. These valued skills are often scarce within the hiring organization and can be related to specific education and credentialing, but at higher levels of management often more directly related to experiences the new hire has had with other companies within the industry, whether competitors, logistic chain allies, or simply organizations which use analogous processes.

Michael Waldron describes his experience when joining Bayview Loan Servicing, a Texas firm that has serviced over $600 million in loans.

One meeting was around an operational issue, and folks were wrestling with how to operationalize a change. They clearly had been at this for some time; there were high-level folks in a room all expressing frustration that they hadn't figured this out yet, despite best efforts. This was very early on in my debut, but I was able to communicate that this was not an issue unique to this platform. There was nothing, as I understood it, being contemplated that others in the industry hadn't already addressed, so there was no reason for us to feel as if we were on our own. I think it gave me kind of an early win right out of the gates, especially because it wasn't a compliance related item. I'm the CCO, but it also showed that I have the ability to add to the business beyond just wearing the legal or compliance hat.

In this example **Waldron**'s expertise extends beyond the ostensible limits of his specific job to include his understanding of the industry, which allows him to contribute significantly to strategic operational decisions.

Show how expertise fits the organization. Good organizations are often proactive in how they recruit for both specific and general industry expertise. Companies may "steal" talent from competitors, or look to allied agencies who have studied their competitors. It is often still up to outside hires to recognize what they are being recruited for and demonstrate this to their new colleagues. This is true not just for the entry position, but also the understanding of the potential career ladder that may be possible if they align their expertise with the trajectory of the company. **Sumit Roy,** President & CEO of Realty Income Company, describes how his expertise as a financial analyst of his future employer's industry led to his recruitment and eventual rise to the top.

I was in investment banking at UBS, covering commercial real estate companies, and my UBS colleague John left for Realty. He reached out to me for a strategic capital markets discussion, which quickly turned to a pitch for me to join Realty. I think fundamentally why that conversation happened was that the company was going through a changing of the guards, if you will. Tom had been the CEO since the company had gone public, the company was just coming out of the Great Recession still very solid and at a point where succession planning was being contemplated. My previous role gave me industry insights.

When I first joined Realty we were about 70 people and $6 billion [enterprise]. Today we are a 163 people, $22 billion enterprise, so we've gone through a major metamorphosis. There was anticipation that this growth could happen and that's why people like me were being brought in, to help this company take this journey, to build off the advantages we had and to accelerate the pace. Then when I was *allowed to take leadership, I was probably the only one qualified to run the transition. I think that people could see what I brought to the table, and it confirmed their original beliefs. This put me on a very solid footing.*

Similarly, the Parkinson's Foundation CEO **John Lehr** found himself in high demand due to the unusual combination of relevant experiences in his background, which he had to demonstrate through his recruitment and subsequent actions upon hire.

When I was being recruited for my current position, the board was very interested in three things in particular. One was that I had merged two nonprofit organizations before, which is not done often at the national level. Also, I knew how to organize a volunteer-driven organization to change the course of a disease. Finally, I had run a $175 million major giving campaign at the Cystic Fibrosis Foundation. I don't take credit for its success. I had a role in it, and with an amazing team it just came together. But that was the thing that was so interesting to them, because the Cystic Fibrosis Foundation is widely acknowledged to be a model of success in the disease-specific space. They thought, "Well, this guy knows how to do some of the things that we want to do." So I think coming in from the outside with a fresh perspective and a certain skill set is what helped win the role.

Give input with empathy, sensitivity, and caution. **Ed Ahn**, speaking in relation to his former role as Chief Technology and Strategy Officer at Anika Therapeutics, stressed that it was important for an incoming leader not only to mine their new company for information, but also to acknowledge the work and passion of those who had been working in the organization prior to the leader's arrival.

I would say that patience and compassion is important to leaders coming from outside. There is a pre-existing culture, and others may have had a very different way of approaching leadership. You may not be able to accomplish as much as you want, because there is a collective of people that are making decisions that I don't have control over.

Similarly, **Michael Waldron** discusses situations, noted through his work as outside legal counsel, where the outside hire must demonstrate sensitivity in building support and implementing changes that he or she was brought into enact.

Leaders brought in from the outside are hired with expectations that they will accomplish specific goals, so should bring as much change as is necessary to achieve success for their new organizations, but with sensitivity to their new colleagues. The idea is first to leverage the good done by those who have gone before, making sure that changes are actually improvements, whether focused on gaps or different philosophies. Then, make changes where needed, but always with an understanding that many of those who will be helping to implement those changes could be the same people who structured the operation initially.

Effectively, external hires must consider limiting or buffering their direct critiques of prior managerial practices, at least in consideration of those of their new colleagues who may have been aligned with the outside hire's predecessor.

Finally, it should be noted that the line of caution may be taken not just to benefit the new leader, but also the organization. A CEO of a midsized medical company, who preferred not to disclose his identity due to the sensitivity of who he refers to below, explains

I think where I struggled was just trying to work within the organization. I knew that the previous CEO had a reputation for being difficult. So my role as a C-level executive was to buffer him, and to protect the rest of the organization from him. There was a lot more that we were doing as damage control, rather than leading.

3.1.3   External Networks

Hiring from outside the organization yields not just leaders with their own talents, but also with their professional and personal networks of contacts. These networks represent sources of information and support, not only for the new hire, but also for the organization. Many of the new hire's contacts are likely to be in comparable or complementary organizations, providing opportunity for innovative ideas and useful comparisons. As **Michael Waldron** discusses, he was able to help Bayview Loan Servicing through the connections he had built at earlier stops in its career.

There was a real ability to leverage my own industry relationships, due to having previously been in other shops. I think most importantly and most formative having been outside legal counsel and an advisor to the industry and having the experience of literally counseling hundreds of different companies. I could reach out to former clients and industry friends to survey how they've handled this issue, then come back to my leadership team with some industry intel. They saw very quickly that there is value in those types of relationships.

The value of this network may be augmented when hiring across industry lines, such as from government to corporate. The contacts that a new hire brings with them, as well as their specific knowledge of how things get done in allied or dependent organizations, will often save the hiring organization resources that they would have otherwise spent on expert consulting. Experts hired from senior levels of government agencies or Congressional staffs, for instance, are likely to have a deep understanding of policy issues and an extensive network of contacts within the government. **Shawn Whitman**, Vice-President of FMC Corporation and former Chief of Staff to two US Senators, explains:

> *Working on the Hill[2] gives you a vast collection of relationships, a rolodex. The key when coming into FMC was finding relatability of this Washington DC world, establishing and explaining what the political world means to my new colleagues. If someone is head of supply chain and is facing new tariffs on key products, I explain how the process works with the US Trade Department, including the decision points and influencers. This opens their mind to the art of the possible and unlocks my value for them.*

Utilize and share network relationships. Leaders coming from outside the organization should use their networks to increase their own effectiveness for the betterment of the organization. Leaders can probe for areas of need in the organization and match with their external connections. **Tami Majer**, Chief Human Resource Office at 24HourFitness, believes that leaders should use their networks as mentors and guides, helping to plan their strategic moves, and continue to develop them further both inside and outside the organization.

> *There should be a balance between flexing your muscle – showing what you know – and having patience in the learning process. It's really important to take the time to form a good opinion on the nuances of the organization you enter, understand the formal and informal power networks, and start to build relationships. When hired as a senior leader, the temptation is to start too fast, getting ahead of your skis before you really understand the organization and the consequences of your actions.*

Majer goes on to suggest that a way to better understand is to

> *balance your agenda with relationship building. What I tried to do was to take time to listen, learn, and build relationships. Get to know others on a personal level, not just a professional level; really invest in your team.*

---

[2]The term "Capitol Hill" or "the Hill" denotes working with U.S. Congress in Washington DC.

Leaders may also choose to share these valuable ties with their new colleagues. It should be noted that there may be some risk in disclosing ties and making connections. A network tie carries not only information and access, but also the reputation of each person involved, and therefore must be treated with caution. To address this, leaders should first focus on developing trusting relationships with those with whom they would share, and also to assess appropriate need for access.

In crossing over to his latest leadership path, as externally-hired DeVry University President and CEO **Tom Monahan** discusses how his background and network of relationships has value in his new role.

> *I took what I learned from my time at CEB, where we helped evaluate tech sector careers, to connect to the mission of DeVry. The core of what we do here is pretty cool; we help our many non-traditional college students to get better jobs. Higher education as a sector can do better on employer connectivity; I can leverage my background to lead the effort here at DeVry.*

As referred to in Chapter 2, our Appendix tool 2.1 Personal Network Analysis and Action Plan can help newly hired leaders to assess the network that they bring to their new organization, accounting for its reach, strengths, and any gaps that should be filled.

3.1.4   Perception of Earned Hire

By virtue of being recruited, with some presumption of the value of the perspectives and expertise described above for the organization, leaders entering as outside hires are often deemed worthy of their positions or at least will be given opportunity to be successful within their role. As one executive who we interviewed describes,

> *Coming in from the outside, people look to you as the leader. There is a credibility from the organization for knowing the industry. They know that you were brought in because of general expertise, but they are waiting to see how you apply it in a particular context.*

Explore reasons for hire and how they were communicated. To leverage this presumption of value, externally hired leaders should offer their input within their clear areas of expertise, particularly early in their position. Building on her clear expertise in legal compliance, **Stephanie Davis** used this earned perception to enhance her effectiveness at Volkswagen.

People respected where I was before this; my KPMG legal background [where Davis was Director of Regulatory Compliance] makes them more apt to listen to me although I am very young for this role and often the only woman in the room. I've never had anyone question why I was here or not take me seriously. However, we previously had someone in a similar role, who came from the head office in Germany on a three-year contract, and he was not really taken seriously, in part because he was an insider. I think that coming from the outside for this particular role was absolutely necessary. I have earned authority because I am an expert in the field; no one questions that.

Align ideas with strategy. To truly excel, such leaders should leverage their opportunity to introduce new ideas early in their tenure, when their halo may be relatively untainted. **Jeff Nally** suggests that one way to address this is to clarify the core issues and speak to the strategic center of the organization, aligning with those who can help achieve the change that the leader is hired to enact.

Being hired as an external person, it was "we need what you know and what you've done, because we don't have that here." When I moved to Clarcor from Commonwealth Aluminum, it was a much smaller manufacturing firm, but they had bought six competitors and were bringing six different brands of air filters together. So the notion was "who can lead HR across 13 different organizations with 13 different HR managers and think like a large, huge manufacturing for profit publicly-traded company?" And that was me. So I got a grace period. HR was run at the locations by 13 different people. So my modus operandi was "how close can I get to the President, and the senior leadership team, to make the new strategy happen?"

Leaders in this position might benefit from the use of a tool mentioned earlier, 2.3 My Personal Onboarding Plan.

Leverage the surrounding talent. **Mike Nolte** relates that his skillset, built through prior leadership positions in healthcare business and consulting, gave him credibility as he began the CEO role of Influence Health. He later became CEO of Signant Health. At Influence Health, he leveraged his background through the somewhat uncommon tactic of retaining the former CEO in an active management role.

He actually still works for me, which is a little bit of an unusual dynamic. He was fundamentally a sales guy, a really strong leader, but essentially the complexity of the business had gotten to a point where they needed someone else. During the transition we made a play to keep the prior CEO on board as the chief customer officer, running sales and client management. We did that with, as you can imagine, a reasonable probability of not working out great. But it's actually been fantastic, so far for 18 months.

As **Nolte** intimates, there were risks inherent in keeping the former chief executive around in an active role, such as potential for divided loyalty among the employees or the threat of undermining his own authority. However, **Nolte**'s strong standing as an outside hire with needed skills enabled him to successfully navigate roles for both executives.

3.1.5   Been There, Done That

While few words from a new employee may grate like "at my last employer, we did things *this* way," it should be obvious that external hires will be expected to draw on knowledge gained in their former roles and organizations. For the leader, bringing in past experience must be done skillfully, choosing moments and giving credit to what has gone before. As outlined by one executive who was spent 20 years being promoted through the ranks at one company, only to take a mid-career move to a rival later in his career,

> *It took me a while to assimilate this. When you join you need to respect what is, understand what has gone before, create hope and then your twist of what more you can bring. But don't think the first thing that an organization needs is the "new" that you can bring. First, they want to be respected for who they are already, and I learnt that the hard way.*

Understand the relevant factors in the new organization. The tendency to act according to the dictates of his or her experience may also pose a challenge to an outside hire who may too quickly believe that their past successes provide a perfect template for addressing issues in their new organization. **Jay Hammer**, CEO of Theralogix, points out that even when organizations that may look similar from the outside, leaders should be careful of assuming that they operate in the same way.

> *When I went to Gap, it was clear that they were a big organization just like Macy's, where I had grown up in real business. Those companies shared a lot of the same operational, organizational, and hierarchical structures. Yet at Macy's, I was responsible for the very lowest level even with an MBA. I was still opening up boxes in the housewares department, and if all the pots weren't facing in the right direction, that was my fault.*

Gap was different. I was intentionally hired as a reaction to a completely home-grown kid who started as a stock person, who was tough and street smart. I was essentially the antithesis of that, as the preppy MBA who had already excelled in another organization and knew how to run a team of several hundred people. So it becomes important when you're hired from the outside to take the time to assess – "what are the norms that I can't mess around with? What are the performance metrics that aren't going to change?" There's a lot more assimilation, more inflexibility. and there's a lot more self-reflection that you have to do about "how am I going to get done what I think I've been hired to do?" and what I want to do in an environment that is already established.

It is apparent that new leaders must give close attention to the idiosyncratic factors and practices in their new organizations, rather than assume they can simply duplicate practices from their former organizations. This awareness, combined with developing a competitor profile, will enable leaders to develop their core messages. The tool 3.2 Competitor Profile found in the Appendix can help leaders to organize insights about how their new colleagues view other organizations, including points of admiration, critiques, and cultural comparisons that can serve as a basis for leveraging the competitor experience for the good of the organization.

3.1.6   Willingness to Take Risks and Make Changes

One clear advantage for the external hire, in many cases built upon the opportunities discussed above, is the license to take risks and make changes. Leaders hired from the outside can capitalize on this opportunity, particularly during the grace period that is often granted in the first few months on the job. In this time frame, changes may be expected or at least accepted from newly hired Outsiders, and missteps may be attributed to a lack of familiarity, with forgiveness more likely. But the willingness to take risks when needed can help the leader to make changes when strategically useful. For instance, **John Lehr** tells of his entrée into the Parkinson's Foundation, where his past success in merging non-profits and his lack of favoritism for either of the component organizations buttressed his ability to broker the merger. Further, as a new leader from the outside he was not beholden to the inertia of earlier decisions, so was more willing to take risks without this historical baggage.

As an outsider coming in, I saw that they have these assets; a center of excellence network and a Parkinson's outcomes project. But what's the impact of that? How are they helping the greater community? They were still in their initial stages and needed to ask "okay, what's next?" So my strength was that I had no allegiance to either of the legacy organizations, and could think about the broader goals. I think that was helpful in winning over the team.

As Outsider leaders initiate changes, especially when entering more traditional organizations, their intentions are likely to be questioned or even assumed. It is therefore critical for such leaders to center themselves in what they believe is truly best for the business. **Jack Potter**, President and CEO of Metro Washington Airports Authority and former US Postmaster General, believes that values such as integrity should drive any attempts at change, which helps to balance out and calculate the worth of risk undertaken.

People in these big organizations were traditionally rewarded for being "yes men." It takes courage for a leader to step outside of the mainstream. There are pre-requisites that you need to establish in order to have credibility. You have to have integrity. You have to do your homework. You have to be a performer. Those credentials enable you to introduce change. If you don't have that foundation, you're not going to succeed. People respect a person who performs, is serious minded, and gets things done. This enables that person to promote change because there is a confidence that it is a betterment, rather than a sales job or a "program of the day." Allowing people to engage in conversation about the merits of how things should be done, and being flexible about how to achieve a goal, keeps everyone focused on the mission as opposed to the politics of who's leading the charge.

As we have seen, the Outsider path is filled with opportunities that leaders can leverage to achieve success:

- Leveraging new perspective, expertise, networks, and perception to provide insights that fit the organization's direction, while being careful not to overly criticize nor to assume that it should be automatically accepted or without criticizing past work.
- Familiarity with ideas, processes, and systems that with care can work in the new organization.
- Willingness to take steps that insider colleagues may believe to be risky, as long as they are planned to support the organization.

The Listening Tour Action Plan referenced earlier (see Appendix 2.2) may be especially useful for leaders who are outside hires, providing a tool for leaders to get to know their stakeholders, probe for existing practices that are working well or that need revision, and assess receptivity for new ideas.

Next, we will discuss the challenges that the Outsider may encounter along the hired path.

3.2 Outsider: Challenges and Strategies of the Hired Path

Table 3.2 Hired path: Outsider challenges and strategies

Hired path challenges	Strategies for managing
1. Cultural assimilation	• Get involved (e.g., well-planned listening tour, observation, ask questions, engage informally)
2. Not knowing: Who and what	• Proactive approach to relationship development
3. Organization onboarding deficiency	• Own your onboarding • Identify and reach out to key stakeholders
4. Identification with former organization brand (especially competitors)	• Work intentionally to earn trust of colleagues • Show objectivity with regard to former company
5. Lack of support from rivals	• Emphasize the value of potential rivals on the team
6. In the fishbowl (visibility)	• Plan and intentionally manage impressions when entering the new organization

Leaders hired from the outside often have many strengths desired by the organization, but in order to effectively use them, they should be mindful of a number of challenges. As they transition from outsiders to members of the organization, leaders may encounter limitations related to their own knowledge and experiences, or of the perceptions and beliefs of others. As shown in the hired path "Challenges" table, these limitations relate to the leader's understanding of the organization's culture, their relationships within and knowledge of the new organization, their process of learning, and their identification with their past employers. The way newly hired leaders are seen by others also relates to this identification, as well as support from rivals, visibility, and unknown or emerging reputation (Table 3.2).

3.2.1 Cultural Assimilation

When new leaders enter an organization, they are faced not just with tasks and responsibilities, but also with understanding the less explicit norms and expectations of how the people of the organization work together. In the recruitment and selection process, the incoming leader and the organization would have been likely to each assess their fit with one another, but it is generally difficult to fully acculturate until a person is immersed in the everyday working environment. Similarly, organizational members will make their own assessments about whether the new leader fits their expectations. Becoming acclimated to a culture is then more than just learning the ropes; it is accepting the values, goals, and the organization's means of fulfilling them. While this does not imply that the leader's values will merely come to duplicate those of the organization, because there is typically room for some diversity in values and approaches, the desirable result is for leaders to be clear on how they will support and extend the organizational culture.

Culture goes beyond the strictly operational work processes to include more subjective and sometimes personal standards and expectations for behavior that give an organization its own particular style. One senior executive describes learning this, soon after being hired as an executive at Nike.

> *Nike was a harder transition for me coming from my previous employer, a large family-run company, because it was a much more hierarchical organizational structure than I had ever experienced. My previous company was very flat and egalitarian. At Nike, others might be a bit reluctant to give you time in onboarding if you weren't clear on how you might benefit them. This was hard for me in getting to understand the business. It also challenged my ability to feel connected with the culture.*

While organizations often make an effort to assess their hires for cultural fit, external leaders often find themselves in the situation that the executive above describes. It can be difficult to adjust to new organizational assumptions, prompting some to question whether the move was the right one for them.

The words used by an organization, including technical terms, titles, and buzzwords, as well as styles and speaking mannerisms, can seem like a barrier to those who have not quite crossed the threshold to be an insider. The language and manner of expressing ideas may represent how people in the organization expect to be treated. As **Stephanie Davis**, who generally found that she fit in well with Volkswagen of North America, relates,

> *Early on I found that I wasn't speaking the language of the organization, maybe not knowing where the pressure points are. So if I offhandedly said something like, "Well, clearly we were doing that wrong in the past" I wouldn't know who I'm insulting. That's been tough for me because this company, more than many*

companies, has its own shorthand. They typically don't really like outsiders; it's very insular.

One senior executive's experience in joining a Fortune 100 American firm from one of its European rivals had some similarities. He found the executives and company culture to be very impressive, but different from what he had been used to.

The executive who recruited me was pretty heavy hitting, the most senior woman [in the company] now. She and I got off to a difficult start. We couldn't find common ground and I think some of it came down to accepting the language in the way the business talked about itself, and therefore speak the language of business, stop fighting and rebelling against it. Even though I found it eccentric to start with.

He found that acclimating to the culture at his new firm was worthwhile, however.

If you know [the company], it is by all accounts one of the top tier most difficult companies to join in that it has one of the strongest cultures. It can be very polarizing and the success rate for staying up the two years is actually quite low. Yet they have success in long-term retention.

This executive points out that there is a skillset needed for those who come from the outside, in order to successfully socialize by gaining new skills and shedding some former practices, as part of adapting to the new organization.

I'll say that I completely undervalued the skill needed in leaving one company and joining a new culture. So to some degree you just get knocked off until you're more in the mold of what the culture wants. At 12 months in, I had to ask, do I stay, or do I go?

He found success in socializing to the strong culture, and as of this writing has remained with the American company, continuing in his position as an operational division president.

Job moves across industries and geography can increase culture assimilation difficulties, as related by **Sumit Roy** of Realty Income.

There were many changes, some anticipated, some not. The biggest challenge I faced was how long would it take for my family to adjust to a new environment, and also for me to adjust to the differences between an investment banking lifestyle versus a senior level management team.

What exacerbated the situation was the geographic move to San Diego. We were uncertain that it would ultimately be a good thing but really it was just a question of how much time would it take before we all settled in. I recognized that things were going to be somewhat more deliberate in a corporate environment than it had been in investment banking, so just learning how to adjust to that pace, learning how to sort of slow down and really connect with people, building relationships. I'll tell you now on the back end, it was one of the most satisfying journeys that I've undertaken.

Another potentially important factor influencing cultural assimilation is that of visually apparent or personal background differences. This may be particularly salient for those leaders who embody historically underrepresented demographic categories, such as gender, racial, or ethnic identity. As discussed in our Promoted Path chapter, being a "first" may amplify the apparent differences, providing significant checks on acceptance and assimilation. Similarly to our recommended strategies for promoted leaders in general, outside hires who are part of an historically underrepresented group may want to find opportunities to share their expertise, and find people outside the organization who can serve as a sounding board.

<u>Get involved (well-planned listening tour, observation, ask questions, engage informally)</u>. To address the challenge of cultural acclimation and assimilation, we recommend tactics that are in many ways similar to those of leaders on other paths: conducting a listening tour of internal stakeholders, spend the time observing and asking questions, solicit and accept invitations for interaction, find ways to engage informally, and learn the language of the business. **Tami Majer** of 24HourFitness describes her approach when moving between executive positions at Mars and Danone.

I was pretty equipped to understand the Danone organization because it's very much like Mars, so I knew culturally that it was a very relationship-based organization. The way you had to network was to figure out who the stakeholders were, getting on their calendars. The White Wave [the company merging with Danone at the time] side was a little different, a bit more traditional, formal, and not quite as open. Very friendly people though, so not at all suspect for a newcomer, but a little bit less used to the "walk in my office and have a chat" approach. It was more about getting through the gatekeeper, the administrative assistant and booking time on the calendar. It was deemed a little odd that I just wanted to walk in; they thought that was a bit forward.

As **Davis** worked through the language issues and spent time communicating with her colleagues at Volkswagen, she realized that she had more in common than she first knew.

> *I've been very pleasantly surprised at how quickly they have adjusted to my presence and to the role of compliance in the organization. I'm sure part of that is because there's a lot of Germans on the executive team who value directness. I've been someone my whole life who kind of gets called out for being direct and so much to the point. We kind of make jokes that that's the reason the Germans loved me. And the reason that Americans think I'm a jerk [laughs].*

The work involved is to connect to the culture and the people in the way that best fits their expectations.

3.2.2   Not Knowing: Who and What

A significant difficulty for new leaders coming from outside is to capture enough of the organizational story to be effective—learning the players and their proclivities, the key stakeholders and processes, the tasks and the operations of the business.

Getting to know the specifics of the organization's purpose, mission, and operations is no easy task. **Jack Potter** of MWAA suggests that one tactic is to simply ask employees directly, particularly if they are chafing with ideas that they have not been able to test in the past.

> *In my experience, one of the biggest mistakes made by leadership is consulting everybody except the people doing the job when they want to affect a positive change. The best way to improve an operation is to ask the people performing the operation how they could make things better. In short, listen. Then, if what they say makes sense, let them do it. In the best-case scenario they now have ownership and have been successful. In the worst-case scenario it doesn't work and they are open to new ideas. Using that methodology, I took a small geographic area in the Postal Service from worst service to best in the country, and all I did was embrace the ideas that made sense and that people already wanted to do.*

The leader can also use this knowledge to determine how they fit in and provide value to the people of the organization. This can be particularly challenging for Outsider leaders who cross industry lines, where formerly familiar markers of value are no longer well-understood. **Shawn Whitman** of FMC recounts his experience in moving from government staff to corporate environment.

Coming into private sector organizations unfamiliar with government affairs, there is a lack of understanding about you and your capabilities. The importance of your previous relationships on the Hill may mean nothing in your new environment. Your former boss may be an influential Senator and chair of an important committee, but that won't matter to your new colleagues if they don't know your boss and haven't heard of the committee. That can be a humbling reality to feel like you've fallen from the heights of politics and now be at the bottom.

Given its importance and relatively large challenge, we offer strategies for learning about the people and purpose of the organization. At heart, leaders should take a proactive approach to relationship-building. This encompasses a few methods, simple to understand but often difficult to successfully accomplish.

- Outsider leaders should seek to build currency with new colleagues, getting to know their needs and matching it with what the leader can offer of value to their work tasks and concerns.
- Conducting a well-planned "listening tour" can be a useful step.
- Leaders should seek to act with humility, deferring to insiders when possible, and showing appreciation for their support of the leaders' acclimation and learning process.

The leader must adjust in order to be successful. It may be useful to find a guide to help in this process, a mentor inside the organization, an affinity group based on some shared interest or background attribute, an external association or sounding board, or an executive coach who can listen and provide tailored feedback.

Getting to know the organization goes beyond the formally espoused targets and practices. Sometimes it is necessary to get creative to meet the company's goals by determining where compromise may actually be helpful. For instance, **Jay Hammer** shares his dilemma at Gap where the directive for each store manager was to reduce both payroll hours and shortage (essentially, theft from retail shelves by "customers").

Early on I decided that I would make the tradeoff by blowing the payroll goal. I thought those were too tight and I understood that I could pay for it with an improvement in shortage. I tracked it; every extra hour I added in people above the base resulted in a bottom line saving because less was stolen. So I repeatedly blew my payroll goals, but made my profit goal by increasing or decreasing the shortage in my stores. For some people in the organization, the operations and loss prevention unit, that was still bad. So I was a hero, but for the operations guy who wanted me to come in at 7.8% instead of 7.9%, I was a goat. That was OK. When you're brought in from the outside, it can take time to figure out where you can go.

Hammer had a very successful career stint at Gap, perhaps in no small part because he determined which measures really mattered, and planned his actions accordingly.

3.2.3 Organization Onboarding Deficiency

The process of moving from outsider to insider, described as socialization or onboarding, varies widely in its degree of structure and formality. For many leaders, the experience is more self-service than catered to their needs. As one executive puts it,

> *Coming in from the outside, no one can teach you how the business runs. You have to learn that for yourself. At some point you must actually demonstrate that you know how the company makes money, how value is created.*

This executive espouses that even when organizations offer onboarding jump-starts, such as a standard orientation program, they are likely to focus on what happens within the business, it is still up to the leaders to onboard themselves. This self-guided process is necessary and somewhat idiosyncratic, even for seasoned leaders who have successfully acclimated before, because each organization has its own culture, practices, stakeholders, and touchpoint issues.

Sometimes the leader's self-journey is necessitated by a lack of organizational resources, whether due to internal or external factors. **Tami Majer** tells about her experience joining Danone in the midst of its merger with White Wave.

> *There was zero capacity for the organization to plan my arrival, so I was a little bit on my own. When you're coming into a senior-level role you have to take ownership of your onboarding .... So I just set about figuring out who the stakeholders were and got on their calendars.*

In this example, outsiders may need to put on the hat of an insider, who could be more expected to initiate and manage their own onboarding. With this mindset, such leaders can overcome the lack of formal onboarding by taking the reins themselves, proactively seeking the information and support they need to hit the ground running.

Own your onboarding. It's clear that in many cases, organizations do not, and perhaps cannot, tell a leader coming from outside exactly what is most important for the leader to learn. The steps to be taken for an outside hire to plan their own onboarding are perhaps not surprising, but the perspective shift needed to truly take ownership of the process is important. Once a goal for the onboarding experience is set—such as learning how value is created, as suggested above—the steps will include identifying key stakeholders and proactively reaching out to engage them in a version of a listening tour. The manner in which outside leaders engage is also key; as one executive puts it, they must have *the humility to relearn and readjust.* The very act of completing this process, connecting with new direct reports, colleagues, and other stakeholders, will give space for them to view the outsider as a legitimate leader.

Whether onboarding is led by the outside hire or not, one human resource executive in our sample favors any process that will slow down the transition enough for the leader to deeply engage in it. Like many of our other interviewees, he suggests that creating a plan for the first 90 or 100 days may be a good start, but that a true onboarding experience lasts much longer. Some, like **Tami Majer**, suggested that six months is more realistic; others stated that it never really stops. One suggestion was instead of teaching incoming leaders about the business through standard orientation, programs should be more focused on forging relationships among company leaders.

3.2.4 Identification with Former Organization Brand (Especially Competitors)

As human beings, and generally as good employees, it is natural to feel some affiliation and identification with organizations where we have worked. We gift employers not only with our time, but invest talents and energy into our work, often also developing collegial relationships along the way. When we transition across organizations, this overlap of self-concept with a former employer becomes a challenge. Leaders hired from the outside may still think of themselves as members of their previous employers. Even if they do not feel the affiliation, a leader may simply be accustomed to their former ways of doing things. At the same time, members of the new organization may also identify the leader with his or her former organization, whether this is accurate or not.

For example, one executive mentioned above made a big move between rivals, crossing the Atlantic Ocean in the process. He admitted to incongruous feelings about his new position, even when he knew he was giving his best effort.

> *So I'm bringing as much as I can to the job, but then find myself almost like an organ that's being rejected by the body. From the most simple vocabulary that I used, not understanding acronyms. For the first four months felt like I was sleeping with the enemy.... I completely underestimated the skill of managing the emotional states of leaving something that I loved and joining something that I had been forced to beat.... I'll never forget the first time I saw my email address with [my new employer], the company I spent 10 years hating. The enemy had me, it was mine.*

Some who face these challenges manage to effectively adapt, as did this executive. Our strategies below offer steps as to how this may be successfully accomplished.

Work intentionally to earn trust of colleagues. The strategies for addressing the challenges of identification involve demonstrating to new colleagues that the leader is serious about his or her new organization and can be counted on to work for its best outcomes. This means that the leader should not only seek out ways to earn the trust of new colleagues, but in most cases to be very candid about it.

- For instance, outside leaders could explicitly state intentions that are in line with their new organization's interests.
- When referring to the leader's former company, externally hired leaders should show objectivity, rather embellish its performance. This will help to manage colleagues' perceptions that the leader is still an "Outsider." This may take the form of acknowledging deficiencies as well as positive characteristics about the leader's former company, and by outlining the differences between the organizations that may influence effective implementation of benchmarked practices. Finally, it may be good to refrain from overly referencing the leader's previous organization when possible, and instead develop a habit of speaking about ideas from multiple other organizations.

The process of working through disidentification, and adoption of a new organization identity, can also be beneficial to the leader. As **Tami Majer** tells it,

Sometimes you can reinvent yourself when you start fresh with a new company. If you're smart about it, you can let go of things that have haunted your past; you come in with a fresh start. Everyone has developed a brand that they carry around. Sometimes it's hard to shake that brand, but probably it's a good time to shake it when you start with a new company. Do your own personal inventory, decide what is it about your brand that you want to take forward and what is it about the brand that you want to let go.

3.2.5 Lack of Support from Rivals

Sometimes when you come in from the outside, you're replacing someone who had performed very well. Sometimes you're replacing someone who is being transitioned out.

As **Michael Waldron** intones above, outside hires are typically walking into a situation where others have tried, sometimes failed, and sometimes succeeded. In most cases, the incoming leader was not the only candidate for the role, officially or even in the minds of employees who were already there. Some variant of this situation has been examined across several paths in this book. The special twist for the outside hire is both a threat and an opportunity. The outsider does not necessarily know the lay of the land with regard to those who may not have championed his or her arrival, which could keep the new leader from seeing passive sabotage or other acts of resistance. On the other hand, being hired from outside means he or she will be less likely to carry the biases or hurts related to power dynamics rooted in issues before his or her time.

The best strategy to mitigate this situation may be to simply focus on the collective goal that the leader was hired to address. Following the principles outlined above, leaders should <u>emphasize the value they bring</u> through their perspective, expertise, and networks, using these to craft a positive vision with steps toward the future. **John Lehr** sensed some rivalry when he took the top job at the Parkinson's Foundation.

There was a senior leader on the team interested in becoming the CEO. He was running big programs, but was not necessarily thinking about how to translate those for greater impact in the community. I saw it as my job to move from value to broad impact, and to ask him to take it to the next phase. Lots of programs have value, but not all have lasting impact.

3.2.6   In the Fishbowl (Visibility)

Generally, company leaders will have eyes on them as they go about their jobs. For outside hires, this may be exacerbated due to their novelty, as well as for the expectations placed on them by virtue of being handed the keys to a business that they are just joining. Since outsiders do not typically cut a fully formed image in the mind of their new colleagues, early actions will have an outsized role in filling in the missing information. Therefore the image of incoming leaders, and to some extent their subsequent effectiveness, may be defined by their initial actions and first measures of performance in their new roles.

Probably the most visible first moves of outside leaders will be how they build, retain, and structure their teams. Our tool 3.1 Talent Assessment Action Tree, located in the Appendix, can assist with the process of diagnosing and deploying the leader's team, including identifying the goals and expectations of the team. These early talent decisions build numerous potential narratives such as:

• The leader is focused on themselves OR the leader shows interest in my career growth and advancement
• The leader is willing (or is not) to make the hard talent decisions
• The leader is able to retain (or not) the team's most valuable talent
• The leader is bringing in their own team (or sticking with the inherited team)

By assessing the talent situation early and acting in ways to support their vision for the team, leaders will quickly send the key messages and ideally set themselves up for a successful transition.

This is a particular challenge when the new hire is placed in a situation where immediate action is necessary. **Jack Potter** of MWAA uses decisive leadership tactics, following a code that fits with his organizational values and goals that he believes his organization should track. These decisions are not always what is expected of leaders in his industry, but his direct style and consistency sell them well, and a short while after his arrival, his employees knew what to expect.

While running a Postal Service field operation that had the worst service in the country, I was criticized for not following the usual corporate route of engaging consultants who had been hired by headquarters to conduct process improvement studies. But the recommendations were trying to fix a field problem using an unnecessary level of sophistication; we might use them at some point, but we had to do even more basic things before we'd be ready for their ideas. So, I said to him, "This consultant is brilliant, but he's trying to tell me how to take the top apple off the tree without doing any damage to it. But to the average insider the problems and solutions were obvious. So here I was in the orchard with fruit falling and hitting my head. I didn't need charts, graphs and programs. I just needed a basket to catch the fruit before it hits the ground."

For two years afterward, they left me completely alone and we rose to become the top service area in the country. What made it work was empowering people. I would tell them what needed to be done, they would tell me how they planned to make it happen, and I would say, "hey you got it; we don't need consultants, just go do it." I viewed my job as eliminating distractions from getting the job done. The consultants had become a distraction. When one supervisor told me that they under-performed because they were never trained, I established a two-day training for over 1000 supervisors and all were trained within a month. The excuse/distraction was eliminated and now the supervisor could be held accountable.

These fishbowl effect can bolster these decisive actions, because it is in line with the expectations of the Outsider. As **Michael Waldron** points out, outside hires are often brought in for a particular reason, or at least to take action of some kind.

When you are hired from the outside in a leadership position in the business, the expectation is that you're not going to sit on your hands. You have a voice that's different from others.

Making visible decisions is indeed expected of the newly hired leader, stresses **Tom Monahan**, a seasoned CEO and board member. Further, the decisions may be expected to proceed along particular lines set by those who hired the leader.

If you're being brought in from the outside, it's because we needed, in developing specifications for the new CEO, direction where they want the business taken and the associated need for skills and perspective – operational versus strategic, domestic or global, growth or maintenance. The person stepping into that role must under-stand that, while as an outsider you have a lot of permission to act, it must be within a specific strategy vector for which you are being hired. Further, should you decide to change course, it will require significant conversation and buy-in from the Board.

For example, a Board envisioning growth from M&A may select a CEO who has experience leading growth through acquisitions. There may be times, however, when the hired CEO may not agree with the board's preferred strategy after spending some time at the company. Why? It's simple math. In the best cases, Board members spend 1-2 days per month thinking about the company. After 100 days in role, the new

CEO has already spent the equivalent of four years of a Board Member's time on company business. The new CEO may decide that growth through acquisition is not the right approach because more organic growth is possible or because the company's infrastructure does not yet support it.

As an executive, I have always said, "you can fire me on the spot if I propose something big without starting with the phrase 'As we have been discussing…'." The beaches should be well softened before big decisions. It is critical for a successful CEO to create a shared context with the Board.

Plan entry and intentionally manage impressions. Given these perspectives about the need to take visible actions, sometimes quickly and decisively, there are a few simple strategies to consider. First, before starting a leadership position with a new organization, the outside hire should take the time to consider and plan their entry strategy. This includes the normative plan for the first 90 days, but also may represent a reset from previous roles, and should cover tactics and initial decisions that will intentionally produce a set of first impressions of the leader for the organization, especially key talent decisions and investments. Beyond this initial phase, the outside leader should then reflect on and consider how to further build and manage their own personal brand, creating a development plan that builds on their previous organizational success and challenges.

3.3   Navigating the Outsider Path

In this chapter, we outlined factors that influence the success of hired leaders and strategies to maximize opportunities and address challenges. As with the other paths we describe, some factors and strategies will be familiar, while others are more specific to those leaders who have been hired from the outside.

As one executive cautions,

When coming in from the outside, the higher you go, the riskier it is. I can tell you from my time at [multiple Fortune 100 companies]; the data shows that it can take years for an outside hire to be able to get to the same level of performance as those that are promoted from within.

Hiring leaders from the external market is often the best strategy for organizations to change and grow into what they want to be. For the organization it is a potentially perilous decision, as the incoming leader may have incompatible values, goals, and methods of guiding the workforce. For the leader, there is room to maneuver but also a tight window for success.

Reflection Questions

- Given that outsiders are hired for a reason, how can you best plan for your success in leveraging your external perspective and talents, while making sure to fit well into your new organization?
- What is the organizational story around your hire? How was your arrival positioned with your new team and new peer group? How will that narrative support (or deflect from) your leadership?
- What relationships can you bring with you to your new organization and how will you build your new internal network? What will support you in developing these relationships?
- How can I best use this opportunity to re-set and apply what I have learned from past leadership roles? How can I prevent making the same mistakes and take a new approach?

4

Representative: The Elected Path

When **Connie Morella** changed her party affiliation so that she could vote for a friend in the Republican primary, she never expected to one day run for office. In a few short years, however, she began her 24-year journey as an elected leader, first in the state-level House of Delegates, then representing Maryland's 8th district in the US House of Representatives. As a Republican representing a liberal district, she gained credibility and power as a moderate, voting with Democrats as often as with her own party. **Morella** closed out her political career as US Ambassador to the Organization of Economic Cooperation and Development. As she recalls, Ambassador **Morella** did not intend to seek elected office, but was inspired by social inequalities such as those highlighted by the Equal Rights Amendment (ERA) movement:

> *I couldn't get a credit card without a man signing for me. This was in 1972. Think of what that did to prevent women from any kind of equity, independence, entrepreneurship, etc. So it wasn't until the Equal Credit Act that was to come about. Many professions, many companies would not hire a woman who might have a baby. Or she had to sign an affidavit that if she did have a child, she would be terminated and lose various benefits. Not until the Pregnancy Discrimination Act did we have that change. I remember looking at the newspaper, and there was one section on want ads for women: secretary, clerk, maybe a schoolteacher in a rural section, maybe a nurse. Then I looked at the men's opportunities: construction work, engineer, doctor. Therein you saw a difference. So I became committed, and Maryland did pass the ERA. Second, the women's movement put the movement into me. So that's how I got started. I used to use the expression: if you want to*

M. A. Clark and M. Persily Lamel, *Six Paths to Leadership*, https://doi.org/10.1007/978-3-030-69017-5_4

make things better for the country and your area, you need to have a seat at the table, or you might be on the menu. I ran in 1974.

Ambassador **Morella**'s story, while unique to her circumstances, resonates with the journey of many elected leaders. Those on this path often take their first steps in response to a burning issue or personal incident, channeling this desire for change through even the smallest opportunity to vie for a position on the ballot and a subsequent elected position. As elected leaders, they are voted into their position as representatives of a particular set of constituents, characteristically serving a finite term and often as members of a political party. While we may typically think of those on the biggest stages, such as US Congress and the Presidency, this special brand of leader may be found in city council chambers, school boards, county commissioner offices, professional associations, and elsewhere.

This chapter reviews factors that influence the success of elected leaders—opportunities and challenges—inherent in the elected path. We build our ideas from many sources, including one author's extensive consulting experience with elected officials and their staff, interviews with elected officials at various levels of government, including seven members of the US House of Representatives, one US senator, one state senator, a mayor and county executive, and a city council member. Many professionals who have been congressional staffers also offered insights, including **Brad Fitch**, president, and CEO of the Congressional Management Foundation.[1] Needless to say, there are nearly as many stories of success and failure as there are leaders. Rather than cover all of them, we offer a core set of opportunities and challenges, paired with strategies revealed through our research to leverage and mitigate as needed. As in other chapters, many of the lessons learned from those elected can help understand leadership across varying paths.

---

[1] www.congressfoundation.org.

4.1   Representative: Opportunities and Strategies of the Elected Path

Table 4.1   Elected path: Representative opportunities and strategies

Elected path opportunities	Strategies for leveraging
1. Leader as the entity	• Know vision and know who they are (purpose, values, and skills) • Choose a "role" and practice it • Personally connect with staff, constituencies, and peers (commitment, humility, respect)
2. Clearly delineated authority based on position	• Clearly communicate the services the leader can and cannot provide • Identify creative ways to enhance leader influence, outside of designated authority
3. Power to convene; a seat at the table	• Pursue passion and prioritize impact • Differentiate formal structure and leader interests
4. Responsiveness of stakeholders	• Strategically manage stakeholders; access pre-existing and new networks • Proactively communicate with constituencies and colleagues
5. Ability to help people maneuver the government bureaucracy	• Celebrate wins regularly • Leverage this ability to support those without access
6. Exceptional talent availability	• Hire the best; complement leader skill set and thinking, align with core values and character • Do not hire anyone who cannot be fired • Invest in staff; intentionally manage composition and culture

4.1.1   Leader as the Entity

Perhaps the most striking and distinguishing characteristic of the elected path is the manner in which the leader embodies the path's purpose, operation, and resources. The elected leader is the entity, in terms of being the product and the organization through which their work is accomplished, to a degree beyond most other leadership paths.[2] The persona of corporate leaders such as Howard Schultz and Bill Gates, for example, generally will not stop consumers from buying a Starbucks coffee or using Microsoft software. In elected positions, however, as former Representative **Russ Carnahan** (D-MO[3]) points out, "*those who fail often do not have the right personality or skillset to be an effective legislator,*" which can serve as an entity to drive success on the path (Table 4.1).

The process of being elected may reinforce that the leaders are products to be packaged and marketed according to their attractive features, resonating with particular constituencies. Once elected, they are the visible means and evidence of campaign success as well as the name associated with votes and authored legislation. Even their staff members, through campaigns and while in office, will weight their choice toward working with candidates with whom they personally resonate, as opposed to targeting a company with a particular product line or brand. Elected leaders work with and through other entities, whether City Council or US Congress, but their own organization rises and falls with them. An example of this is the late US Senator John McCain, whose position, expertise, and credibility were dependent on who he was as a person, according to **Brad Fitch** of the Congressional Management Foundation:

> *John McCain had an outsized voice on military matters. He earned his stripes in a prisoner of war camp and in the military. That carries a lot of weight in the legislative process and other areas; usually, it's deeply respected.*

As the entity, the elected leader must have not only vision and skills, but also the confidence of personal self-worth. **Cathy McMorris Rodgers** (R-WA), US Congress representative since 2005, spoke of understanding not only that she was the entity, but that being herself was enough for the job.

> *[Speaker of the House] John Boehner called to ask me to give the response to the State of the Union in January of 2014. I had just given birth, so thought he was calling just to say congratulations. He asked, and I was surprised and uncertain. Because for all those years that somehow I thought I needed to be just a little bit different, act a little bit different, dress different or a be smarter or more articulate*

---

[2]Some parallels as entity exist for other paths, typically to a lesser degree, such as founders and family legacy leaders.

[3]In this book and especially in this chapter, we use the convention of identifying elected leaders by their party and the entity represented. For instance, party abbreviations are "D" for Democrat, "R" for Republican, or "I" for Independent. The entity represented is typically a US state (e.g., NY for New York).

or give a better speech or whatever it was. You drive yourself crazy, just being so critical of yourself. So I said, "Well if you think so, I'll do my best."

He responded, "Cathy, don't overthink it. Just be yourself." That was really a transformational moment in my life. It was significant just to be able to say to myself, "Okay, Cathy, you are here. You are representing these people, you're doing a great job being you, and doing it your way. Don't be so caught up in how others might do it. They are doing it their way. Just be you. You work hard, and know that you have something of unique value to offer." That's been revolutionary for me because since then I've been able to embrace more of who I am and be more confident in my ideas and my vision.

Because an entity drives and personifies the destiny of their organization, it is essential to not only recognize, but also to proactively plan, how the elected leader presents to others. **Barbara Sexton Smith**, a City Council member in Louisville Kentucky, refers to this as the "personal brand" and suggests that it should be specific, authentic, and consistent.

Your personal brand becomes who you are, no matter where you are. You have to use words that you want the world to use when describing you; if you don't, the world will brand you as it sees fit. I selected six words that I wanted everybody to say about me and I became those words: authentic, believable, connected, determined, energetic, and fun. And it works beautifully because it's really me, 24 hours a day, seven days a week.

The opportunity associated with viewing the elected leader as the entity can be leveraged by many strategies, including self-knowledge, choice of roles, and personal connections.

Know your vision, know yourself. **Doug Duncan**, who spent 24 years in elected leadership including County Executive of Montgomery, the largest county in Maryland, Mayor and Council member of the city of Rockville, advises that elected leaders must have something beyond a desire to run or to be in charge.

To me, the big thing especially is "what do you want to do?" Some may run just because they want the title, to be in charge. You've got to have a vision of where you want the county to go and you've got to be able to bring people along with you.

As the entity, it is critical for elected leaders to have a vision and to know their own values, interests, strengths, and limitations as applied to every aspect of their role. Leaders must keep in mind their personal and professional reasons to be in their role.

Sometimes the values that a person holds may close some doors but open others. Former Massachusetts State Senator **Bill Golden** (D) entered politics somewhat accidentally, just out of Yale University, through a stint in President Nixon's administration. **Golden**'s disagreement with Nixon's core policies meant that he would refuse a political appointment on principle. However, his support of the administration's desire to act on environmental issues led him to accept a civil service position, which in turn allowed him to play an integral role in the formation of the Environmental Protection Agency, which in turn offered visibility for his aspirations of elected office. Golden learned early in his career the importance of knowing his own values, acting politically without compromise, yet pragmatically seeking a place where he could influence progress related to his values. This served him well in his later political career, when he was known for a willingness to work with either party if they were aligned on an issue he cared about. As he states,

You have the ability to file legislation, you have the ability to put together alliances that are with other public officials and private groups, and you have the ability to generate a dialogue with your constituents. You do two things. You show that you care, but you also have the obligation to set an agenda that is based on your own personal views.

Representative **McMorris Rodgers** refocused her office around values to help herself and her staff to remember their reason for being there.

It has been transformational in my office, and it's countercultural because Capitol Hill is more about checking boxes, getting bills through, even if you push a lot of people out of the way to get yourself to the top. We counter with our values to say, "Okay, every day, every phone call, everybody matters. Everyone who walks through the door, every meeting. A meeting is a moment. It's about building relationships."

Beyond the need to understand their own values, elected leaders should also be aware of their skills. It should be noted that personal preferences are not necessarily the same as skills; the latter may be improved through training or practice. For instance, a leader's preference for introversion does not preclude him or her from developing skills normally associated with extroversion, such as proficiency with meeting people, public speaking, and related actions. Another area which may require a delicate balance between personal preference and outward practice is that of ego versus humility. Our interviewees mentioned the need to have a strong ego, or at least the confidence that goes with it, to drive through arduous campaigns, debates, and public criticism. However, the showing humility, and actually believing it, can be critical to being accepted by others. **John McHugh**, who spent over 20 years serving New York as a state senator and US Representative before six years as Secretary of the Army, would tell elected leaders "*Hold your principles and your core beliefs dear, but recognize you don't know everything.*"

Ambassador and Congresswoman **Morella** relates how the self-deprecating interpersonal skills of President George W. Bush made him a valuable ally, even when they often disagreed on policy.

> *George W. did a fundraiser for me. I very reluctantly let him do it, but my staff said he'll come through. One of the things he said was "She's been a fine congresswoman. She votes for me when she thinks I'm right, and she votes against me when she thinks I'm wrong, and she does a lot of the latter. She used to teach English, and there are those people who think I should take lessons from her." So what I'm saying is he knew his audience and I think it's one of the criteria for leadership: know your audience.*

Morella extends this idea of understanding others to a more general notion for leaders:

> *Leadership means you have to know your people, get to know something about them personally. Our first President, George Washington, wrote the book <u>Rules of Civility and Decent Behavior</u>. His rule number one: when in the company of others, act with respect for those who are present. So my motto is listen, learn, and lead.*

Once an elected leader understands his or her own values, vision, and skills, they can begin the sometimes-difficult journey of building a consistent strategy for leading. The late Senator Paul Wellstone (D-MN) advised, "*Never separate the life you live from the words you speak*" because he knew the difficulty of paring oneself with one's actions. (See Appendix for tool 4.1 <u>Elected Leader Strategic Plan</u>, which can serve as a north star to guide the leader when bombarded with the many requests for time and energy.)

<u>Choose your role and practice it</u>. Knowing oneself not only represents an idealistic view of the purpose of elected leaders, but also a pragmatic necessity for making an impact and building a career where that impact can be sustained. Leaders must connect their self-knowledge to an understanding of their context and stakeholders, so they will know best how to apply their vision and skills. **Barbara Sexton Smith** states that it starts with understanding the basics of government and your role within it.

As a newly elected official it is critically important to understand the full scope of power and authority that your elected position has, and that of your legislative body. Whether you are Council member in Louisville, Kentucky, a state senator, or a Congresswoman. Next, you must understand the relationship between your legislative body and the executive branch. Then you must understand how your body interacts with the third branch of government, the judicial branch. Each is powerful and works best when operating within their respective scope of authority. When you don't understand these basic differences, you will waste everyone's time – yours, your constituents, your peers, and all citizens.

There are a variety of ways to create success as elected leaders. In their publication Setting Course: A Congressional Management Guide, for instance, CMF outlines **five possible roles** (see the table below) for members of US Congress, noting that each elected official should pursue one primary and one secondary role. The idea is for elected leaders to become known and navigate their careers through making choices among a focus on legislative expertise (developing and passing laws), party politics (ideology and structure, may involve elected or appointed positions among the elected leaders), ombudsman (resolving issues for direct constituents), statesman (broad policy for the good of the public), or outsider (critic of the system or a particular issue).

The five unique roles of a member of congress	
Legislative	Developing and passing laws
Party	Ideology and structure, may involve elected or appointed positions among the elected leaders
Ombudsmen	Resolving issues for direct constituents
Statesman	Broad policy for the good of the public
Outsider	Critic of the system or a particular issue

Source Congressional Management Foundation

These roles provide opportunity for elected leaders to capitalize on their own strengths and skills while setting a strategic course for their careers. **Brad Fitch** gives the example of Rosa DeLauro (D-CT), in Congress for over 30 years, in illustrating how such roles could develop.

DeLauro had a couple paths available to her. One was the more political that could lead her to leadership, and maybe the speakership, and the other was legislative, which would lead her to chair of appropriations. She dabbled in the leadership one, lost in a leadership race by one vote, and then pivoted and said, 'nope, I'm going up the legislative path.' She became chair or first ranking member Chair of the Labor HHS subcommittee, at the time the most powerful, influential subcommittees in the Congress.

In 2021, Rep DeLauro was elected to Chair of the powerful U. S. House Appropriations Committee.

Be personable, make connections. A consistent theme among the elected leaders we spoke with was the importance of interpersonal skills, as mentioned above, to develop personal and professional relationships. As the "entity," the influence of elected leaders often depends on their ability to get others to personally connect with them. Senator **Golden** describes how he builds relationships:

> There are three things that I think you need to do if you want to be an impact player. The first is to listen carefully; listen to what people want, what they know, and why they think that opinion or belief is good for them. Then you should show basic respect, that you understand what they're saying and that you care about their concerns. Third, you have to show that you care enough that you're willing to and can do something about it.

It is critical to nourish connections with constituents, donors, fellow elected leaders, and members of their staff, and to realize that the manner of supporting these varied stakeholders may differ. As Representative **Carnahan** states,

> I've been describing the phases to work together in a diverse coalition, in your official capacity as a legislator. But there's a whole other skillset, outside of that in terms of how you communicate with your constituents. Yet another skill set is needed for the mechanics of how you do that.

Efforts toward collaboration must not only find common ground, as in **Carnahan**'s example but should also include the possibility of actual compromise. Secretary **McHugh** drives this point further.

> Remember what you told your constituents, but remember as well that to make progress, there's got to be some kind of give and take.... If you're going to move the ball down the field, you have to give to get a majority of the votes. You have to give the other side something to vote yes for.

4.1.2 Clearly Delineated Position-Based Authority

While leaders in most fields must spend time developing and defining the scope and implications of their authority, elected leaders begin with an almost enviable level of clarity. The role of the elected leader is typically defined by statute or policy, whether in the halls of Congress, the Governor's mansion, or other contexts. The basic authority of US Representatives, for instance, springs from holding a single voting right for any bill that comes before the House legislative body. Governors and presidents, as executors of the law, typically have broader but still defined powers. Similarly, city mayors and other elected officials have authority defined by others, although there tends to be considerable variation in these positions across geographic areas. **Doug Duncan**, who served in several elected roles across city and county government, remembers,

> *My first run for elected office was Rockville City Council. The mayor was just sort of the chair of the council, setting the agenda, because we had a full-time city manager who ran things. When I was on the city council, what struck me was that people asked, "what issues did you study?" and "what bills did you pass?" Then I ran for mayor and the first thing I noticed when elected was that people looked at me differently. Now they were asking "what did you get done?" So it really was a different kind of leader, a noticeable difference, and I developed this real sense of urgency to make things happen.*

One key is first understanding and using the clear formal base of authority. Legislators have that single vote, no more or less than their colleagues, regardless of party affiliation, tenure, or popularity. This can be reassuring during the potentially overwhelming early months in elected office, especially if the voting schedule is intense and leaders are required to quickly get up to speed so as to vote on issues they had not previously researched. Because many constituents hold high expectations for help from their elected leaders, sometimes beyond the leader's control, it can be useful to communicate the limits of purview along with clear statements of what services the leader can provide.

It is for this reason that many legislators step heavily into their constituent service role. A legislative vote, while critical, often does not have the impact that elected leaders strive to make on the everyday lives on their constituents. Proceeding from that base, the next step involves exploring how leadership influence can further develop. In particular, elected leaders can draw on the entity-related strategies discussed earlier to extend their influence and plan where they can make an impact on their priority issues. For instance, leaders can extend their reach by leveraging professional relationships through elected colleagues, through authorities resident at other levels of government, through donors, and through the knowledge and connections of their own staff. Being creative in ways of extending influence beyond simple authority can extend opportunities to serve the public and maximize the reach of the leader's role.

Vic Snyder, who spent 14 years as a US Representative (AR-D), intoned one of the main opportunities of an elected leader, reflecting both the delineated authority and its extended reach: *"People pick up the phone when I call."* This segues nicely into the next opportunity, access to others.

4.1.3   Power to Convene, and a Seat at the Table

One of the greatest assets of elected office is the very real ability to convene others and to sit at tables where important topics are raised, regardless of whether the leader has formal authority to make decisions or implement action. This power can be realized through formal mechanisms of the leader's government position, such as House or Senate committees, but may be equally effective through working with communities, targeted stakeholders, experts, and other partners. Convening through these less formal means may even serve the leader's professional interests more directly.

As Representative **Carnahan** describes,

> *As a member of Congress, you can go out and vote and advocate for things in Washington, but one of the things that was really an indirect benefit was the power to convene. I could form a task force, on local foods or health care or seniors, whatever the issue was at hand.*

Some elected officials take full advantage of this opportunity, surrounding themselves with experts, inserting themselves into policy conversations, promoting their involvement to the public, and using their pulpit as pressure on public institutions. Others do not leverage this capacity, often due to a lack of strategic planning, or because their time is spent reacting to the many draws on the schedule of elected officials.

One first-year member of Congress who worked with co-author Meredith was passionate about energy issues, but was a bit frustrated about not being on the top associated committee of jurisdiction (Energy and Commerce) where he could more easily propose legislation. In working with his staff, Meredith recognized that his desire was not specifically to influence legislation, but was targeted at the lack of industry innovation. He then leveraged his status to convene traditional and alternative energy company representatives to share ideas and identify opportunities for collaboration. His shift— from wishing for a committee role to finding ways to leverage the influence of his existing role—was critical for his future. When the Congressman ultimately made it onto the Energy and Commerce committee, he was able to leverage the experiences from those early months of his first term.

Pursue passion and prioritize. With a more considered prioritization of what is truly important, versus what is merely urgent (often stimulating a reaction, whether or not it is really needed), leaders may find that convening or joining such collectives will better align with their personal and professional goals and objectives. As Congressman **Snyder** advised us, "*think of where your interests are, and where you want to make a difference.*" He describes how his interest in foreign policy, and learning about culture through travel, moved him to join Congressional caucuses for countries around the world. These caucuses, essentially groups of Congressional representatives who had policy or related interests in a particular country, involved meeting with their ambassadors and industry leaders as well as occasional travel. **Snyder**'s list of countries that he caucused with seemed impressive—Algeria, Armenia, Azerbaijan, Ethiopia, France, Greece, Jordan, Morocco, Poland, and more. However, these foreign interests did not at first necessarily line up with those of his constituents. Snyder made it work:

> We set up speaker series with ambassadors, officials, and others. I would invite them to Little Rock, and since they were always looking for ways to promote their country, we started getting this little trail of ambassadors coming to Arkansas. This turned into some economic development that went really well for the region and my constituents. Not only that, but my young staff came away with a sense that there is a lot of nuance in the world, particularly with regard to international issues.

This story should be told with a cautionary note as well. While Representative **Snyder** successfully married his interest with the benefit to his constituents, not every interest of elected officials will be viewed as important by their voting community. Becoming a leader involves finding the value for all parties, communicating this well, and stitching these interests together while also not neglecting other core issues.

Similarly, former Congressman **Mike Honda** (D-CA) utilized his seat at the table to promote the values, developed over a lifetime that included confinement in World War II internment camps as well as a 30-year career in education, that he believes were shared by his constituents. One of the themes he expresses is that "*an important part of leadership is responsibility.*" For **Honda**, this means doing what he believes is right, and calling out priorities that otherwise receive little attention. He relates two incidents where he believed that workers on public projects were being put in danger by a lack of investment in personal protective equipment, in which **Honda** used his platform in Congress to call attention to the situation. Because the incidents were both high profile—one was a large public works project clearing an asbestos-laden tunnel, and the other was the cleanup following the 9-11 terrorist attack on the World Trade Center in New York—**Honda** knew that he was drawing attention to potential failures of oversight by his Congressional colleagues. However, his passion for protecting vulnerable populations overrode any desire to protect the institution.

Formal structure and leader's interests. One category of seats at tables is that of the committees or other subgroups that are part of the elected leaders' organization. Elected legislators must be proactive to ensure assignment to powerful and relevant committees, which develop the legislation, fund initiatives, and otherwise direct the policies of entities within the legislative branch. For statewide and federal officeholders, positional power and influence can be dramatically affected by how the leader is aligned with the majority party (or parties), which also influences voice on the committee. Members of a minority party, for instance, could be assigned to a politically divided committee where their influence is limited because they do not control the agenda, regardless of whether their position could result in a majority vote.

Elected leaders at other levels of government face similar challenges within their own contexts that may be resolved through the power to convene experts or rally the public around a policy direction. Mayors and governors are executive leaders charged with coordinating an operational administration, can differentially give time, resources, exposure, and other support to those that are most in line with their constituent needs or campaign promises. **Doug Duncan** describes how, very early in his county government administration, he had to convene parties across the community to eliminate a large, long-burning fire in an illegal dump in North Potomac's Travila, a toney area of the Washington DC suburbs. The previous County Executive had not resolved the issue, and organizations from the various jurisdictions involved were either in stasis, or in denial of their responsibility. Duncan convened several meetings, first with his county services.

We go back to my conference room, there's like 30 people there, all at this big conference table. I'm at one end, at the other end is one of the Fire Department chiefs. I said, "You know, we have the authority to put this fire out." Literally, it was the sixth time I said "just put the fire out" that the chief said "Are you telling us to put this fire out? Ok, we can do that"

The method of putting the fire out involved moving a lot of the material to the other side of the county, where it could be safely disposed. **Duncan** needed to involve multiple fire departments, get permission from the power brokers across the county, then sell the plan back to the original community.

> *I said "I need your permission to move this dump here; thankfully they said yes. I went to the Travila community and said, "Here's our plan." People were screaming at me. Within a week it was out, while they had projected it was going to burn for months. It was a great way of coming into office. We're going to get things done.*

4.1.4   Responsiveness of Stakeholders

The newly elected leader's world changes overnight. Suddenly, people quickly return calls, take meetings, and become very accommodating of the leader's schedule. The elected leader will be invited to enough events to fill every day, multiple times over. This responsiveness can be valuable when it supports the direction of the leader's goals. It is up to the leader to shape this direction; their response is only as powerful as the request. These leaders must be cautious of being so responsive to others' requests that they lose sight of where, and with whom, their time is best spent.

Senator **Bob Corker** (R-TN) shared that the greatest advantage in the Senate was

> *being able to talk to anybody… You've got a platform to speak from and you've got the ability to reach out and touch almost anybody in the world.*

He leveraged that advantage to invite the representatives from Volkswagen while in Washington DC down to Chattanooga, Tennessee, where he had been mayor. He invited these executives to his home, along with Senator Alexander and the Governor. This meeting led to VW establishing its US operations in Chattanooga which is now on its third expansion and a significant employer in the city. **Corker** further explains, *they wouldn't have taken my call as a mayor like that, you know, being a senator made a big difference in that effort.*

Leaders on other paths typically have to earn such a level of responsiveness. Elected leaders certainly can have challenges, such as the continuous election cycle, especially when fundraising. One day the potential elected leader would be chasing after stakeholders, but the pattern changes as soon as the votes add up to a win. **Vic Snyder**, who retired after 20 years in elected office (6 years in the Arkansas state senate and 14 years in the US House of Representatives), laughs about his new career in the private sector and how different the treatment is:

> There are people who still recognize me from the old days. I think for most of them it's a positive memory, so that still is a door opener. But the negative side of it, that handful that do recognize me also know that I'm no longer in office. "You don't return my calls anymore," right? They can turn around to walk the other way if they want. I mean I'm a has-been, I know I'm a has-been [chuckles].

It is often asserted that elected leaders must have strong egos, needed to fuel their fire to run for office in the first place, and to endure the slings and arrows that come with a job in the public eye. If the leader is not careful, the natural tendency to feed such egos may also limit exposure to a more diverse set of stakeholders, beyond those who may simply reinforce the leader's existing viewpoints. While some attention must continue to be given to those stakeholders who are already supportive, elected leaders should find ways to stretch beyond the viewpoints and resources that these constituents offer.

Congressman **Snyder** had more progressive views than his district of Little Rock, Arkansas. Yet his constituents, and even the media, grew to appreciate his consistency and conviction. In fact, the conservative editorial Board of the Democrat-Gazette newspaper once wrote,

> While we abhor some of his political stances, there is no doubting the sincerity with which he takes them. Or his patriotism....We're endorsing an honorable opponent today, not his politics.

By definition, all leaders are visible to some stakeholders, but elected leaders may be unique in the prominence of their profile across multiple audiences who believe, with some credence, that they are owed accountability and oversight privileges. Those walking the elected path defer in some way to a majority of their voting constituents, at minimum, as well as to their party leaders, donors, media, and others who shape the confines of their journey. Understanding, balancing, and ultimately leveraging the interests of these stakeholders are essential for long-term success. The process of stakeholder analysis turns the challenge of a reactive stakeholder strategy into an opportunity to align your stakeholder outreach with your priorities. In fact, through this process, you may determine that the group you are avoiding because of an inability to meet their top priority could be an essential ally on another. (See Appendix for tool 4.2 Stakeholder Analysis, used to prioritize stakeholders and means of proactively engaging them more objectively.)

Instead of staying in the passive mode, elected leaders ought to build on their distinctive strengths to create different approaches to how they develop their own networks. In the best case, leaders use their networks to extend their reach to varied stakeholders, to increase the flow of novel information, and to connect them to resources that they would not otherwise have. Well-constructed networks can offer something that is often difficult to find among higher-echelon leaders: an honest evaluation of the leader's ideas and actions.

Accordingly, there are some common mistakes to watch out for, such as building networks predominately with those who are similar to the leader. As **Fitch** puts it,

> *Lawmakers' stakeholder networks can be invaluable, but sometimes they don't build the right ones. It's a question of, "Do I build networks with people who will give me honest advice, say no, and speak truth to power, or am I just going to get an echo chamber?" It's interesting that elected leaders often are more likely to respect people who come from their own world. So the businesspeople listen to other businesspeople, leaders from the military listen to the military, teachers listen to other teachers. On some levels that's a disadvantage, right, because you're limited to a contained culture.*

Carnahan also warns against relying too much on pre-established networks. Relationships built prior to an elected leader's entry into public life, especially those based on family connections or prior public service "can be a double-edged sword. Remember, you'll inherit both friends and enemies of those you associate with." Having several family members who held high public office at the state or federal levels—his grandfather, both parents, and a sister— **Carnahan** knows this intimately.

> *In my experience, the good far outweighs the bad, but it was best described as opening a door or having a good introduction. It was really up to me to really build on that, then make it my own.*

Similarly, many of our interviewees stressed the importance of building connections with other elected leaders. As **Carnahan** points out, "*You are only one vote, which doesn't pass anything. You've got to use your committee, your party.*" Although he is speaking primarily about legislators, this may apply to other elected leaders who face the challenge of getting others on board with their policy choices. **Carnahan** also warns against polarizing tactics, saying "*If you are hyper-partisan, it will come right back at you.*" Instead, he recommends finding common ground, such as in this example of legislating funding for multiple sclerosis research, which involves the sometimes politically sensitive use of stem cells.

My first term in Congress, there was a lot of debate about stem cell research. We had a bipartisan group that was led by Michael Castle, a Republican, and Diana Degette, a Democrat. We had regular weekly meetings, Democrats and Republicans, and some of the more conservative Republicans often identified with pro-life positions. Our bipartisan work was epitomized by Orin Hatch from Utah. He said that his vote for stem cell research was the most prolific thing he'd ever done. This was because a lot of these people had a family member or friend or acquaintance that had MS or other diseases that could benefit from stem cell research. And it opened up a lot of minds and got people to think outside the box in ways that they might not otherwise do.

Efforts toward collaboration must not only find common ground, as in **Carnahan**'s example but should also include the possibility of actual compromise. Secretary **McHugh** drives this point further.

Remember what you told your constituents, but remember as well that to make progress, there's got to be some kind of give and take…. If you're going to move the ball down the field, you have to give to get a majority of the votes. You have to give the other side something to vote yes for.

It is also important to get to know the specifics of how power is assigned in the elected leader's organization. **Carnahan** describes how members of Congress are assigned to committees, where much of the legislative and budget power resides. Essentially, each party has an internal leadership system, and that leader makes committee appointments through consultation with the Policy & Steering Committee. Thus, it is important to become visible to the leaders and the committee members. **Carnahan** recommends that members *"tell the leader or committee what you can bring to the table"* in terms of your reason for wanting the appointment, your external connections, influences on the votes of others on key issues, and other resources.

4.1.5 Ability to Help People Maneuver the Government Bureaucracy

The elected leadership path holds an advantage that may be truly unique from other paths—the authority and the means to help constituents maneuver through the government bureaucracy. People who do not often have need for government services are not as likely to be familiar with the best way to navigate the system, but an elected leader not only has insights, but also can cut through red tape. Each level of government, including the various state and federal agencies, has liaisons with elected representatives. With good staff support, the elected leader can develop and leverage these relationships to achieve great wins for their voting public. Whether it is owed benefits such as social security payments or veterans' insurance, a tour of the Capitol building, or a 24-hour turnaround on a passport for a family emergency out of the country, leveraging this access can relieve stress and bring joy to the voters.

This advantage can be valuable for not only constituents, but also for the elected leader. While many aspects of elected leadership may be frustrating—members of Congress who lament that their one vote is not enough to make real change in a timely manner—performing constituent services can feel like a real win. The constituents may also transfer their satisfaction into future support and votes. In this manner, elected leaders who focus on constituent service are able to better leverage their current and future position.

Robert Taub saw this in action during his time as chief of staff for US Representative **John McHugh** (R-NY). He discusses the need for elected leaders to have the ability to pivot between the roles of serving the public directly—"*in the customer service business, where the single constituent is the priority*"—and walling oneself off from the immediate needs in order to perform the other parts of the job, such as researching positions, negotiating with colleagues, and developing legislation, and oversight of government agencies. For the former, **Taub** believes that the desire to serve must be a sincere part of the leader's makeup:

> *It's on-the-street constituent service. A lot of this was just John [Rep. McHugh]. He was not out there for the Watertown Daily Times or to be on Fox News, so we had the luxury of focusing on the home district issues. He didn't mind you sitting on the phone for an hour with some crazy constituent. That is just part of the job, and his bandwidth for it was huge.*

McHugh picks up this train of thought:

> *Certainly after your first election before you accrue a record, your constituents have to be your first concern. After that, I think a lot of Members of Congress do get a little insulated. You've heard about the inside the beltway mentality. Well, when you're going through the same committee two or three times a week, when your whole perspective is trying to do the best bill you can, you may lose sight of the fact that the folks back home are counting on you to do something maybe entirely unrelated to your committee. So, keeping that constituent connection is important. When you hear people do 58 town halls in a month, you know, it's an effort laudably to try to stay connected at the same time.*

In order to succeed in the latter parts of the job, however, elected leaders must prioritize their own time and resources, of course. **McHugh** compares some competing priorities,

> *As a member of the Armed Services Committee, I did feel that the men and women in uniform were stakeholders of what we're doing. My total focus was to do the best I could for soldiers and their families. That is easy in that generally what you are doing for one soldier will be well-received by another. Whereas, what you're doing for one constituent may not be so well received by someone with another interest.*

When balancing constituent's immediate needs, versus the longer-term duties of the job, one strategy for success is strategic deployment of their staff. This presumes, of course, that the staff has been planned and selected accordingly, which relates to another opportunity for the elected leader.

4.1.6 High Level of Talent Available for Staffing

There is considerable cachet associated with working on Capitol Hill, in the Statehouse, or in working in the upper echelons of almost any level of government, and effective elected leaders make the most of it. Despite the long hours and limited compensation, the best and brightest still seek entry level staff positions, in hopes of one day writing policy that may have a positive impact of our society. As **Brad Fitch** of CMF puts it,

> *A legislative assistant opening in a House Representative's office will easily get 100 to 200 resumes. This kind of job is still a merit badge. Everyone wants it on their resume, and everyone wants to serve. I still see really great people, great public servants who have been very successful in other parts of their career and their lives willing to make the sacrifice to work for Congress. I was Tammy Baldwin's [now Senator from Wisconsin] first Chief of Staff in the House of Representatives. She was the first openly gay or lesbian leader elected, and we had 1200 applications. Representative Alexandria Ocasio-Cortez [D-NY] had 5000 applications for her office staff.*

Hire the best, complementing leader skills, aligning with culture, core values, and character. Given the talent pool, elected leaders can be selective about those hired and importantly, ensure that the staff have the skills needed to support the leader's direction. At the federal executive level, presidents generally find talent from many walks of life, but may become known for sampling more generously from particular areas. For instance, President Obama famously pulled many staff members and appointees from academia, including two professors serving as Secretary of Energy. His successor President Trump found many department heads from private sector business, such as Goldman Sachs CEO Gary Cohn and ExxonMobil CEO Rex Tillerson, and the military, such as his Chief of Staff John Kelly. Members of Congress, while for junior staffers often hire young, eager people educated in fields related to political science, for their senior staff often draw from other professional ranks. Senator Rob Portman (R-OH) plucked Marc Isakowitz, founder of one of the top lobbying firms in DC, to serve as his Chief of Staff. As a Senator, President Obama hired Ian Solomon, who had been a consultant with McKinsey & Company and an Associate Dean at Yale University, for a Legislative Counsel position.

This wealth of talent, managed properly, can be a considerable asset to an elected leader. Senator **Corker** put considerable thought into building a high-quality staff whose members understood his approach and was rewarded by being able to trust them with implementing his vision. As he recalls from his 12 years on Capitol Hill,

> *Sometimes you forget the lives that you touch when you're in the Senate. You realize that your staff extends your reach, because it was really them touching people, although it had my name on it.*

Given the importance of an elected leaders' staff, there are further strategic caveats to consider.

Do not hire anyone who cannot be fired. First, never hire anyone who cannot be fired if the circumstances call for it. The Congressional Management Foundation dubs this the number-one hiring mistake on Capitol Hill and generally refers to situations where a personal relationship, favor owed, or complex situation gets in the way of making employment decisions based on strategic need. It is certainly not difficult to understand how elected leaders might find themselves in such situations. While this is not dissimilar to entrepreneurs who face challenges of keeping their early employees when the venture may grow beyond their capacity, or to legacy leaders hiring family members, elected leaders may face an extreme version of this situation. Elected leaders generally have the freedom to hire as they wish, and due to their reliance on so many in their journey to electability, they may be expected to reward their supporters. A campaign includes volunteers who may consider their contribution of time and effort to be a down payment on landing a job on the other end. This may be quite problematic for newly elected leaders who need their staff to support a successful launch.

Complement leader skill set. Second, leaders should be careful not to necessarily hire staff members who are overly similar to themselves. As famously modeled in President Lincoln's "team of rivals" approach, incorporating diverse perspectives and even at times differing goals can add resilience to a staff team. This caveat must be tempered with the elected leader's place as the "entity" discussed earlier. It may be useful to consider that the entity is not just the person of the elected leader, but can be considered to be the future of the leader, whose continued development depends on incorporating and managing multiple viewpoints.

Invest in staff; intentionally manage composition and culture. Third, the importance of the staff in implementing and extending the elected leader's vision implies that each person must be valued, treated fairly, and in many cases nurtured. Staff members have their own goals, whether for themselves and their future, or related to their belief in the policies directed from the elected office. Leaders who support their staff, such as in the example shared earlier in the words of Representative **McMorris Rodgers** and Senator **Corker**, reap great benefits. Those who place themselves above their staff members, engage in unfair practices, or create a culture of fear, often reap negative returns. Further, word travels in staff circles across offices. Those leaders who have a reputation for not treating their staff well may have difficulty retaining valuable staff members, or hiring in the future.

Elected leaders who best leverage this opportunity see building their staff as a strategic and genuine part of their professional identity. This means first understanding the needs of their office, such as building expertise in a given area, networking with the appropriate people, or gathering particular resources. The leader should also understand their intended office culture, and how they will prioritize their work. Each of these necessitates the leader's self-knowledge, including expertise, values, shortcomings, and blind spots. **Tonya Williams**, a Director at Softbank Group who served as then Vice President Joe Biden's Director of Legislative Affairs, recalls,

I don't think there was any better example than Vice President Biden when I worked for him. For him it's personal, and the work is deeply personal as well. He does this amazing thing where he spends a lot of time with each hire, to get to know what he believes in and why. You spend time with his family, you get to know and love the person, so much so that I think that's a huge part of the followership and the reason why there is not a lot that he asks of people that they won't do.

The process of recruitment can then be one of finding the right candidates and complementing the leader's strengths and preferences. In this way, the talent of the staff will align with and enhance the strengths and values of elected leaders, preparing them for the different viewpoints that will be encountered outside of the office walls. Former Representative **Mike Honda** emphasizes the importance of creating a culture where the staff can be openly critical of his actions. He describes how this works in their staff retreats.

> *I had to figure out exercises that allow them to say certain things about our office without them being identified. So I use that technique where everyone writes "the thing that bothers me about Mike's leadership..." or "what bothers me about Mike..." with a blank for them to fill in. The next part is "I wish he would...." So they fill it in, then put it in the center of the room. Everyone grabs one randomly and reads it. It's tough to go through, but it helps to improve myself and the office. And it teaches them to be able to do the same thing.*

This last point exemplifies the importance of elected leaders hiring staff members that they can trust, in terms of both relying on their expertise and sharing a vision of why the leader ran for office in the first place. **Sarah Bittleman** draws on her long experience as a Congressional staffer to point out,

> *You need people around you who can have real conversations with you. If you are incapable of having real conversations with your closest staff you are just in it on your own.*

Elected leaders who prioritize hiring of a capable, dedicated staff will never have to feel like they are on their own.

Perhaps because the elected leader is the focal entity for most stakeholders, staff members are not as visible as they are actually important. **Fitch** ranks building the staff—planning, recruiting, hiring, and managing—as possibly the most critical task for a newly elected leader.

> *Your first 90 days, you have got to set up a small business called the Congressional office. Yes, it might be fun to, for instance, examine the latest Middle East peace deal, and talk to people in that area. But members who are really smart set up the apparatus, like the Donna Shalala's operating model, that can function effectively six or seven months in. Or else, trust me, when you're eight or nine months in, it's just going to be a mess.*

Representative **McMorris Rodgers** uses the process of strategic values alignment to promote inclusion of her staff and get their input on the direction of the office.

We developed values for my office around having fun while we SERVE: Seek excellence, Everyone matters, Responsibly own it, Vigilant integrity and Embrace change. At every staff meeting we spend time reflecting on the values. We do "shout outs" recognition for staff members promoting the values. We hire and do staff reviews to the values. So for every person that we hire, now we are all sharing our values and asking them what they think about each one of these.

Many members of Congress have used tactics to highlight the importance of staff members which also serve to sustain connections formed in the office. The late Senator Ted Kennedy (MA-D), for instance, would regularly hold staff alumni events, which helped to keep social and professional networks alive. Representative **Mike Honda** (CA-D), a former high school principal, told his team members that his goals included developing staff members to go on to bigger and better things, and spoke of his pride in those who moved on from his office to pursue jobs with even more impact. For example, he states,

I had two senior staffers in particular, my Chief of Staff and Senior Science Staff who were exceptional and critical to our office's success. They, and many others, continue to grow professionally and increase their scope of influence.

Generally, it is essential for elected leaders to plan and communicate how staff positions will be offered, especially when working with volunteers and supporters during the campaign process. These tactics help to keep loyalty beyond a mere transactional employment relationship and can be vital support for the entity of the elected leader. **Tonya Williams** described how Vice President Biden approached his employees.

I'll never forget that when I went to work for the Vice President, in an early chat he said, "You know, there are very few things that get you fired around here. But one for certain is if I find out that you are neglecting yourself or your family. Nothing that you're doing here, no matter what we're doing, is so important that you should risk those." It actually came up when I had a slipped disc, and I was at work taking medicine. I was trying so hard to get things done. And the Vice president heard about it, came to my office and literally told me to go home. He gave me a big old hug on the way out, because he cares about you.… It's a loyalty that really is a two-way street.

As shown above, the Representative path is filled with opportunities that elected leaders can leverage to achieve success. They can use their personal and position power, to clearly articulate a vision and role which can be used to connect with constituents according to the needs and interests of all parties. They also have the ability to access high levels of government, including its resources and talent pool, to get things done.

Next, we will discuss the challenges that the Representative may encounter along the elected path.

4.2   Representative: Challenges and Strategies of the Elected Path

Table 4.2   Elected path: Representative challenges and strategies

Elected path challenges	Strategies for managing
1. Term limits and fixed terms	• Ensure staff is in place early to quickly operate • Leverage the re-election campaign process to align staff, reinforce your purpose and strategic focus • Develop a fundraising strategy that aligns with ethical and political considerations
2. Constituent expectations and public exposure	• Set boundaries and rules of engagement • Practice transparency about what can and cannot be delivered, and honesty when mistakes are made
3. Associations with party leadership and expectations to toe the line	• Leverage the advantages of party association while maintaining independence when necessary • Choose your battles and explain them to stakeholders
4. Tenure matters for elected leadership positions	• Do work that does not interest others • Choose a road less traveled
5. Schedule, travel, family toll	• Find mentors who can share their strategies • Encourage a strong relationship between staff and family

While there are many advantages on the elected path, it also includes several important challenges that are unique to elected leaders, reviewed below along with strategies for mitigating their potential negative effects. While there are likely additional strategies for managing these challenges that are not outlined below, we share some successes that elected leaders have had in managing the critical challenges along this path (Table 4.2).

4.2.1 Term Limits and Fixed Terms

The position of an elected leader is typically characterized by a relatively unique boundary—a fixed term of office with clear process of renewal which may or may not match up with doing the job well. Leaders on some other paths may have more uncertainty in the longevity of their positions, but do not also face the need to constantly interview and be hired for the job. In some circumstances, elected leaders may not be given the opportunity to reapply for their position, as when terms limits[4] are in effect, and in rare instances may be "fired" early, typically when faced with a recall vote[5] or possibly through impeachment. While others may be asked to resign if they can no longer be effective due to a scandal or some other discovery. In the more common situation, these leaders must be re-elected to continue their position, a process which includes many challenges.

The process of being re-elected is not limited to the election itself, of course. Depending on factors such as the visibility of the position, the competition, and the length of term, the election cycle can include significant time spent on fundraising, networking, campaigning, and related tasks. In the case of Representatives to the US House of Representatives, the two-year term creates an almost constant election process, in contrast to the six-year term of US Senators and four-year terms of the US President and most state governors. It can be difficult to be strategic when the term of office stifles long-term plans. All these leaders must balance their beliefs and goals with the actions needed to assure re-election in the short-term. For those in a highly contested or holding a relatively "unsafe" seat, the scrutiny can be intense as their strategic choices, voting record, alliances, and general activities either solidify their chances or put them at risk for the future. More importantly, they are more likely to be affected by "waves" that tend to follow national trends.

---

[4]"Term limits" refers to legal restrictions on the number of elected terms that an official can serve.
[5]Other removals from office may occur, for instance, when found in violation of the ethics or standards, as in an impeachment conviction.

To mitigate this circumstance, elected leaders can engage in strategies both to prepare for the election cycle and term restriction, and to use the circumstances to plan their own course. The preparation should begin, as outlined above, with the recruitment, selection, and development of a strong staff with clear goals, roles, and assignments. For instance, staffing divisions should balance the need for connection with the various stakeholders in an elected leader's orbit—constituent voters, donors, party leaders, politically influential partners, and others. **Brad Fitch** of CMF recommends that elected leaders prioritize putting together their staff in their first 90 days of service, even when other duties may seem more pressing, because a strong staff will be needed to keep ahead of the leaders' many obligations. A well-organized staff can, for instance, separately and effectively work to understand pressing voter issues, especially in the swing portions of a constituency, develop potential donors and fundraising partners, research the matters most pressing for action, respond to constituent mail and requests, and help the leader to navigate their sphere, whether the Town Hall or the halls of Congress.

At times, the perils of an unsafe constituency, such as typically measured for Congressional seats as the number of likely Democrat and Republican voters, can be mitigated by the personal popularity of a candidate. Representative **Morella** enjoyed relative safety as a Republican in a largely Democratic district for most of her time in Congress, largely earned through her credibility with her constituents, even those who disagreed with her. **Morella** explains,

> *I always said you voted on the basis of your country, your constituency, and your conscience. I was always aware of my constituents and my country. At one point, one of the stats was that I had the most Democrats in my district of any Republican. How do you stay there? You explain.*

Morella relates a story wherein she calls a voter who left a strong message disagreeing with her position on an issue. She calls him back to talk about it, still maintaining her disagreement, but he is so happy that she called that he becomes a big supporter afterward. "*People want to feel that they're being listened to. But you have to do your homework.*"

Elected leaders can also use the process of re-election efforts to engage in visioning, goal setting, and even soul-searching to determine how best to position themselves through a campaign, and to maximize their time in office. It can be an opportunity to consider why the leader is seeking elected office in the first place, and what it means if he or she wins or loses. This introspection can be prodded from the outside, as when the political winds changed for a senior member of Congress, a client of Meredith, who faced an unexpected primary challenge in his formerly safe district. Working with his staff to rethink and prioritize, he found that the reoriented direction of his campaign gave him a new "North Star" to guide his continued work. Like many leaders in relatively "unsafe" seats, he used the opportunity to re-engage with his reason for running for office in the first place and hone his message with various stakeholders.

Short election cycles, such as those in the US House of Representatives, are often considered to be a burden for Congressional members. The fundraising may feel like it never ends, and most representatives would rather be working on legislation. However, as Congressman **Mike Honda** (D-CA) points out,

> *the two-year election cycle is tough, but it allows you to stay connected to your district, learn what the people are thinking, and to develop deeper relationships with the community we represent. As a teacher, I was accustomed to evaluations. The Congressional cycle was like an exam assessing my worth to the district.*

It is also worth considering that there is some power in being faced with this restriction on eligibility for re-election, most specifically that a term-limited leader may be free to act according to the dictates of his or her conscience. No longer constrained by the need to consider the needs of, for instance, a small number of constituents who hold outsized influence, a leader can push decisions and resources toward goals that are more central to the long-term good or that are necessary yet unpopular among voters. This power to act may be mitigated by other factors, of course, including the leader's future career plans, concern for other members of the party, and such. The simplest example of this is that an outgoing President is expected to purchase upgrades to Airforce One, as not to burden the next President with spending taxpayer dollars on something seemingly unnecessary to many constituents.

At times, the reconsiderations of political stances, pivot points, and even positions that completely reverse over time can create a perception of a politician who is more interested in being elected than leading well. While we recommend that leaders should ultimately stay true to their values and goals, Representative **McHugh** offers a pragmatic take:

> *So, I've always been amused by people who say, "Well, all you're doing is politics." What's the core of politics? The core of politics is getting elected and generally you get elected because you do the job that people want you to do.*

Because of the constant need for campaigning and the importance of financial contributions in order to rise in party leadership, members of Congress spend on average 15-20% of their time on political and fundraising activities.[6] In swing districts, the burden is even greater as Congressman **Carnahan** explains,

> *One of the biggest disadvantages is the amount of time you have to spend on fundraising. For myself and other members, it's not unusual to spend anywhere from a fourth to half of their time any given day on fundraising. So you oftentimes find yourself wondering, what else could I be doing to help my constituents or work on an issue if I didn't have to spend a third of my time every week on fundraising? That's a lot of time. But that's the reality of most members, being in seats we had to run every two years.*

Carnahan further explains the additional complexity whereby

> *… third party independent groups often will spend more than your individual campaign on your opponent's campaign. This completely independent attacking you never know until the last minute, if and when that's going to happen. So part of it is the time consumption issue and also the risk and uncertainty involved.*

As elected leaders develop their approach to fundraising, it's important to develop a fundraising strategy that aligns with ethical, and political considerations. While there is no magic bullet to managing the stresses of fundraising for elected leaders, there are some principles that have been consistently effective, which we developed here as "Guidance for Managing Fundraising Pressures on Elected Leaders."

> **Guidance for Managing Fundraising Pressures on Elected Leaders**
>
> 1. Identify the stakeholders that both fund campaigns and align with your values and priorities. Target these groups to support your work and position yourself for committee membership where these priorities align. For example, a labor supporter may seek union fundraising support whereas a pro-life member might seek support from anti-abortion groups and their supporters. Resist the temptations to change your core values in the interest of easy access to funds.
> 2. Develop your fundraising philosophy carefully and in an informed manner. For example, be careful in the campaign process of which moneys you

---

[6]"Life in Congress: The Member Perspective," Congressional Management Foundation and SHRM, 2013.

welcome and/or reject. It's important to fully explore, for example, the pros and cons of accepting corporate Political Action Committee (PAC) donations.
3. Seek mentors that reflect your fundraising strategy. Some of the younger members of Congress are showing how social media and small donations can support their fundraising goals while not sacrificing their political positions. Whereby other members may start a PAC of their own to help fund candidates they support.
4. Align your official staff, campaign staff, and fundraising consultants on your fundraising strategy. For example, what are the goals and how will you achieve them? Avoid staff conflict over where and how you should spend your time when fundraising and official business compete for your attention.
5. Do not get too wrapped up in the numbers. Consider your campaign strategy and caucus strategy in order to set realistic targets that align with your strategy.
6. Be sure to clearly delineate your fundraising/political work from your official business both for yourself and for staff. Seek early to deeply understand the ethical lines and reinforce them continuously.
7. Set time blocks to devote to fundraising, often referred to as "call time," to more efficiently fundraise and to not distract from your official work.

© 2021 Six Paths to Leadership

4.2.2 Constituent Expectations and Public Exposure

While in the United States there are clear delineations of authority (see opportunities) for different political offices, rarely do constituents fully appreciate the distinctions between county, state, and federal officeholders. Further, stakeholder groups may expect their member of Congress to attend their 4th of July picnic every year because "they came last year," not recognizing the size of the district (and therefore number of picnics requiring attendance). Finally, when constituents come to the state or federal capital, they usually expect a meeting with their elected representative, regardless of the work calendar and other priorities. Adding to these pressures, so much of the elected leader's life is now exposed through the media and even more so with public media. This exposure further elevates expectations and/or interactions that require some sort of timely response, which becomes more difficult as the volume of constituent interactions increases. For example, according to CMF, in one Senator's office the volume of mail on the topic of education alone increased from 1000 to 45,000 messages in January 2016 versus January 2017.

Not only might constituents lack an understanding of what is a realistic expectation of an elected leader, but the leaders themselves often stay within their own orbits and fail to reinforce the roles and accountabilities.

County Commissioner **Doug Duncan** decided to take this head on to better develop relationships between the transportation and police departments. He explains,

> *When I was first elected as County Executive, I was talking to a transportation division chief and a police department representative, both who served over 20 years and were in the top 200 leaders in the county. There was such a stovepipe structure that they had no clue who each other were. The system was set up for them to care about their own department, rather than the county as a whole.... So I instituted leadership forums for the top 300 managers in county government once each quarter. We had a Q&A with me, we had speakers come in. I forced them to sit with people from different departments and it drove them crazy. For comparison, in my time at AT&T, you're going to know someone at a high level because AT&T shifts you around every two years. .... So then we created sort of a senior management service for folks to encourage them to move between departments to learn from each other.*

Given the quantity of expectations as a result, **Fitch** declares,

> *One of the most important leadership qualities that we see in successful members of Congress is those that say "I'm going to be a particular type of member. I'm going to focus narrowly. I'm going to be an expert in this area..." Make these tough choices and decide to be a leader on these issues. Say no to everything else, or you become one of two types of members of Congress. If you're in a safe district, you'll be an ineffective member of Congress. If you're in an unsafe district, you'll be a former member of Congress. Which do you want to be? ... That is an important part of leadership, being able to say no, and identifying what you're going to focus on so you can be a leader in that area.*

For Senator **Bob Corker**, the transition from the executive branch as Mayor of Chattanooga to serving in the US Senate was significant. After just six weeks of a Senator schedule, he realized he needed a better strategy for personal success and fulfillment. While Senators may fall into the trap of just accepting meeting after meeting, Senator **Corker** established his own boundaries and rules of engagement. He further sought ways to leverage his background and prioritize his impact while in Washington.

> *For me, the secret to being somewhat successful in the Senate was to begin to realize that I'm not going to have 28 meetings a day, like I was having the first six weeks. We're going to have a lot of meetings because we need information, but we're going to focus on a few things and really try to make a difference. After six weeks of being there, I literally called "timeout." We had a meeting, and I told my Chief of*

Staff "I'm not doing this anymore." I meant; I'm not having a bunch of superficial meetings every 15 minutes. I want to be a real senator, so I focused on a few things and gained some expertise.

One difference is that as a mayor you set your agenda. As a senator I had to develop a vision and then put the pieces in place. In the Senate, you have to wait for the opportunity. The first opportunity came for me with a financial crisis where even as a junior senator I was able to have an outsized impact because I knew a lot about the topic. I got a call one night at 10 pm to show up the next morning with Hank Paulson, Ben Bernanke, 33 Republican senators, three Democratic senators. From that point on, I played a big role. And that was heady… that was exciting.

Former Representative **Dan Mica** (D-FL) reinforces the importance of transparency about what you can and cannot deliver, and honesty when mistakes are made. This will prevent disappointment among your stakeholders. He explains,

I also believe in - and this was a big issue in my third career - transparency. A number of members of Congress and a number of elected officials don't want to tell the full story. Democrats and Republicans, both, they want to just get enough out there that makes them look good and so on. Sometimes you need to say "hey, I screwed up, I made a mistake here."

4.2.3 Associations with Party Leadership and Expectations to Toe the Party Line

In a two-party political system, party association holds many advantages, including preference for committee assignments, fundraising support, and political alliances to pass legislation or fund priority work. However, the association also brings expectations to vote with the party and take stands that the leadership recommends. That said, either for personal or constituency differences, elected leaders may choose to diverge from leadership at times. The elected leaders we spoke with emphasized the importance of, when diverging, to communicate plans early, explain the rationale and be discriminating.

Even when elected leaders mostly associate with their party and only exhibit independence in order to better represent their constituents, they are often caught up in party "waves" that tend to be in reaction to the president's popularity more than any particular local position. The most recent Democrat waves were 2006 and 2018, whereas the Republican waves included 1994, 2006, and the 2010 Tea Party takeover of the Republican party.

More recently under the Trump administration, many Republican party members have adapted to Trump policies, many which did not reflect a traditional Republican agenda. **Mica** (D-FL) explains further,

> *Obviously, in Washington now there are an awful lot of people who are "politically right" but really not "correct right". I have a number of Republican colleagues who I stay in touch with who are really disappointed in Trump, but they're doing the politically right thing. They're not shy about telling me that they don't support him. If you build credibility, the first few years, you may have to sacrifice to get some votes. But once you build credibility, there are people who will give you the latitude to vote differently than what the majority wants because they trust your judgment. So I guess part of it is building that credibility in a way that people who work for you will trust your judgment and try to be straightforward with you.*

Connie Morella recalls how she maintained her independence from her party, but also how she managed these differences by explaining them to her party colleagues, as a moderate Republican in a majority Democrat district just outside of Washington DC in Montgomery County, MD. She shares her story.

> *My party was a barrier to a degree. But on the other hand, it also allowed me to change legislation and make it bipartisan and to get some of the nasty elements out of the legislation. For instance, consider the appropriations committee. I was told, "Connie, there would be times when you would have to vote against certain things that would help your district, so we don't want you to be in that position" Well, BS. But my point was that they even tried to be nice to me. I mean they tried to say, "we value you, we think you're doing a good job, but appropriations would be tough for your district and with your colleagues." I just think if they want to know [why you are for or against something], you tell them why.*

Ultimately, despite her popularity, **Morella** lost re-election after 8 terms in the U.S. House, likely due to her party affiliation. Her affiliation ultimately would serve to be a vote for a Republican Speaker of the House, which was not in the interest of her democratic-leaning congressional district. In fact, **Morella** has so far been the last Republican to hold this seat in Congress.

See our Appendix tool 4.3 Party Affiliation Venn Diagram to help to identify where and in what manner the leader and the party are similar, and where they differ. This sets the path to engage in these conversations and develop a collaborative strategy, as well as helping elected leaders know where to diverge when needed.

4.2.4 Tenure Matters for Many Elected Leadership Positions

When each member of the Democratic leadership in the House of Representative and across the committees was over 70 years old in 2020, it was no accident. While House and Senate Republicans have term limits for their committee chairmanships, on the Democratic side, the work is most rewarding after years of seeing others exert additional power through their leadership positions. For caucus and conference leadership, there are term limits. However, the top three positions are not term limited and without an election loss, we see very little turnover in these positions.

Cathy McMorris Rodgers was elected to the Washington Statehouse at just 26 years old and went on the fast track in leadership at the state level and then again when she arrived in the US Congress, becoming Republican conference chair in 2013, the fourth highest position in House Republican leadership. While there are many potential reasons for her ascent, including some great mentors, she cites her willingness to take on assignments that did not interest others, do the work, and take risks. McMorris Rodgers further explains,

> *I was willing to take assignments that others may have shunned. I remember taking on a task force on water rights. Not necessarily what I really wanted to do, but there was a need. Taking the assignments that I was asked, and doing them well, has served me well. I was appointed [to a vacant seat] in December of 1993, and the Republicans won the majority. 1994 was a big Republican year; we went from having 33 Republicans in the State House to 62. So I was chairing a committee in my second year in the statehouse. Again, it wasn't the committee that I would have picked....*
>
> *So I look back on it, and even though I might have been hesitant, I was willing to take a chance and take on an assignment that maybe wasn't what I had imagined. When you get into elected office, there's a lot of issues that need to be addressed that you may not have a background or a lot of knowledge, but you have to dig in.*

Given the importance of both tenure and fundraising, elected leaders may choose a road less traveled in order to ascend in leadership. Many individuals run for federal elected office because of common signature positions on popular issues like healthcare, education, and taxes. Yet when they get to Congress they realize that the coveted Ways and Means Committee in the House or Finance Committee in the Senate holds the majority of power on these issues because they require government spending. Leadership positions on these "A committees" takes many years to achieve. Those elected leaders who instead target the less popular committees may ascend to leadership positions much more quickly.

4.2.5 Schedule, Travel, Family Toll

The schedule and travel of most elected officials are extremely demanding, such as the frequency of meetings, events, and flights, as well as the long periods away from home. Most federal elected leaders maintain a second home, sometimes shared among junior members of Congress, in Washington DC. The stressors of elected office can take a heavy toll on family and loved ones, and elected leaders are aware of this issue. Elected leaders should seek out mentors who can provide guidance on the different ways to "make it work."

A study cosponsored by CMF found that while 68% of members of Congress cited "Spending time with family" as very important, only 16% were satisfied with this aspect—giving it the lowest satisfaction rating among all 25 aspects studied for the elected positions.[7] Congressman **Snyder** weighs in on how to succeed in these circumstances.

> *I think that you've got to have a really strong marriage and family support system. Hopefully you've made enough money [*before running for office*] to have your family come up for visits, so that they can start participating in that life…. Families have to make the decision knowing that they are going to be separated a lot. It helps to have FaceTime and Skype and those things. But in my experience while in DC is that when you call home and your four-year-old is reading a book or playing Legos, they have no interest at all talking to you. It's just that's not what their life is about.*

Work-Life balance is one of the most overwhelming challenges for the elected leader as they not only lose control of their schedule, but they are constantly under public scrutiny. This challenge moves beyond the leader to their entire family. Staff members who support elected leaders can benefit the leaders and their families by developing a strong relationship between the staff and family, engaging around important questions about expectations and working relationships. In the Appendix, we offer tool 4.4 Managing the Family of the Elected Leader for supporting a constructive working relationship between an elected leader, their family or partner, and their staff, where appropriate.

---

[7]"Life in Congress: The Member Perspective," Congressional Management Foundation and SHRM, 2013.

4.3   Navigating the Representative Path

While the Representative Path is one of the least traveled paths, the exposure and impact of these leadership positions make their navigation especially challenging. As elected leaders embark on this journey, they should step into the tremendous opportunities to have a seat at the table, hold clear role authority, and act with the power to convene. They do this along with the ability to attract top-notch talent, maneuver through the government bureaucracy, and get the attention from an array of stakeholders. To fully leverage these opportunities, those elected leaders who have spent the time to know their purpose, prioritize their efforts, and connect with their constituencies will not only be more successful but also better enjoy the position and the experiences it brings.

As elected leaders leverage the power of the position, they may confront unique challenges along the way in the form of party affiliation, term limits, fundraising expectations, and a tremendous toll on their personal lives. Knowing their north star and identifying how to achieve their impact, while staying aligned with their values and ethical compass, will set these leaders apart from others. Indeed, the regular need to run for re-election is not only the test others will impose but also the one for themselves and whether this path is where elected leaders most want to be.

Reflection Questions

- Why did I run for office? What will make this journey fulfilling?
- Where will I target my political capital? What do I want to be known for?
- What are my strengths? Where do I need support? How do I build a staff organization that can best support and challenge me to maximize my position?
- How did my stakeholders position my ascension to political office? What do I want to emphasize and where do I want to create an alternative narrative?
- How will your relationships change as a result of taking elected office? How will you manage them differently than you did in the past?
- What personal sacrifices am I willing/not willing to make while in elected office? What boundaries are important to me?

5

Proxy: The Appointed Path

*When then-Congressman **John McHugh** was appointed by U.S. President Obama as Secretary of the Army, he brought with him **Robert Taub**, his chief of staff from McHugh's years in Congress, to serve in the equivalent position. Robert had no military experience himself, nor had he expected a move into the Executive Branch of the government. Nevertheless, he had a critical skill: the trust and respect of Secretary McHugh. For his part, McHugh knew that he would be more successful with Robert by his side. McHugh and Taub had each represented the 23rd district of NY of Fort Drum and served on the House Armed Services Committee for many years. They had a lot to bring the office of the Secretary, but also a lot to learn!*

Both Secretary McHugh and Chief of Staff Taub became political appointees of President Obama, as two Republicans willing to serve a Democrat administration. Taub and McHugh had been an effective team in Congress, and that team was now going to serve as the key liaison between the Obama White House and a critical branch of the US Military. Everything would be different from their years in elected office. The stakeholders were different as were the processes, demands, and opportunities. Where to begin? How would they earn the respect of the career military professionals? McHugh's former peers in Congress would now have oversight of his role and be responsible for funding his organization.

After two years at the Department of Army, Taub would be appointed as a Commissioner of the US Postal Regulatory Commission, taking an open Republican seat on the Commission. His ability to lead a bipartisan commission further led to his appointment as Chairman of the Commission, where he began serving in 2017.

© The Author(s), under exclusive license to Springer Nature Switzerland AG 2021
M. A. Clark and M. Persily Lamel, *Six Paths to Leadership*,
https://doi.org/10.1007/978-3-030-69017-5_5

Overview of the Proxy: Appointed Path

Most leaders will never cross the *appointed* path, due to the relative scarcity of the position, which goes along with its frequently high profile and impact. This path exists primarily in government and on boards of Directors[1] of privately-held companies and not-for-profit (NFP) organizations, and lasts for a fixed term. Despite their low numbers, many people will be influenced by appointed leaders in their working life, making it helpful for all of us to understand the characteristics of this path. Just among the US federal agencies, over two million employees are led by political appointees.

Characteristics of Appointed Leadership Positions

- The power of the position comes from the principal, the person or body (e.g., a board) who appointed the leader into the position
- There is legal or governing authority of the position in legislation or governance documents
- The principal who appoints the leader sets the agenda for the appointee to execute
- Appointed leaders are often brought in for their specific expertise or their connections to their patron, to the organization, and/or to the organization's stakeholders
- There is a set term for the appointment, sometimes renewable

In this chapter, we will focus primarily on the public sector appointees (i.e., federal government) because their description applies generally to most appointees, while calling attention to specific differences with private sector appointees as they arise. That said, there are a few major distinctions between typical government appointments and their counterparts on private sector boards, including:

- Government appointees often are charged with operating an organization, including general responsibility for a workforce, whereas private sector boards are less likely to supervise budgets or employees, generally exerting their governance collectively through the board and interacting primarily with executives. Thus, board members, perhaps especially those in for-profit enterprises, are often limited in their scope of understanding or attention to the operational aspects of their organization.

---

[1]Although many top executives and contractual employees are called "appointments" we do not include them in this path, because they generally follow the pattern of "hired" or "promoted" paths.

- Government appointees often are expected to serve only while their political patron is in power, while corporate and NFP board members often outlast organizational executives, clients, and sometimes owners.
- Board members of for-profit enterprises often are owners or their representatives, with fiduciary responsibilities, while government appointees cannot own nor profit from their public sector agencies.
- Board members, whether for-profit or NFP, often represent marketplace partners, constituent populations (such as those who benefit from the services of an NFP) or other stakeholders. In the public sector, there are disclosure and ethics rules that prohibit gifts, nepotism, and other forms of profiteering from government contracts.

For this book, we interviewed a variety of individual appointees across an array of organizations, largely in the federal government and corporate boards. The range of titles and settings included:

- Secretary or Director (US federal agency)
- Political Appointee, e.g., Chief of Staff, Deputy, Communications Director, General Counsel, Legislative Affairs, Commission Chair or Czar (US federal or state agency)
- Director or Trustee, Board of Directors (private-sector for-profit or not-for-profit company or organization)
- President or Provost (University)
- Ambassador (USA government)

In addition to the position holders, we also interviewed individuals who interact with appointees and therefore offered valuable insights. For private sector board appointees, we learned from a highly-regarded board advisor and from executives who work with boards. They were particularly helpful in clarifying the limited time and scope that board members have to understand the operational aspects of their organizations. For example, our board advisor was Executive Insights company founder **Rich Schroth**, who serves as a leadership fellow of the National Association of Corporate Directors. **Schroth** explained,

> *Boards hire me because most that I work with do not trust their management team enough to tell them the truth about the condition of the company. The executives filter things, and the board does not know what kind of questions to ask.*

The senior employees encountered by members of boards of directors and other non-government appointees will most often be top company executives such as chief executive officers, presidents, and divisional directors. Our sample includes members of these categories. For public sector appointees, we gained additional perspectives through focus group interviews of a US federal government "career" professionals who report to appointed leaders and, importantly, typically outlast their tenure. Those participating were senior civil service employees near the highest "general schedule" (GS) job classification; GS-14, GS-15, or Senior Executive Service (SES). This classification reflects a pay scale that begins at GS-1 and includes nearly the full range of federal employees. SES employees represent the next step up, higher in pay and typically higher in responsibility, and may include some who are directly appointed by the President. More generally, Presidential appointees are in another category termed "Executive Schedule" employees, which is the highest level of officials in the executive branch.

The presence of these long-term senior employees contributes to a unique dynamic for the appointed path in the public sector. Essentially, the employee will have a longer view (both historically and into the future) than the appointed leader who is tasked with guiding both the organization and the work of the career professional during the appointed term. Understanding this dynamic is essential to understanding the context of the appointed leader. They are visitors; there was a person filling their role before they arrived, and there will be someone after the current appointee. In the meantime, many of the other players—the career employees—will stay the same. In fact, some government career professionals call themselves the "We-Bes" which they explain to mean "We-Be here before you and We-Be here after you."

To a greater extent than for other paths, effectiveness of appointees is strongly tied to the appointing authority. As **Sarah Bittleman**, political appointee in the Department of the Interior under President Obama, stated,

Being an effective leader in managing the agency in a way that fulfills the president's policy directives or policy desires depends on how effective the president himself is and how effective he is at expressing those desires or directives.

5.1 Proxy: Opportunities and Strategies of the Appointed Path

Table 5.1 Appointed path: Proxy opportunities and strategies

Appointed path opportunities	Strategies to leverage
1. Reputation, Power, and Agenda from Principal	• Reinforce the vision of the principal • Embrace and replicate the principal's positive traits • Ensure alignment with the principal • Stay focused on the areas within purview
2. Outside Perspective	• Question the status quo • Act with less historical baggage
3. Access to the Principal and their Network	• Enable access to the principal to build currency • Build two-way communication processes
4. Short Timeframe, Low Expectations	• Focus on what must and can get done • Empower others to act • Take risks

While individuals may be appointed into a position for a variety of reasons, some more noble than others, the appointing authority has selected the appointed leader for discrete reasons. It may be to implement a political agenda, or to bring a certain perspective to the organization. Most likely, they seek candidates who are aligned with their agenda, values, brand, and the priorities of the office at the time of the appointment.

The influence of the appointed leader holds unique advantages we rarely find in the other leadership paths. These positions tend to:

1. Hold clear legal authority—whether a board vote or legal authority on certain decisions (budgets, hiring, etc.)
2. Leverage the authority of the principal. Starting a sentence with, "The President has asked…" certainly carries a lot of weight.
3. Have a clear mandate which enables them to determine where to focus their energies.
4. Access the ear of the principal who also has a high personal stake in the success of the appointee.

These advantages, combined with opportunities that the roles afford, make these positions highly sought after by many exceptional candidates. However, as former Health and Human Services Secretary **Sylvia Burwell** explains, these advantages can be leveraged by appointed leaders only when they are in alignment with the leader who appointed them.

> *Generally speaking, it's about selection alignment. For instance, what Barack Obama wanted from a budget when he appointed me was part of a process. The idea for the appointee is "Don't take the job if you're not well-enough aligned." Appointed and elected paths differ in that you really should be aligned [when accepting an appointment]. Because if you're not, it's not going to end well.*

Table 5.1 outlines the opportunities afforded to most appointed leaders and strategies to best leverage them. Each of these opportunities could also be considered a challenge, or potentially limiting for the leader. Yet, as we see through the leaders' stories throughout this chapter, what could be seen as limiting can become an opportunity depending on how one chooses to approach it.

5.1.1   Reputation, Power, and Agenda of the Principal

Appointed leaders rely on the reputation of the principal—the person or entity who appointed them—to establish their power and authority. For instance, top-level leaders referred to as "political appointees" serve at the pleasure of the President. As a result, they are often viewed as a conduit of the President's agenda, beliefs, and priorities. The principal's reputation, therefore, can be an appointee's greatest advantage or obstacle.

Ilona Cohen, who served in the White House Counsel's office and then as General Counsel for the Office of Management and Budget (OMB), both appointments by President Obama, also discusses this responsibility:

> *For White House appointees, it's common to say that we serve at the pleasure of the President. In the White House Counsel's office, however, there's a tension in that counsel serve the President in office, but they are not the President's personal counsel. White House counsel also feel an obligation to protect the institution of the Presidency and there's always a balance to ensure that the President holding office has the necessary tools at his disposal, but that in creating that space, counsel don't somehow alter or weaken the role for any future President.*

This influence of the principal can also be leveraged outside the confines of the agency employees, to include other stakeholders and decision-makers, as **Taub** attests:

> *For Congress and the administration – to the extent that they're engaged on postal matters – there's that cachet of "we're dealing with a presidentially-appointed, small p, political creature with whom we can have an engagement. So it's important externally.*

Leaders play a key role in <u>reinforcing the principal's vision</u> by outlining how they and their direct reports can support that vision and contribute to the principal's achievements. This means planning their work processes as a cascading system of goals and roles. To further leverage this opportunity, appointed leaders can <u>embrace and replicate the principal's positive traits,</u> serving as proxy or embodiment for the principal's preferred style of enacting progress toward their stated goals. The appointee can also create systems that produce clear policies or products that <u>ensure alignment</u> with the principal's approach. Such systems should include measures of fidelity and feedback loops that will keep the appointee and his or her shop in consonance. For instance, appointees can derive a chart of priorities based on their principal's agenda, using it to rate resource use, staff decisions, and other indicators of progress.

While appointed leaders often hold tremendous authority, they need to understand where their authority starts and ends. It is also critical to understand this dynamic relative to the past, in case the principal defines authority differently. Unlike other paths, the guardrails for appointed positions reinforce the expectation for the appointed leader to <u>stay focused on the areas in their purview</u>, whether as marching orders from the principal and/or the legal authority granted for their position. This may include speaking to their areas of expertise, as when board members are appointed to represent constituencies or domains such as technology infrastructure or finance. For governmental appointees, it may include directives to enact a particular policy or to restructure an agency, for instance. In all these cases, it is important for the appointed leader to lean into their purpose for being there, to make decisions and garner resources to support their mission.

Nicholas Rasmussen served as a US federal government appointee under Presidents G. W. Bush, Obama and Trump in varying national security roles, most recently as Director of the National Counterterrorism Center. Having traveled both the promoted and appointed paths, he earned critical advantages of knowing the stakeholder agencies (CIA, FBI, DHS and military), the job requirements, as well as the key personnel, while also benefitting from the authority provided through the Presidential nominee process. At the same time, having been a key player in the growth and development of the Center, he had to reflect carefully on how his Directorship would differ from the leadership he had supported as Deputy of the organization. There are potentially important differences between this route as compared to political appointees who are brought in from the outside and are therefore often seen as an extension of their principal. For those who are promoted also serve the principal, but may view themselves as institutionalists as well. **Rasmussen** shares his experiences advancing both agendas:

> *Typically someone who is a political appointee first will naturally lean more in the direction of what can be accomplished that is consistent with this administration's agenda during my limited time in office. So I would argue that my priority as somebody who grew up from within the organization is to focus a little more on advancing the objectives of the institution. What can I do to make sure that NCTC is in a position to make even stronger contributions to our counterterrorism efforts? So I would argue that I brought to the job a little more of an institutional loyalty, rather than or focus, rather than a pure political or administration loyalty.*

5.1.2   Outside Perspective

Appointed leaders differentiate themselves from their colleagues with the outside perspective and set of connections that they bring from their past experience. Sometimes this perspective is technical expertise, such as understanding of a particular field, stakeholder group, or target market. **Gaurdie Banister**, who had a successful oil career including as CEO of Aera Energy, was surprised to get a call asking him to consider being on the board of Tyson Foods, Inc.:

> *Fast-forward to when I was recruited to join the board of Tyson Foods. I was CEO of an oil company and had no idea about anything food-related other than that I eat chicken, beef, and pork…. I later found out their criteria for people to join the board - they wanted somebody who was a sitting CEO, so I met that criterion. They wanted somebody who had experience in China; I had just come back from Singapore, had worked in China on a large project. We'd built a gas plant and drilled wells to get gas for the Olympics in Beijing. I am African-American, they obviously were looking for diversity on their board. They had criteria that they were looking for, which I was able to meet.*

In other cases, the appointee may bring a new perspective and process of getting things done. **Ron Klain**, Chief of Staff of US President Biden's administration, describes how he changed processes and procedures at the Health and Human Services federal government agency when appointed as "Ebola Czar"—the federal Ebola Response Coordinator under President Obama:

> *The first was dramatically breaking a bureaucratic norm of how they have their weekly meeting. In the executive branch of government, there are many of these weekly meetings, deputy meetings, principals meetings, and so forth. I used the seriousness of the crisis and the direct grant of presidential authority to break the norms on that, to say we would have weekly meetings of the agencies involved with this one rule: the person who would come to the meeting would be the person who had actual working authority over the problem, without regard to what level they were at their cabinet department.*

This new process enabled the Ebola task force to move quickly, efficiently, and effectively to complete their mission of addressing and preventing the potential health crisis.

Appointed leaders can leverage the opportunities associated with their outside perspective through techniques such as questioning the status quo and acting with less historical baggage. In the example above, Klain was able to use his outsider status to challenge specific protocols and set new procedures that were more in line with his directed goals, rather than blindly following established meeting norms with designated representatives. When employees move up in an agency, they may become overly accustomed to the way work is done, rather than how things work best. As an outsider from the political world coming in with a specific mission, Klain lacked the baggage of those who are promoted up through the agency, whose subordinates could point to previous instances of such insiders following more traditional practices. An appointed leader can question assumptions when entering an organization, without the same long-term relationships concerns that career professionals may hold.

5.1.3   Access to the Principal and Their Network

Appointees, like other leaders, also bring in their network of connections including influencer, experts, and those on the ground who know the important operational issues. **Sylvia Burwell**, who served in multiple positions in the US federal government including Deputy Chief of Staff at the White House and years later Secretary of Health and Human Services (a position that also made her a member of the President's Cabinet), speaks to the importance of networks in managing peers as well as employees. At the broader level, from agency to agency within the government, **Burwell** notes:

The one thing I will say is being a Cabinet secretary who had also been in the White House – that was the biggest gift. In my White House role, I worked beside them and had Cabinet secretaries throwing things across the tram. It makes a huge difference when you know who to call in the White House, you know where to go, you know how to get things done because you've been on the inside.

Prior familiarity with the network of players both inside and outside the organization enables the appointee to prioritize and react quickly, especially when tensions are high, and quick action is required:

There was not a time during my stint at HHS that the command center was not at the CDC. Ebola had started. CDC came in the first day and it was like "We've got to stand at the center." So much of that was just inbox-driven and crisis-driven. But the other pieces of it came from actually listening. For example, implementation of regulation 1557 on discrimination was part of the Affordable Care Act. The civil rights community came in, and these were all people I'd known for years and years. I asked them for what their priorities were, and it went on the list. With that I had a composite of both crisis and proactive items.

Leveraging the access to the principal and their network. The access of appointed leaders to their principal and his or her network should be used to create a smooth path toward fulfillment of the reason for the appointment. Because the principal typically has significant organizational power, the appointee may build currency by supporting others' access to the principal, helping them to build relationships which may be helpful to the others' professional goals and career. Appointees may also find that there are times when mission achievement would be facilitated by short-cutting the bureaucracy, which may be possible for a principal operating at a higher level of the organization.

Appointed leaders are in a position to help the career staff to be successful with the principal. The connection to the principal can help them be successful and get what they need. **Robert Taub**, Chief of Staff to the Secretary of the Army, shares how he used his access to the Secretary to help his team be successful as opposed to name drop to accumulate power. According to **Taub**,

I think people began to appreciate, both on the civilian and military side, that they could come to me with issues that they want to get before him [Secretary McHugh].

Tonya Williams, a director at Softbank, discusses her experience coming in as Director of Legislative Affairs for then-US Vice President Joe Biden. She points out that a leader is responsible for introducing stakeholders where they need to know one another.

A disadvantage of coming from the outside is that people don't necessarily know you. There's a familiarity that folks have with working with people over time. I couldn't just go in and do the work; I had to go to Washington. It was very important for me to get to know them and understand them, and for them to know me. You also have to earn the trust of your staff. I wasn't someone who grew up with them [i.e., as a long-term employee], so they weren't sure of my capabilities. I don't know that that's necessarily a disadvantage, but it is a reality of coming in with a group that is already formed. They question you as part of their professional stewardship. You will need to make good on the promises that their boss made about why we are bringing in a new leader.

Develop two-way communication practices. Creating two-way communication from the onset is essential to building a trusting relationship between the appointed leader and the career professionals. While most senior leaders may have 90 days to interview the key stakeholders, appointed leaders need to focus their first month on soliciting input and building a relationship of consistent communication. A political appointee will regularly give directives from the principal to drive policy and agenda implementation. However, one-way communication is exhausting and disempowering. The appointed leader can initiate a more comprehensive feedback loop to raise the challenges in implementation of the principal's agenda and work on clearing those obstacles.

5.1.4 Short Timeframe, Low Expectations

The short timeframe available to many appointees, especially within federal government administrations, is often seen as a disadvantage to the position. However, this limited tenure can also serve to guide the vision and behaviors of the leader, such that they focus on what must and can get done. This is where the leader may employ authority granted from their principal, assess the resources needed to accomplish their tasks, and direct the workforce toward its new, temporary goals.

Effective leaders will, rather than forcing compliance, will clarify what they expect from their civil service employees, listen to their ideas, and use those to align with planned areas of impact. For instance, the GS-15 group that we interviewed, whose members are significantly involved in working with and implementing dictates of their appointed leaders, had many ideas about how the best-appointed leaders use their limited time.

> *They should get an understanding of your organization, what it's composed of, what its mission is. The second thing is to relook at your assumptions. Not everything done in a past administration is bad. It strikes me that every time the National Security Council changes out with an administration, all the computers and calls are taken away, so the new guys coming in have zero understanding of what we're doing. Don't just start from scratch. There are ways to have continuity.*

While career professionals may expect appointees to push the agenda forward, they do not guarantee followership and often conflict with and/or resist the changes put forth. Appointees challenge the organization's status quo and often ask difficult questions or expect new approaches from a workforce that may be relatively entrenched in its ways. While these efforts and adjustments can result in positive change, the appointed leader should not seek to remedy all organizational processes on his or her own. **Sylvia Burwell**, multiple-time federal appointee and current President of American University, believes that appointees need to hire competent help and underline them to act:

> *These are massive management jobs, which I think many people don't understand. And they have an outward facing component, so you can't whiff on that, which you must balance as part of the management job. That's why you have strong deputies.*

Like other paths, the appointed leader must come in and quickly assess the team and focus on retaining the talent that will support their success. They want and need to hit the ground running. **Nicholas Rasmussen** shares his experience,

> *When I took over as Director I was already working with a whole team of people who knew me quite well which was both an advantage and a disadvantage. I immediately sat down with each of my key leaders at NCTC, who were now my deputies. For some of them I very much wanted to say how impressed I was with their performance and to please stay... For others, "I will be happy to have you at my side for however long my tenure is." For at least a couple of the senior leaders in NCTC, I was thinking about succession, because in some cases they had occupied their positions for an extended period and transition was likely at some point. For*

the team I was inheriting, I knew enough about them and I wasn't interested in trying to create a new book, or bring new fresh blood to my team. I wanted to be efficient.

The short timeframe of the appointed leader also grants a certain license to take risks. They do not have to "live" with their policies and the potential wrath that they invoke. Therefore, the appointed leader may be given mandates that are harder to implement by the career leader. The short time frame also creates a built-in sense of urgency. The appointed leader is able to both present and push new ideas forward more quickly because there is an accepted understanding of the time restrictions on the position.

This is in part because such chance bets are necessary to move decisions along quickly, and also because it is known that the political leader is unlikely to be a long-term leader of that agency in any case. These risks, of course, should be weighed against probability of success and grounded where possible in strategic understanding of the organization.

Having served as deputy for two and a half years before assuming the Directorship, **Rasmussen** had to maneuver a fine line between honoring the work that had been done previously while also stepping into his own authority by introducing changes that he felt would improve the efficiency of his organization. The experience of becoming the President's appointee, then being confirmed by the Senate, empowered him to make these changes.

There is something to be said for knowing you enjoy the confidence not only from the President but also the validation from the Senate intelligence committee confirmation. Having that affirmation was empowering to me and made me feel like these people know what we do in the NCTC, they know our mission and they think I'm the right person to lead this organization. I was the deputy director for the previous director, his full partner, so I wasn't going to come in and turn the organization upside down. I wanted to make a few changes to some of the staff meeting rhythms, some of the ways in which I communicated with senior leaders in the organization…. But I wasn't looking to clean house.

As we have seen, the Proxy path is filled with potential opportunities that leaders can leverage to achieve success, including the reputation of the principal, access to their networks, an outside perspective and a focused goal within a set timeframe. Next, we will discuss the challenges that the Proxy may encounter along the appointed path.

5.2   Proxy: Challenges and Strategies of the Appointed Path

Table 5.2 Appointed path: Proxy challenges and strategies

Appointed path challenges	Strategies for managing
1. Perception of Qualifications and Basis of Power without Merit	• Conduct an early "listening tour" • Create a learning plan • Practice humility and gratitude • Solicit experts and feedback • Identify best contribution
2. Perceived as Managing Up Rather than Leading	• Spend time and connect with staff • Identify early wins
3. Short Time Frame to Make an Impact	• Identify "rocks" and timeline • Identify ways to leverage the team • Address areas where not aligned with career professionals

5.2.1   Perceptions of Qualifications and Basis of Power Without Merit

Because they are appointed on a basis that that does not match more typical merit-based systems for selecting leaders, appointed leaders tend to bring with them a series of narratives that undermine rather than support their leadership. The appointment may be perceived as a political favor, pay-back for donors, or membership of the "inner circle," appointed leaders immediately may feel like they have something to prove to the long-term career professionals who now surround them. Even worse, they may ignore the professionals and fail to see their value.

Ron Klain, who is the current White House Chief of Staff, and also held that position for two U.S. Vice Presidents (Al Gore and Joe Biden), explains this perfectly:

Appointed is much more complicated because, first of all, your authority is secondary. It comes from whomever the appointing authority is, and the propriety of their ability to appoint you may be disputed. The question of how you got appointed, versus someone else, is also in the air. So I think as a premise for leadership, there is a less obvious legitimacy to it.

As can be seen from Table 5.2, many of the challenges of the appointed leader mirror opportunities discussed previously. For instance, the close association of the appointed leader with the principal is seen to reflect on the appointee's qualifications. Additionally, the appointee's power and reputation may be very dependent on the principal. This view may seem to be supported by the fact that, generally, appointees' positions are assigned largely through a political process, as opposed to merit-based selection. This leads to assumptions that the appointee may lack essential capabilities to perform the duties of the position. Those serving in subordinate positions to the appointee—in the federal government, these would generally be non-political civil servants—often view themselves as more qualified for the position than the appointed leader.

Organizational subordinates, as well as some peers and other stakeholders, often assume that the appointed leader is similar to the appointing authority, sharing professional and even personal characteristics. While this can be an advantage when the appointers are powerful and well-liked, it can also be negative if the appointing authorities have poor reputations or suffer setbacks of their own during the appointee's tenure. The appointee could also suffer from failure to live up to the standard of a popular and accomplished principal, or in other ways disappoint expectations through the manner in which the appointee fulfills the role. One of the GS-15s who we interviewed explained,

> One mistake we have seen a lot of political appointees do is try to apply business concepts and processes to the federal process. They come in, they do not try to understand what our baseline process is so that they can determine where the process can and should be changed. They don't leverage the systems that are already in place. They assume an outside system is better. It can blow up in their face.

Given the shorter timeframe and strong mandate for most appointed positions, there tends to be little onboarding. As a result, the leader ought to invest in writing their own Learning Plan. Appendix tool 5.1 **Learning Plan** offers a method for appointed leaders to identify core learning goals that can enhance their leadership and hold themselves accountable. By targeting their learning on the areas required to be successful in the role, the sooner the leader will be able to focus on driving the principal's agenda. There are tremendous learning resources available to appointed leaders. It starts with knowing that while they bring critical talents, the job is likely mostly new to them and they do not have the usual 6–18 months to onboard that other leaders may be afforded.

Practice humility and gratitude. While the first step is knowing what they do not know, the next step is leveraging the talents around them. Secretary **John McHugh** practiced remarkable humility starting his first week as Secretary of the Army. He explains:

> *I think you have got to recognize that under law you may be the most powerful person in the room, but you're not the smartest person in the room, right? I spent nearly seventeen years on the House Armed Services Committee. Honestly, when I first came to the Pentagon, I thought that from a material subject matter perspective, "I've got a pretty good handle on this." But I didn't know anything; in the broader sense, I was 10 miles wide and a quarter inch deep. To do your job, you've got to be 10 miles wide and 10 miles deep.*
>
> *The senior military leaders – three or four stars particularly – who run their commands, have great expertise. What I did was simply try to get to know them on a more intimate level. In other words, not to have them into a conference room with 150 SES [Senior Executive Service employees] in there. Rather, bring them in and ask, "What do I need to know?" They call it an open-door policy. A lot of people proclaim that; I'm not sure everybody lives it. It doesn't mean "just walk in," but if they wanted a meeting and we didn't get them in two days, I wanted to know why. I think I recognized that the first and the best asset I had was knowing that I didn't have that many assets [laughs].*

Whether intentionally or not, appointed leaders send messages to the career professionals that support or undermine their leadership effectiveness. **Nicholas Rasmussen** shares how Secretary of State Tillerson may have unintentionally turned off potential supporters in his early days leading the State Department.

> *I went to a lot of meetings in the first year of the Trump administration and the White House where Secretary Tillerson would invariably bring his chief of staff or his Director of Policy Planning, not the subject matter expert from the Department who would have had line responsibility for the issue on the agenda. I could understand why he would want "his" person to accompany him, but the signal sent to the people back into the department is that their expertise as career officials wasn't viewed as central to the Secretary's preparation or participation in that meeting.*

Solicit experts and feedback Appointed leaders who acknowledge, learn and appreciate the extensive subject matter expertise of the career professionals are better received. When **Ron Klain** came in as the Ebola Czar he did not pretend to be a medical doctor, epidemiologist, or emergency response practitioner. As he tells it:

It was a brand-new position with no precedent for how to exercise the authority. Whatever power or authority I had came from taking away power from people who are doing it until the day I showed up. I was not an expert in any of the disciplines involved. I was not a widely regarded scientist. I was not a highly regarded international development expert. My immediate team, the domain experts who were assigned to me from the National Security Council, I think had some skepticism about the fact that their new boss knew nothing about the things that they knew. So a challenge was establishing what the job was going to be, what authority it would have, and a general challenge of legitimacy in our government that occurs when the White House appoints a coordinator who is supposed to oversee Senate-confirmed Cabinet leaders.

Given the weight of appointed leadership positions, national security positions are known to have advisory groups to help test the leaders' assumptions and ideas. Leaders should access this "kitchen cabinet" early and often according to **Rasmussen**,

For any political appointee, I would try to create for myself some kind of a kitchen Cabinet, to be able to test ideas about changing the direction of the organization or about what you're hearing from inside the organization. We had a Directors Advisory Board, going back to its founding in 2004, which I could populate with people on a quarterly basis, including former directors of NCTC. I could pick up the phone and ask them to meet me for lunch or coffee and say, "here's what I'm hearing, what are you hearing?" I think that was important to me, but it will be much more important to somebody coming in cold into an appointee position, who wouldn't be able to evaluate critically what they're being told unless they have a wider set of sources.

Identify best contribution. **Klain** quickly assessed what he could bring to the team and the role he could play: integrator and convener.

What I really focused on at the outset was identifying the critical problems that needed to be solved with the Ebola response, and what the bottlenecks were to solving them. I made it very clear to people that my job was not to second guess anyone's policy or domain expertise, certainly not to second guess the scientists and doctors. Instead it was to put together a process that would allow them to address what had gone unresolved due to conflicts, or due to a lack of a proper streamlined process; to find ways to resolve the problems. I think this won people's confidence quickly and accelerated the pace of action.

In doing so, **Klain** emphasized that he wanted to clear the path for the experts to do their work, to create "*a proper streamlined process to resolve problems.*" Notably, the approach of placing appointees who are administrative experts, rather than content specialists, must be carefully considered.

Given that the appointed leader often lacks a job description and clear expectations, it is important for these leaders to understand their own strengths and areas needing development. This allows them to design a role where they maximize their contribution to the organization and applies to corporate board seats as well as political appointees. The appointed leader is identified with the principal, so to be successful, appointees should identify which of their own attributes and policies will be welcomed by the organization, and plan to align with those quickly.

Despite the extensive knowledge and relationships he brought with his experience working for the Center for Counterterrorism since its inception, when **Rasmussen** was appointed as Director he recognized his own shortcomings. He knew he needed an experienced, senior leader at his side to fulfill his vision for the Center.

I haven't had a drop of leadership training.... So I selected as my deputy a very senior government official from the National Security Agency [NSA] because I knew he was a subject matter expert on terrorism.... but just as important, I knew that he had been a successful leader at literally every step of his career. I knew he had a proven track record at handling things like poor performers or strategic direction discussions with a subordinate who isn't buying into the plan. I was confident there wasn't any sticky personnel or HR problem that my deputy somewhere in his 30 + years at NSA hadn't confronted. Toward the end of my tenure my deputy left to go back to his home agency. In hiring a new deputy I conducted a very different search because I had been in the job for three years. By then, I was comfortable with my leadership style, so I looked at some out of the box choices.

5.2.2   Perceived as Managing up Rather Than Leading

Due to their close connection to the principal and the focused mission for the organization, appointed leaders may be perceived as gazing upward for guidance, rather than looking inside the organization for the expertise of those on the front lines. In response, some employees may feel undervalued as they perceive that their leader is not looking out for their interests. This has great potential to hamper the ability of the appointed leader to connect to his or charges and motivate the workforce. The titular followers are also less likely to be invested in the leader's success, due to this perception, which further exacerbates a difficult situation.

<u>Early Listening Tour</u>. Appointed leaders in such situations are advised to employ a few basic strategies to mitigate this challenge. First, appointees should prioritize an early listening tour, creating opportunities for members of the workforce to be heard both formally and informally. When planning these tours, the leaders should make sure to include subordinates and colleagues who may hold varied perspectives and represent multiple divisions and positions within the organization, before the transition if possible. Pre-transition listening tours are not always viable, politically or practically. For instance, it is typical for U.S. federal government agencies to set up transition teams, with incumbent employees compiling critical information and holding meetings to share further point with the incoming administration, generally regardless of political party. However, the administration of President Donald Trump rejected this transition norm by disregarding offers from the prior Obama administration,[2] and largely refusing to cooperate with the next administration of President Biden.

It is important to understand the general history of the former occupants of the position and their work. Whether a Board of Directors or Government agency, both entities have complex histories that require learning. Leaders will want to avoid stepping on the same landmines as their predecessors. **Marla Blow** (founder of FS Card, currently President and Chief Operating Officer of Skoll Foundation), who held appointed positions at the federal Consumer Financial Protection Bureau as well as on multiple boards of directors, told us that she conducted an initial "listening tour" starting her first day on the job, sitting down with her colleagues to learn their concerns and priorities. The follow-up to this was just as important, so she would go back and ask many more questions about the organizational history, instead of focusing only on the present and future.

Ideally, the leader will query others about their thoughts for the organization and for themselves, as well as asking what support they think is needed to pursue their desired direction. As one of the GS-15s that we interviewed expressed,

> *I think early on they have to find a way to connect with the staff. Either an all-hands meeting when everyone introduces themselves and what they cover, so they know what their staff offers them and aren't learning it the hard way after a crisis.*

---

[2]Lewis, M. (2019). *The Fifth Risk*. Norton & Company.

Once the listening tour has gathered insights from employees, one GS-15 interviewee suggested sharing the results in an organized format.

> *To add to that, they should produce a document reflecting what the staffers said, "Here are the issues we work on, here are the concerns, here's what's successful." Just a high-level, two page document saying, "This is who I am, this is my portfolio, and here are my issues and here's what I can offer you." We did that for our political appointee, and it's been very successful.*

Beyond the initial listening tour, appointed leaders should continue to prioritize means of spending time and connecting with their direct reports, working with them and learning how the organization functions well. This not only will continue to build support as employees feel appreciated from their work, but also increases the appointee's familiarity with the workforce and its operation. Former OMB General Counsel **Ilona Cohen** shared that she went into a career professional's office to ask him his opinion on a matter. His response was, "*This is the first time that someone in your position has come to me, instead of calling me into their office.*" **Sarah Bittleman,** formerly appointed at the Department of the Interior, further explains that the career professionals have insightful opinions and information and bringing them into those critical conversations not only enables higher quality work but also shows them the respect they deserve.

While ideally, the appointed leaders will proactively reach out to their new staff to develop relationships and learn about their roles and contributions. At an organizational level, a lot can be done as well. Our GS-15 interview group suggested connecting appointed leaders to civil service employees through existing onboarding practices:

> *One thing my agency did is political appointees have to go through new employee orientation. I don't know what other agencies do, but that forces them to be in the same room with GS 9s and 7s and 15s. So they get an introduction to not only the agency, but also the staff.*

Many appointed leaders may feel like they do not have the time to go through such a formal onboarding process. However, these opportunities to connect to the broader organization and learn the culture and structure will undoubtedly benefit them as they seek to maneuver through a new, likely complex bureaucracy.

Identify early wins. A last strategy for managing the perceptions of those within the organization is for the appointed leader to point out early wins of the internal workforce, so as to keep the focus on their success. Our GS-15 group pointed out that the agency itself can support this, paving the way for the appointee's success, which in turn can engender appreciation for the civil service employees on the part of the leader.

> *The most successful career staff have been able to assess the motivations and the needs, anticipating what we will face with a new administration. Coming into this administration, we took a lot of time to look at political speeches and other materials. We knew that right after Inauguration Day that there would likely be a hiring freeze or a pay freeze. Not surprisingly, on the Inauguration Day, word came down that there would be a hiring freeze. And because we were anticipating that, we were able to provide information about previous freezes and actually shape this new hiring freeze in a way that is least harmful to the federal workforce. If we hadn't anticipated that, helping our leaders to provide planned leadership, we wouldn't have been prepared, the impact would have been a whole lot worse.*

5.2.3   Managing the Bureaucracy in a Short Timeframe

The job structure itself also brings with it a set of challenges. The legal authority of federal government-appointed positions often includes a tremendous bureaucratic administrative workload. Whether it is approving company budgets or reviewing policies, communication, or other duties, the need to sign-off on the many items that cross the appointee's desk can be quite overwhelming. All efforts must be accomplished within the available timeframe, often 3–5 years within federal government appointments, which limits what appointees can get accomplished as well as how others view the appointee.

The appointed leaders we spoke with were clear about what they wanted their legacy to be for the agency. Whether as Secretary of HHS or now as President of American University, **Sylvia Burwell** shares that it is essential to know:

> *What are the priorities? That doesn't mean that you're not doing the other things, but it is being willing to have your list of big rocks. I have it. It's like the list of the big rocks for the first six months.*

The "rocks" refer to the demonstration made famous by Seven Habits author Stephen Covey, where when faced by a task of placing a varied set of rocks in a container, prioritizing the bigger rocks allows all to fit. If the pebbles are added first, they may take up the available room, rather than fitting in the spaces around the larger rocks.

Burwell further explains that as HHS Secretary,

> *You can imagine that I knew what the president's largest priority was, which was "get this thing working". In everything about the selection for the position, about me - was about that. But also in the case of an appointed leader, I knew that I was busy working on the president's second term management at OMB. That's what I was working on when all of a sudden, I needed to turn, shift, and think differently. The president passed the health care bill. The whole ACA[3] and everything he'd done, was all about affordability, access, and quality. So I needed to get that fixed, which was weighing us down. I didn't even need to ask him.*

Identify priority "rocks" and timeline. As **Burwell** expressed, it is essential to identify the big rocks in order to set priorities. Given the short-term nature of most appointed positions, it is helpful to divide up the responsibilities across them so that some individuals focus on the day-to-day, where others can be more strategic at looking at the full term. Further, appointed leaders say that their relationship development should be focused on the long-term stakeholders as opposed to other appointees.

Perhaps most important is to decide where the appointee focuses their efforts, considering in advance what the appointee's legacy will be. When **Jessica Smith** began as head of Public Affairs for the Federal Emergency Management Agency (FEMA), a job that is literally concerned with fighting fires, she knew that she needed to carefully plan if she hoped to make a positive long-term impact on the agency. As she put it,

> *It would be a miserable 18 months if people just were waiting for me to leave. You want to be able to make an honest contribution to the job and you want to feel like you're there for a reason. You want to be a leader.*

After three months of listening and asking questions to the career professionals, she picked her focal project—to reorganize the department in order to create new efficiencies. **Smith** shares the story of how she managed such a large endeavor within the limited timeframe of her FEMA position, especially considering the cooperation from staff that she would need to be successful.

---

[3]ACA refers to the Affordable Care Act passed by U.S. Congress and signed into law by President Obama in 2010.

I had to put together a rollout plan for this re-org because people weren't excited about it, or they were working in the agency leadership for seven years and they were waiting for their promotion within the leadership. And the idea that I was going to move them over to a new division called "strategic communications" made them feel uncomfortable, if they were getting off course or I was going to screw their trajectory within the organization.

Identify ways to leverage the team. **Smith** also managed up, leveraging senior administrators to help craft and sell her program.

I got buy-in from a lot of the senior staff in the organization: the chief of staff, the deputy administrator, and they actually helped message with me. Once they were bought-in I had them have conversations with others, then I had one-on-one conversations with people. …The deputy is never a political appointee. Deputy is the career position - they want the number two in any department to be somebody who has institutional knowledge because the number one person may rotate in and out. So that number two has to be an established veteran.

My deputy was very involved in the process and helped me think through the rollout, and I had to get buy-in with her too. I was there for 18 months, and I'd say nine months of it was re-org and buy-in from the people who actually do the disaster response – those who put the trailers out and send out supplies – and putting people on notice. When I did my re-org, it messed up who liaisons to which offices, so I needed their buy-in too. I'd say, "don't worry, I'm going to take this person away from you, but I'm going to give you somebody equally good." There was a lot of internal buy-ins that I had to get. It was a long process.

Perhaps the greatest reward for Smith was that the re-organization that took so much effort and buy-in lasted beyond her term in position.

(See Appendix tool 5.2 **Project Prioritization** for a tool to help appointed leaders align their agenda with interests of the principal to manage their short timeframe and impact.)

Similarly to leveraging those areas where the leaders are aligned with the career professionals and historical players, leaders should also develop a clear strategy for areas where there is not alignment. Here, leaders should bring in their influence skills to the table. Some appointed leaders go wrong by assuming that their authority will suffice to move the organization. It is not easy to overcome the relatively passive resistance to change which occurs when the workforce is not aligned with the leader's vision. One appointee told us, *"We call that the 'agency Yes' where they say yes to your face, then go back to doing things the way they always did."*

The goal of an appointee, like other leaders, is to bring people along to support the organizational agenda—as we've seen, in the appointee's case that agenda may be narrow and conferred from above. The workforce that lives beyond the appointed term must be given or encouraged to develop a reason to support the appointee's success. If appointed leaders demonstrated that they are invested in the success of the rank and file employees, whether through access to the appointing principal or by supporting employee career growth and interests, they will be more likely to help the appointee to be successful.

The appointed leader's relationship with the career professionals can be extremely challenging. Starting with perceptions of you as a deserving leader, but with regard to their interest in your success. In the federal agency, these relationships tend to start at a major trust deficit, and many times, these are never overcome (especially when interests are not aligned). One GS-15 commented that it was hard enough for an appointee to gain followership of career employees when their interests were aligned. He could not imagine the level of difficulty for Trump appointees whose agenda was in conflict with the missions of the agencies. Further, another GS-15 describes the influence on civil service workers from words which may be political rhetoric:

> *I think political appointees also have to be careful about the language that they use when describing federal employees. A specific example of that would be the "drain the swamp" term which many political appointees spew in the national news media from the beginning of this [Trump] administration. That's very harmful to the relationship between the political appointee cadre and staff.*

Specific mismatches of assumptions about work practices can also be detrimental to effectively leveraging the federal workforce, as another GS-15 professional expresses:

> *The other senior advisor and I both saw this political [appointee] completely shut out the civil service. After that, no one listened to what he was saying. He thought that he knew best, and civil service was part of the problem. We started to read the tea leaves and separated ourselves politically from him and this institution because we knew his days were limited. In fact, he ended up being put in charge of closets after his first year.*

5.3   Navigating the Proxy Path

Life as a political appointee is not for everyone. The work demands can be overwhelming, and the compensation can be a struggle especially for families requiring additional childcare due to the long hours. As one former appointee put it, *"for me to go back, the mission and the impact would have to be so attractive that I simply couldn't pass it up."* The short timeframe in these roles has much to do with the pace required of the leaders. That said, many former appointees fondly remember the amount of impact and miss having that level of influence in their later roles. Whether it's negotiating global agreements, setting rules to protect consumers, or implementing national policy, appointed leaders can have an impact well beyond their years of experience and unparalleled to other industries. That draw will be forever enticing to leaders desiring to have a significant impact.

While appointed leaders may be on a short timeline, patience is required when leading career government professionals who may be asked to pivot very quickly, yet are operating on a much longer time horizon than their new boss. **Rasumussen** explains,

> It should be expected that we could have an administration change and a new set of appointed leaders, and the policy direction of the government could change. For political appointees, it's important to balance change with regard for career individuals. In a place like the State Department, those individuals [may be] taking new marching orders where the policies that they were energetically promoting six weeks ago are antithetical to the President and his new team.

The GS-15 interview group offers still more suggestions on what helps to make effective appointed leaders.

- *Political appointees who have been in prior administrations are much more mature. They've been around the block, know the importance of civil service, and take time to talk. It is the new politicals who we think "Don't they teach you anything?" They are just assumed to have leadership skills and political acumen when they arrive, but they don't.*
- *Successful appointees connect. They take the time to meet people that are working for them. They have staff meetings where they actually sit down and listen to ideas that are coming from the civil servants, policy officials.*
- *They have an appreciation for history and the long game.*
- *I think all political appointees should meet with their predecessors from an opposite party and administration.*

Reflection Questions

- Why did you seek/accept this position? What are the principal's expectations for you and how does this align with your goals?
- What expertise, talents, and relationships do you bring to your role and organization and how can your new stakeholders benefit from this expertise?
- What knowledge and expertise will I rely on others for? How can I maximize their value and contribution?
- Given the likely short timeframe of my position, how will I define my success in the role? What do I need to put in place in order to achieve these priorities?

6

Creator: The Founder Path

Seth Goldman had a vision of a healthier way to enjoy refreshing drinks, to create pure and drinkable goodness beyond the sugared chemicals he saw dominating the soft beverage market. This vision inspired him to travel the world in search of the best natural sources of tea – he relates his journeys to tea fields in Asia in his standard backstory discussions and speeches, and it is a story worth hearing. He and partner Barry Nalebuff launched Honest Tea in 1998, and the resulting range of flavored low-sugar teas met eager consumers in the form of $70 million in sales in 2010, then investment and eventual acquisition by The Coca-Cola Company ($43 million investment in 2006 for 40% of Honest Tea, followed by total buyout in 2011). Unlike many founders who have sold their ventures to a larger corporation, Goldman maintained leadership and operational control of Honest Tea as a quasi-independent brand and business unit. Working from a small office in Bethesda, Maryland, he had to adjust some of his management approaches, but Goldman largely kept true to his original vision for Honest Tea. In 2015, he stepped away as "TeaEO" and became TeaEO emeritus until he resigned at the end of 2019 to pursue other ventures in the healthy food space.

Founders of businesses and other organizations hold a much-admired, enviable place in the eyes of the world. They are the creators and the visionaries that many of us see when thinking of the "ideal" leader. Admired as risk-takers, even idolized for their fearless journey through the start-up world, they often mold their companies in their own image, breathing and bleeding their own brand.

© The Author(s), under exclusive license to Springer Nature Switzerland AG 2021
M. A. Clark and M. Persily Lamel, *Six Paths to Leadership*, https://doi.org/10.1007/978-3-030-69017-5_6

Within the broad strokes, however, every founder paints their own picture. They vary in the inspiration, the selection of colors and shapes, and the story outlined in the sketch. The founders are artists who diverge as do their creations. Some dash off a sketch before moving to the next subject, others nurture the assignment and create a space for it in the world, still others swirl colors and add layers until achieving a masterpiece that changes how others appreciate their art—in whatever corner of the world their art lives, through a product, service, or technology.

In this chapter, we will share and discuss factors that influence the success of leaders inherent in the founder's path. For our purposes, we consider founding leaders to be those who begin a new venture, generally in the private sector,[1] and develop it to the point of financial sustainability or acquisition by an allied entity. We use the founders' own stories and words to convey the opportunities of their path, and how these can be leveraged. We also review challenges that founders may experience in their journey, how these can be managed or mitigated, and where mistakes may lead to temporary setbacks, missed opportunities, or longer-term failure. While the founders we feature have had considerable success—almost a given for most "how-to" leadership books—each has also encountered difficulties and disappointments along the way.

To understand the founding leader's path, we spoke with many founders, investors, and "early" employees hired as part of entrepreneurial start-ups. We will introduce you to several founders, many of whom have started multiple successful (financially, creatively, and/or influentially) and recognizable companies. The majority of our interviewees have the same title— "founder"—although many have added other titles as their companies grew, such as CEO and President. Our interviewees discuss their ventures across the multiple industry sectors in which they operate, including consulting services, education and technology, energy, engineering, financial services, and food and beverages.

---

[1] We did speak to leaders who launched new government agencies, but generally do not draw upon them here.

Very typically, founders encounter the limits of their own talents in perfecting a product or service, and in building a workforce. Founders sometimes face the necessity of "killing the baby" in scrapping early attempts that may have represented significant blood, sweat, and tears, but that simply are not performing. **Goldman** reports the failure of many tea flavors, multiple packaging ideas, and—early on—refusals of shopkeepers to stock his products. They may find that early hiring selections based on friendship or proximity must be reversed, often painfully. To get through, founders rely on their vision, passion, credibility, know-how, tireless dedication, and through strong relationships. Good leaders find ways to leverage their founding advantages, garnering and controlling resources needed to further their vision, building appropriate roles into their workforce, and supporting transparency to carry their vision to others.

As leaders of their own ventures, founders draw from advantages which are inherent to their position. They may lead with aspects that suit their personality and their venture—vision, passion, and credibility through know-how, tireless dedication, plus a thorough understanding of the reach and limits of their authority. Good leaders find ways to leverage their founding advantages, garnering and controlling resources needed to further their vision, building appropriate roles into their workforce, supporting transparency to carry their vision to others, and building the relationships needed to empower others to help build their organization.

6.1   The Creator: Opportunities and Strategies of the Founder Path

Table 6.1   Founder path: Creator opportunities and strategies

Founder path opportunities	Strategies for leveraging
1. Personal Vision and Values	• Clearly communicate their vision to their employees, investors, and customers • Communicate, support, and enact personal values to establish a resonant culture • Ensure that employees understand connections among vision, values, and steps to achieve them
2. Founder Passion	• Tap into the employee passions to ignite their motivation • Showcase passion in how approach to work • Use performance management to shape the workforce
3. Credibility: Commitment, Knowledge, and Authority	• Demonstrate commitment to the venture • Establish a clear governance structure that holds oneself and others accountable • Willingness to learn about and participate in all aspects of the business

6.1.1   Personal Vision and Values

At their essence, founders may be epitomized by their personal vision of the organization, product, or service that they will build, and their ability to translate this vision into reality. When their vision is clearly communicated and connected to the people of the organization, it helps to illuminate not just the end goal, but also the guideposts and many decisions along the path to success. As will be discussed below, to succeed this vision must be paired with resources, sold to organizational stakeholders, but before any of that, the venture begins with the founder's personal vision—the concept, foresight, and imagining of what could be (Table 6.1).

This primacy of vision can be seen in **Seth Goldman**'s story of healthy, drinkable goodness, especially following the acquisition of his enterprise by Coca-Cola. Seth insisted not only on minimizing the sugar content in his teas, but also in developing marketing materials that emphasized the contrast with less healthy, more sugary drinks that dominated the market. In other words, he emphasized the downside of sugar within a company that thrived on sugar's addition to their core products. He explained,

> *I would highlight the difference in sugar levels in our drinks – I launched Honest Tea because I wanted a less sugary drink. For me, I'm driven by the mission of the work, the impact of the work.*

The personal aspect of the vision may be inherent in the will or skills of the founder, in the sense that founders believes that they can do the job more ably than others, or even that they would just rather not have others tell them what to do. For **Selim Chacour**, founder of American Hydro, it was a bit of both. He explains his work for a large capital-intensive manufacturing and engineering firm, just after he had been tasked with returning profitability to a failing division.

> *One day they said they could not afford the division I led "Even though you turned it around, your next goal is to sell it." At that moment, I decided that I would help them sell the division, but I wouldn't be part of the deal. So I called them to say, "Yes, thank you, but I'm not going to continue with the company. I've decided to go out on my own." Everybody was laughing, and they said if anyone can do it, it's you guys, but look at the odds.*

Those laughing at the time may have reconsidered their skepticism in just a few short months, when American Hydro began winning contracts and looking like a formidable industry competitor. Certainly, they grew to respect the venture as it flourished, employing over 240 people with annual earnings of $45 million when they were acquired by Finnish energy company Wärtsilä Services in 2016.

The vision can also be about the people of an organization, or at least how to accomplish the vision through the workforce. The late Tony Hsieh of Zappos[2] relates this as

---

[2]Raz, G. (Zappos: Tony Hsieh). (2017, January 23). *How I Built This* [Audio podcast]. https://rad iopublic.com/HowIBuiltThis/s1!574ab.

Imagine a greenhouse, at the typical company where the CEO is the strongest, and tallest, most charismatic plant that all the other plants might strive to one day become. I think of my role as more about being the architect of the greenhouse and all the plants inside will survive and flourish.

This is a powerful vision and one that may resonate with employees as they realize that the founding leader has their well-being in mind.

Personal values. Many founders discuss the relationship of their own value system—their beliefs and ideas about what is important, as both end goals and instrumental paths—to the culture and operation of their venture. The extent to which these values are shared, communicated, supported, and enacted among the leaders and members of the workforce is known as an organization's "culture." Generally, such values can emerge from many organizational sources, such as an influential set of leaders, but in entrepreneurial ventures the values commonly begin with the founder. Founders have the unique advantage of setting the values for their organization, rather than buying into the values of an organization or leader. As they set these values, they can establish the type of culture that energizes them as long as they work with employees to enact those values through organizational practices wherein they know their leadership and their employees will thrive.

Marla Blow, as founder and CEO of consumer credit company *FS Card*, relished the opportunity to shape an organization in line with her vision, target market, and beliefs about the role of how an organization should operate, such as in the realm of work-family balance. **Blow** began FS Card in 2014, soon acquiring $40 million in venture backing, and then raising $150 million in credit financing in 2017. Her vision was a company that reached underserved consumers, "*re-imagining the small-dollar lending landscape and working to meet the needs of a customer base that has been poorly served by existing credit options,*[3]" often for families and minorities who more typically must deal with the higher risks and interest rates of a sub-prime market. In 2018, she was honored as *EY Mid-Atlantic Emerging Entrepreneur of the Year*.

Blow realized that in building her own business, in contrast to her experience as an executive with Capital One and an appointee at the federal Consumer Financial Protection Bureau, she could "*put my thumbprint on it, and make exactly what I wanted*" especially in terms of family-friendly policies. This included family-friendly policies in line with the importance **Blow**

---

[3] https://markets.businessinsider.com/news/stocks/fs-card-inc-closes-150-million-credit-facility-to-continue-its-build-card-product-expansion-1005338030, accessed January 2020.

places on supporting families, aligning her personal and organizational values, such as by allowing parents to bring their families to work on occasion and having work-related social events during the day instead of on employees' personal time. Blow clearly signals the importance of family by ending work-related events by 5:30 pm (even if she would be up working until 2am, after putting her son to bed). We will have "*no forced corporate fun,*" she intones.

See Appendix tool 6.1 **Establishing a Value-Based Culture** for a tool to support founding leaders to intentionally create a culture that reflecting their personal values, establishing clarity about these values related to norms, practices, and policies for their organizations.

At times, there may need to be a limit to the extent of founder values, alignment, or identity with the organization, at least in the eyes of some founders. **Chip Paucek**, co-founder and CEO of educational technology company 2U, puts this clearly:

I'm hopeful that the culture reflects 2U, not me. I think that's really important. I've intentionally focused on the culture. I believe each of the guiding principles. But I guess I would give the distinction that if I got hit by a bus tomorrow, I believe 2U survives. I believe 2U is not about me.

So, for the health and sustainability of the venture, at some point the founder may want to consider just where they begin, and the organization ends.

Strategies for leveraging vision and values. The advantage of a founding leader's vision is not merely that they understand the picture of the future business, but also that they are able to share it in a way that both communicates the ideas and gives room for others to be recognized for their contributions. **Marla Blow** tells us that to share the vision, leaders must find room to reiterate—"if saying it once is not enough, say it with enthusiasm!" Blow initiated a weekly lunch together in the office, wherein a standup followed the meal: what's going on, working on, feel good about, worried about, open questions—plant Qs if needed. She also used these meetings to recognize people formally for good work.

Rob McGovern, founder of CareerBuilder.com (launched in 1995 and sold for $200 million in 2000) characterizes the process of turning vision into reality as a personal and professional challenge to "*prove something*"—make an advance in technology, achieve a meaningful level of financial return, build a high-performing team, deliver an "MVP product," or generate a customer satisfaction level that gives notice to the other players in the market.

When I arrive on the scene to advise entrepreneurs they score too high on hopes, not on entrepreneurial competence. One example is, if I've said this one time I've said it 10,000 times to entrepreneurs: "Just prove something." Don't try to change the world, prove something. Because if you prove something you raise more capital, and you can prolong this game. … Here is a real-world example. I always tell entrepreneurs that after you raise capital money, the very first meeting should be with all the staff to have them say "What do we have to prove with this money?"

This use of vision includes a measurable outcome which also functions as a subsidiary goal and feedback device for progress along (or deviating from) the path. When shared with others, it serves as a guidepost for involvement from organizational members beyond the founder. The best founding leaders know the reach of their vision, its potential limitations, and have a plan to make their vision a reality for their markets, employees, and other stakeholders. They employy strategies that extend their vision to others, and help them to see the picture of the product, service, or organization that the founder aims to create. Good leaders find ways to leverage their founding advantages, garnering and controlling resources needed to further their vision, building appropriate roles into their workforce, and supporting transparency to carry their vision to others.

To augment their vision and build appropriate organizational competencies to enact it, successful leaders must delineate clear tasks associated with the vision, in addition to usable metrics to track progress toward goal fulfillment. **Kevin DeSanto**, a founding partner of KippsDeSanto, a financial services firm, describes a founder's essential tasks as:

1. Recognize opportunity;
2. Surround yourself with experts;
3. Be willing to make hard personal decisions;
4. Sell your vision;
5. Keep your work ethic.

As might be self-evident, it is important that beyond simply outlining such tasks, they must be communicated to partners and employees. In this way, the other members of the venture can share in the founder's vision and work to enact it.

Rob McGovern, who followed CareerBuilder.com with other ventures such as retail data company PreciseTarget, includes his employees in his vision as well:

I was the first employee at Careerbuilder, after writing the company's business plan on the beach. It was a great ride, ultimately resulting in the #1 player in the online jobs category. ...I also learned the secret of being an effective manager: let the inmates run the asylum.

If the inmates are running things as **McGovern** recommends, or if the founder simply intends to empower the partners and employees, it is critical to have clarity of the venture's operation, roles, and duties. **Seth Goldman** gives this advice:

There are basically three duties of a CEO. First, you have to create a distinct and clear vision about what you're trying to do. Next you have to generate the resources to make that vision come to reality, then you hire the people to be able to execute that – obviously hire the right people, give them the right direction and manage the team to make that happen.

Together, these founders make it clear that transforming from vision to reality means delineating clear roles within their founding team, building a workforce of complementary talent, and supporting the development of metrics and competencies that will help the organization as it grows and encounters new challenges.

As we can see through the experiences of those highlighted above, a founder's vision creates an opportunity to specify a goal and illuminate a path to it. Founders can articulate their vision by clearly outlining the end goal and general plan of how to achieve it, through communicating a set of values, establishing organizational practices and norms of operation based on these goals and values, and building a venture consistent with their ideas. Intentional use of this concept along with its associated goals, values, and plans can serve to inspire the workforce and effectively empower them to act in support of the founder's vision.

6.1.2 Founder Passion

Your venture is one bet, and you are all in.
   —**Rob McGovern**, CareerBuilder.com

Another defining characteristic of founding leaders, most often considered to be a strength or advantage, is that of passion. Founders often describe their passion as being connected to their product or service, their venture, or their impact on the stakeholders who they seek to serve. Passion can be realized as the strength of feeling affinity and motivation to pursue an entrepreneurial venture and its components. It can be simple, providing support for the vision, as when engineering firm American Hydro founder **Selim Chacour** utters the classic line "*do what you love.*"

What a founder loves may encompass more than just their own product or service line. In 2008, **Christopher "Chip" Paucek** co-founded 2U, an educational technology company that has grown to a $3.5 billion market capitalization and 2600 employees in 2019. Chip has passion for his company, along with its associated products and services.

> *Be bold and fearless. While I think my favorite guiding principle is 'don't let the skeptic win,' the most important is actually 'be bold and fearless.' What does that mean? It doesn't mean – 'go skydiving'. It means don't do it a particular way just because we did it that way before. Figure out the best possible path to deliver success for each project regardless of what's gone before.*

But while **Paucek** has made great gains in supporting the transformation of online education, and has done well for himself, his passion extends beyond these ends. As he puts it:

> *I'm very employee-focused, by definition. I'm personally motivated by the employees more than I am by my personal wealth – no judgment for those leaders who are wired the other way. It sounds like bumper sticker stuff, but it's really what works for me. We have a deal with the employees overall so that as we do better, the employees do better. Generally speaking, we want our package of both benefits and reasons to work here to get better every year.*

Paucek shares his passion with his employees, using his status as founder and CEO to meet and motivate employees. He talks about shaking hands with each employee on their orientation day, so they can see a CEO who cares about the company and its people. And it does not end with the employee's socialization period; he leverages his celebrity status with, literally, a personal touch:

> *Tomorrow I will go to every employee in the building and "high-five" them. It used to be fast. Now it's like 2.5 hours. But I'll do it tomorrow, and tomorrow night I'll fly down to our new office to meet all the employees. I went to the New York office last Thursday, I do Boca tomorrow, and I do Tempe next Monday.*

Other founders describe their own journeys, going beyond simply creating a product, building a company, or amassing wealth. As **Randy Altschuler**, founder and CEO of multiple successful start-ups including Office Tiger, Cloudblue, and Xometry, puts it:

> … *at some point you make a decision in your life. For me it wasn't so much about money. I was much more interested in building something. That's what really got me excited, it was about starting something and seeing the tangible results of your efforts.*

Still, the passion for creating a new product, building an organization, serving the customers, and benefitting employees and others often starts with the founding leader. This passion shines through not just in words, but also is showcased in how founders approach their own work. **Paucek**, even while prioritizing his employees, still makes sure to put his very best self into his work:

> *I'm super competitive with one person: me. I don't think there is a perfect science of how to become a better leader. Be open, listen, don't presume you know everything, but be confident enough to go for it when you feel like you've got the right. Life's too short. You've got to run at it. I think it's pretty hard to out-drive me. I think that may be my single best attribute, and is what I still bring to this company every day.*

Transitioning from founder to effective organizational leader can be an arduous road, and passion may grease the wheels to help get there. True, deep-seat passion is characteristic of many founders, and their ability to extend it beyond themselves may make the difference for their ventures and the people along for the ride.

The secret for leveraging passion seems to involve transference of the vision and the excitement that drives it. A certain amount of this can be accomplished through the personal magnetism of the founding leader. However, as **Seth Goldman** warns, "*Being charismatic only gets you so far if you can't execute.*"

This implies that passion may be sustained similarly to vision—by having clarity of direction and operation, known roles, and sufficient support. The basics of performance management fit in here as well. Early on, in order to build the organizational talent in consonance with the mission of a growing venture, leaders should plan how they will shape their workforce to be in line with their passion. Ideally, performance management is a process that begins with the venture's image in the marketplace, proceeds through recruitment and selection (communicating clear messages about what the organization is, what it is not, and what it is looking for in its employees), socialization and training, compensation, and other managerial practices. In this way, the organization and those it attracts become clear on what is valued in terms of knowledge, abilities, values, behaviors, and outcomes. The passion, launched from the vision and kindled with charisma of the founding leader, becomes sustainable, directed, and rewarded.

6.1.3   Credibility: Commitment, Knowledge, and Authority

Founders typically are awarded a presumed status of sincerity and loyalty to the mission, of in-house knowledge competence, and of legitimate authority—once the venture is proven viable, anyway. In the eyes of others, such credibility is largely inherent in the founder's position, akin to the goodwill that a parent might have for their family, and is among the most differentiated characteristics of founding leaders as compared to other paths. They use this credibility to attract others (investors, employees, market partners) and to further goal fulfillment for their venture.

Commitment. Founders can extend the effectiveness of their credibility through consistency with their own vision and values, as promoted through their causes. For instance, in the debate over adding "No High Fructose Corn Syrup" on the label of his Honest Kids products, **Seth Goldman** of Honest Tea had to stand up to his corporate parents at Coca-Cola:

> So I said, "We're not going to remove that. It's not that I don't have respect for you or for Coca Cola, but this point of difference is relevant to our consumer." Since then, ultimately we've built something that's 10 times larger than it was when they first invested. People at Coca-Cola know my only agenda is Honest Tea. I'm not playing games, I'm not gonna say things just to get along or to get a promotion.

Founders gain credibility through both the reality and the perception that they have an extreme commitment, built on having a lot at stake in terms of their ideas, talents, reputation, and personal resources.

Knowledge. Founders typically have intimate understanding of the venture and its components, whether in the "big picture" sense or through being acquainted with the details. This knowledge builds and extends credibility, but often does not come as naturally as it may seem to others. At minimum, they are expected to have special understanding of the core product or service and business proposition of their venture. **Marla Blow, Rob McGovern**, and **Randy Altschuler** all brought financial savvy to their ventures, which was especially important for raising capital investment, as well as relying on their executive-level management experience. **Goldman** began Honest Tea with a great business plan, but wanted to immerse himself into each functional area of the venture:

> *Organizationally, when I started out I was literally doing everything. That experience helped give me leadership credibility because I was going into an industry where I had no experience. I can talk about distribution, I can talk about production, certifications, all the different things because I've done all of it. I certainly don't know more than the technical people, but I know enough that I can speak with knowledge about what I've done, and for that matter as I become a board member of other companies.*

In this way, **Goldman** is essentially cross-training himself to be fluent in every aspect of the business—a practice that he continues to this day.

Authority. It may seem obvious that being a founding leader confers authority to make decisions, allocate resources, and generally direct the organization. However, as a venture grows it acquires more stakeholders, some of whom invest financially, some with their blood, sweat, toil, and maybe tears. The founder can use their vision, passion, and other aspects of credibility, while also tempering authority with a balance of what is good for the organization and its stakeholders, for both short and longer term. **Blow** her success in balancing her decisions on the values and clarity of communication within her organization and across the needs of multiple stakeholders. She explains:

> *I really wanted to serve all of our stakeholders. So considering the employee, our end customers, our investors, and our partners who made it possible for us to issue credit cards. Everybody is probably a little bit unhappy, which means that we're likely doing it mostly right. So that was one of the things that I very clearly articulated at FS Card. It was one of the values that we actually had up on the wall in the office, that we seek balance among all of our stakeholder groups.*

Chip Paucek maintains that founders have built-in credible authority both for the idea and for the execution or operational functioning of the organization, and that both matter. The credibility for the idea can be explained in our discussions (above) about a clear vision, shared passion, and the commitment and knowledge aspects of credibility. The credibility for execution goes further, in terms of directing the "how" of thing getting done. It can be accomplished simply in concept, as when founders directly hiring their own team, increasing the likelihood that the members will be aligned to the founder in outlook and likely in direction. The founder also maintains authority through ownership, with a greater portion held equating to less accountability to others.

Credibility relates not only to the founder's core business, but also adds a sheen to seemingly unrelated professional and personal areas. **Paucek** certainly enjoys his ability to inspire his employees just by establishing a personal contact through handshakes and high-fives, but at times he also wonders why his presence means so much to employees. **Paucek** does not want to be a celebrity in his own company and in fact relishes his longer-term employees in part because they do not seem to hold him in much awe, and he puts it clearly:

> *I will tell you also that the day I leave, no rose petals. If you start thinking it's more about you, you need someone to knock you down a couple notches.*

Strategies for leveraging credibility. The strategies for leveraging credibility can be seen in the words of the founders above, in that a founder can increase credibility through demonstrating commitment to the venture through knowledge of critical areas relating to the product and the operation of the organization, as well as through demonstrating authority by establishing clear governance lines. Sometimes, as in **Goldman**'s case at Honest Tea, credibility was enhanced by accessing financial resources to get the venture through lean times. His cofounder, Barry Nalebuff, while not pouring funds into the venture, "*had the ability to write a check to keep us afloat.*"

Founders interviewed discussed building their knowledge-related credibility of the organization and its operation by participating in all aspects of the business—including getting their hands dirty. As discussed above, **Goldman** mentioned that he cross-trained himself across his organization's functional areas early in its history. Although **Goldman** has become wildly successful by the hopeful standards of many entrepreneurs, this manner of building credibility does not stay exclusively in the past.

> *It was important to really be engaged in the work. For example, earlier this week we had a load of tea delivered to the back, just to use as samples. The CEO or the founder wouldn't typically help unload the pallet. but I was down there unloading pallets. It's all part of the business and you never want to get too far away from any part of this, and especially not the sales. I think that sometimes founders have to keep a little part of the business operation, that they really love to take on.*

The Creator path is filled with opportunities that leaders can leverage to achieve success. Their venture is often built on the founder's vision, passion, and expertise, which if leveraged properly may grow into larger, successful organizations. The better entrepreneurs will communicate their vision and their passion for the venture, personalizing it for other stakeholders. They build credibility through sharing ideas and know-how, and leverage the talent around them by developing skills in managing performance and connecting with employee motivations rather than simply assuming that others will have the same fervor for the venture. Next, we will discuss the challenges that the Creator may encounter along the Founder path.

6.2 Creator: Challenges and Strategies of the Founder Path

Table 6.2 Founder path: Creator challenges and strategies

Founder path challenges	Strategies for managing
1. Resource Scarcity	• Continually seek funding, selling ideas, and demonstrating success
2. Founder's Personal Limitations	• Surround yourself with complementary talent
3. Sharing and Giving up Power	• Plan for how to distribute authority and decision responsibility
4. Engagement of Non-Founding Employees	• Ensure that employees have a reason to feel connected to the work and the organization
5. Professional Relationships versus Friendships	• Make the difficult talent decisions
6. Celebrity Status and Approachability	• Build a system that provides honest feedback

While society admires famous founders, in spite of this path's inherent advantages, they have quite an uphill road to climb. Challenges can emerge from the market—resources, investors, consumers, opportunities—as well as from the organization and the people who become part of it. Founders must often make tough decisions on what to keep and what to cast aside, including about early companions who may not be suitable for the continuing journey. Challenges abound as the ventures find success and growth, creating barriers and diversions, some of which offer alternative opportunities, but many of which threaten the viability of the venture (Table 6.2).

6.2.1   Resource Scarcity

A common refrain among the founders we interviewed was the need to garner financial support for their venture—as **Marla Blow** phrased it, "*how much runway do we have?*" for the vision to take off. Even with success such as increased sales, founders often needed large investments to support their growth. Most founders experienced common areas of need as their ventures grew, such as support of an increasing number of employees, infrastructure, marketing efforts, and client care. This continual fundraising was a challenge that some welcomed, while others reported it keeping them up nights. For instance, the nature of **Blow**'s industry required more liquid investment to cover the consumer credit debt that her firm offered, making her constant dilemma "*how can we use precious capital and where can we find more?*"

Other founders who also found great success reported that there was little time to rest. **Seth Goldman** of Honest Tea, for example, reported that he was constantly chasing performance and resources:

> *People in Honest Tea who thought that they had job security for the first 10 years were kidding themselves because you just don't know how the business is going to do. So you have to perform, and if the business grows and it hits one of its goals, only then do you renew your license to keep growing.*

Over time, the positive growth of his venture within Coca-Cola afforded him the resources and autonomy for brand control, but he knew that Honest Tea was potentially one bad financial quarter away from losing its autonomy. Back in 2019, **Goldman** said:

> *I always tell people that growth can cure a lot of ills, so don't take it for granted. We're now back up into a 25 percent growth rate, which is fine. But it's not just leadership; no matter how charismatic I am, if we're not growing, we don't get to keep doing this.*

Strategies to mitigate resource scarcity: **Blow, Goldman**, and other interviewees reported similar strategies for mitigating scarcity—including a constant search for further funding and other resources—with some nuance within industries. Several founders discussed the move toward profitability by demonstrating success and market share beyond a "proof of concept" to denote a viable and sustainable line of business which would be ripe for acquisition. In these examples, the funding model was not necessarily built on a long-term view, at least not from the founder's perspective.

Although similar in some ways, **Blow** and **Goldman** demonstrated distinctive approaches. **Blow** sought supporters not only financially, but also selling her ideas—the importance of her mission to provide low-interest credit to underserved minority populations, which helped her to attract investors, establish a viable product, and ultimately sell to a larger investment bank. **Goldman** relied heavily on his brand purity and the mammoth leverage of a larger organization, taking advantage of product placement available to his Coca-Cola division. This allowed Honest Tea to achieve growth in new markets once the thirst was satiated in a given area.

6.2.2 Founder's Personal Limitations

I was going into an industry where I had no experience. So by definition was hiring people who had more experience.
  —**Seth Goldman**, Honest Tea

An important theme discussed by the founders we interviewed was the challenge of understanding, and dealing with, their own personal limitations. At its simplest level, this can refer to the fact that no founder can do it all, whether due to deficits in knowledge, skill, or experience or in the sheer number of tasks which must be completed to run an entire organization. Eventually, nearly all organizations will grow beyond their founders' reach. **Carl Grant**, a serial entrepreneur and investor in start-ups, likens the mix of talent to a bakery:

A successful startup is like making a cake; they need to have all the ingredients. Very seldom do you have one person who can build the product, sell the product, manage the business, and do everything right. You fill those gaps with other resources.

Strategies for addressing limitations. In fact, every founder path leader we interviewed made a priority of compensating for their own inexperience. **Blow** emphasized hiring people who complement your deficits with talent, as well as who are a match for the kind of organization you are building. **Selim Chacour** of American Hydro said to hire the best, not "yes men," and gave a way to do so:

Develop relationships with a banker, a lawyer, and so on; select the best, not the cheapest. Approach the best from other companies, and be direct. Tell them "I like you and want you to work for me."

Or, as **Rob McGovern** puts it: "*I want to be the dumbest person in the room.*" Seek out people who are not looking for a job. Weed out bad hires quickly, and expect to fail in your hiring ("4 out of 10"). Keep high standards, because good people attract others: "*they want to hang out with other cool people; don't hire the weak.*"

(See Appendix tool 6.2 **Founder Self-Assessment & Action Plan**, which helps founder leaders to self-reflect on where they are strongest and weakest, providing the foundation for determining the best way to supplement their leadership.)

6.2.3   Sharing and Giving Up Power

A natural corollary of addressing resource scarcity and personal limitations is the need to share control, whether in the form of **investor expectations** or **employee empowerment**, both of which have been referred to as "giving up power" in the words of our interviewees. Although in some sense a challenge, giving up power can be a gift to busy founders who want to leverage their own talents. However, it can also become a threat to the venture if not managed well. For instance, Susan Tynan,[4] the founder of Framebridge, at one point found that she was spending more time managing investors than running her business. She had to reassess and then re-prioritize her time and energy toward the business in order to survive. Other founders report the need to learn to trust their employees, who often do not immediately share the vision or commitment of the venture, as discussed next.

Strategies for sharing power. The founders we interviewed shared several ways of successfully managing the sharing of power with investors, employees, and others, some of which are explicated among the other areas. **Blow** had good general advice for how this might be done, and not surprisingly it involves intentionality and planning ahead. **Blow** advocates planning a governance structure and process for distributing decision responsibility before launching the organization. Making an actual plan, she cautions, involves "*more than just theory of doing the right five things, but is instead about the real-life management, how products and services are delivered to the customer.*"

Goldman agrees with this general approach, describing how it worked at Honest Tea:

---

[4] Raz, G. (Framebridge: Susan Tynan). (2019, May 6). *How I Built This* [Audio podcast]. www.npr.org/2019/04/26/717496919/framebridge-susan-tynan.

Before we launched, I spent a day with Barry, my cofounder, so we could be totally clear about roles and how it was all going to work. We discussed the big picture, like, what are we doing this for? What are our personal and life goals? What do we hope to get out of this? What does success look like to each of us? How would we handle disagreements?

That said, **Blow** acknowledges that there are limits to what should be shared, and with whom. Transparency can be useful in mapping out roles and directions, but she found that after leaning toward full disclosure early in her venture, she had to limit it as time went on: "*People think they want to know, but they don't always want to see the sausage made!*"

6.2.4   Engagement of Non-founding Employees

Founders reported that there is often a disconnect between their own view of the venture's priority—often as personal to the founder as "my baby"—and that of their employees, especially those hired after founding, who were sometimes more likely to consider the venture as "just a job." The strategies to deal with this included many of the key advantages of founders—sharing their vision in a personal way, exuding passion, and embodying credibility. However, those factors were sometimes not enough. Whether through compensation packages or other means, for the talent they want to retain, these creators need to ensure their key employees have a reason to stay and feel connected to the work and the organization.

Strategies to build engagement. Many founders recognize the importance of rewarding employees, as in **Paucek**'s 2U example of improving employee pay and benefits every year. Some go a step further, offering company performance-based bonuses, stock options, or outright ownership shares. This may not be simple, however, especially in highly leveraged ventures who must maintain equity for current or potential investors or who are otherwise operating on thin profit margins. These factors make it all the more important for founders to involve key employees in the process of creation and extension of their core products and services, building the employees' own passion and knowledge in alignment with venture growth.

6.2.5 Professional Relationships Versus Friendships

What seemed to be one of the more difficult personal challenges for founders was the realization that their relationships within the ventures were not and most often could not be friendships, at least not primarily. This may be particularly difficult for founding leaders, many of whom begin ventures with their friends or close allies—some of whom are also owners. That said, making the difficult talent decisions is a key part of the founder journey.

2U's **Paucek** sadly noted that he'd had to let friends go, especially some who had been early hires but no longer were a good fit for the direction of the company. For FS Card, **Blow** reflected that keeping the good of the organization in mind did not allow for her to make decisions based on friendships. As the organization grew, the roles changed and decisions needed to be made based on functional fit, not personal liking. She also reported that putting business before friendship went in all directions among the stakeholders, including founders, employees, board members, and investors. "*I had to learn how to take a punch in the mouth*" she muses, and how to counter.

Strategies to manage relationships. As **Paucek** and **Blow** advised, it is important to keep the organization's mission and execution front and center. Typically, this means first consider the strategic purpose of the organization and then plan how every resource (people, technology, financing, etc.) should be deployed to further that purpose. In this way, the job comes before the person—once each major task area and job role are planned, only then are specific people considered for their ability to fulfill that job. This is typically best for the organization as well, providing a sustained organization that employs people who understand their contribution.

Founders, especially when being careful not to confuse business relationships with friendships, sometimes find truth in the axiom that it is "lonely at the top." **Paucek** and others recommend finding business confidantes outside of one's own venture. Cultivate friendships with other founders and outside executives, extending your own network while sharing stories, challenges, and potential solutions. Some cities offer such groups through "Founder's Circle" organizations, such as Young Presidents Organization. Other options are to reach out across industries and geographic areas to find like-minded mentors and colleagues.

6.2.6   Celebrity Status and Approachability

As discussed, many founding leaders enjoy high regard within their organizations, a status that often extends to the external world of stakeholders, and even to friends who revel in the founder's success. While such fame can help sell the company vision, opening doors to external and internal stakeholders, it comes at a bit of a cost. 2U's **Paucek** sincerely insists that "*it's not about me*" but he really cannot walk the building or step in an elevator without disrupting the flow around him. While celebrity status may seem like an advantage, it is a disadvantage when it comes to approachability, particularly on the more difficult topics or "bad news." As a result, founder path leaders have to work especially hard to invite this feedback, as **Paucek** notes.

> *What I mentioned earlier about being treated like a celebrity inside the company – it weighs on you. What the company is doing today is big and it's important; it's growing quickly and it's likely to get a lot bigger. But those on our staff who started when it was barely an idea, when we weren't much of anything, just deal with me in an inherently different manner.*

Some of the celebrity issue is merely scale; it's the consequence of growing beyond one person's ability to personally encounter every organizational member. **Paucek** explains:

> *I'll give you an example of something I had to stop. I used to personally write an individual note on each employee's anniversary every year. It got completely unsustainable. It was impossible to do now that we have thousands of employees. But I really didn't like stopping. So what we are focused on now is finding ways to still be high touch and personal, but in a more sustainable way.*

Strategies for managing celebrity status. Holding founder status often confers awe on those around, in addition to that more routinely felt by high-level executives. Employees may not be willing to question or confront the outsized image of the founding leader, which diminishes the value of adding talent to the organizational roster:

> *No one would ever give me feedback on anything if I didn't aggressively seek it. Well, maybe that's too strong, as I have some very good and very senior people. My point is it's harder to come by.*

Sometimes other stakeholders, even investors, may be cowed enough to withhold constructive feedback. As a result, these leaders have to ensure they build a system that provides honest feedback, such as a network of people who will give it to them straight. It may be members of the founding team who knew the leader before the celebrity status kicked in. Feedback could come from an outside source, such as an executive coach. It could also come from a board selected for their willingness to step into the responsibility of comprehensive governance. **Paucek** relies on his board in this way: "*2U has a very high functioning board; they know the business, they're super engaged, they're very available to me. I could literally call any of them on the phone, and they would answer.*"

6.3   Navigating the Founder Path

As founders create and sustain organizations, they must find ways to lead to enable their vision to succeed beyond their reach. This chapter has outlined some of the distinctive opportunities that are important to understanding how founders can leverage their leadership potential, as well as the challenges that may hinder these efforts. We learn how they have opportunities to share their own personal vision, values, and passion, building on their credibility through knowledge, commitment, and the natural authority accorded to those who found an organization. These founders also expressed that they deal with many challenges in bringing their vision to life. They must overcome scarcity of resources and shore up their own limitations. This involved sharing power and giving up control strategically. They must develop tactics for engaging employees even as the organization grows beyond their immediate reach, and recognize that tough business decisions may need to be separated from friendships. As their celebrity status grows within their own organizations, founders must find ways to obtain and manage honest feedback.

Together, these themes provide lessons not just for current and future founders, but also for leaders in other paths. Even an externally hired Outsider leader, for instance, can develop and communicate deep passion for aspects of the enterprise. Legacy family leaders can engage with employees by empowering others to act beyond the family limitations. All paths can learn from the deep commitment and strategic vision of the founder's path.

Motivations Behind Pursuit of the Founder Path. The list of advantages revealed through our interviews is more extensive than the short list reviewed here. Many pointed out, for instance, that an advantage of the founder is that the founder is often in a position to garner high levels of compensation, monetarily and otherwise—it is high risk but also high reward if all goes well. That said, 11 out of 12 start-ups fail, according to Startup Genome's 2019 report. Founders can change roles as they see fit, adapting to their own assessment of what is needed for venture success. Founding leader is in a position to get things done and to tackle issues that are important to themselves—as **Rob McGovern** put it, "*Don't build a company, solve a problem.*"

Reflection Questions

- What will motivate you on this challenging path? How will you stay personally connected to the purpose and the organization?
- How does your role as founding leader evolve as the business moves from ideas, through investment and production, and on to growth?
- Who will accompany you on this journey? Who best will complement your skills, knowledge, and style?
- In addition to the story you want to be written about your company's success and growth, how do you want your leadership story to be told?

7

Legacy: The Family Path

I was called by the family, and they said "Our CEO is 65, he has to retire when he's 66. That's our policy." I asked, "How long have you understood that he was going to turn 66 someday?" They kind of chuckled and told me that they had five candidates for CEO, all family members. They had a 20-person board of directors and so far none of the five could get more than six votes. And this is a billion-dollar company.

I asked, to clarify the point, "This is an open election by the board to see who gets to be CEO?" They replied, "Well, we're trying to do that, but we can't seem to do it."

I came in and spoke with each of these five candidates. I asked, "What makes you the best choice?" Every one of them, in different words, said the same thing: "We've always had a family member as CEO. Yes, we're going to have a family member as CEO, and I'm the least worst of the five of us."

I convinced the business that they needed their first non-family CEO, which we found in their current non-family CFO. About 10 years later, one of the family members did become CEO, but he needed that very focused development to be able to do it. So if the idea is that a family member must be the one to step into a leadership position, that can be dangerous to the business and to the family.

This story, related by family business guru **Craig Aronoff** of The Family Business Consulting Group, illustrates some challenges faced by those who walk the family leadership path. In this case, families may be tempted to confine their talent pool to their blood relatives, and underqualified leaders might limit the success of the family venture. On the other hand, there are advantages and opportunities inherent in the assumptions of these family

M. A. Clark and M. Persily Lamel, *Six Paths to Leadership*, https://doi.org/10.1007/978-3-030-69017-5_7

members. For instance, there is generally a greater loyalty to the family business and a willingness to step up when needed. Exploring the path of family leadership will help us to understand these and further challenges and opportunities, drawing lessons that can benefit family businesses and legacy leaders.

Family businesses are nearly as unique as the variety of families who found, own, manage, and lead them. Some families are very insular, resisting outside influence. Some are more inclusive, welcoming those with talent, perspective, and loyalty into the family without regard for blood relations. Some families rally around the business as a means of extending their legacy, some use the core business as a launchpad for other ventures, while others think of it more like a cashbox to support their lifestyle and interests. As intimated above, this path may apply to family members with various roles—those who own voting shares or hold other interests (such as those who receive annuities), those who hold management or operational positions, and those with broader leadership influence such as top executives or sometimes retired family members. Amid the variations, however, there are clear lessons for leaders walking this path, in the form of opportunities and challenges inherent in multigenerational organizations. As with the other paths discussed in this book, these lessons hold value for leaders walking any of the six paths to leadership.

The sheer number of family businesses in the marketplace also contributes to the broad variance in their operation and character. Considering that those who start businesses often want to share their passion, workload, and wealth with their family members, it should not be a surprise that family businesses create the majority of Gross Domestic Product, jobs, and for-profit organizations in the United States and globally.[1] While not all who are members of family businesses take a leadership role, those who are called to lead typically take on responsibility beyond simply running the business. They must account for other family members who have other roles: those who maintain ownership, those who work for the family business, and those who have a less formal stake but who still care about the legacy. The family business leader may find that these roles may be difficult to disentangle, in that often their own name and personal reputation are synonymous with the company brand.

In preparing for this chapter, we drew these and other themes from discussions with legacy leaders as well as with family business experts, framing the resulting opportunities and challenges with strategies for success. For our purposes, we consider family leaders to be those **members of a second generation or beyond who hold a formal position charged with handling**

---

[1] www.gvsu.edu/fobi/family-firm-facts-5.htm, accessed January 2020.

the family legacy, whether through ownership, management positions, or other leadership influences. The businesses of these leaders represent a variety of family ventures—from billion-dollar corporations and high-stakes investment funds to smaller ventures that have a visibility in a geographic area or industry sector—and the roles, relationships, and inherited knowledge within them. We also spoke with those with significant legacies beyond for-profit ownership, including political families.

Strategies addressing opportunities and challenges. Our thematic analysis identified four key opportunities and four challenges of the legacy path. While in most other chapters we shared strategies to specifically leverage each opportunity and challenge, in this case, we found that the family leaders use strategies more to collectively address multiple opportunities and challenges. We therefore will outline each opportunity and challenge, followed by the collection of strategies to leverage them.

7.1   Legacy: Opportunities and Strategies of the Family Path

Table 7.1 Family path: Legacy opportunities and strategies

Family path opportunities	Strategies for leveraging
1. Family Brand	• Record the family narrative
2. Culture of Family Values & Founder DNA	• Clarify and instill family values into all parts of the company
3. Passion & Shared Commitment across Generations	• Provide and support early-life mentoring
4. Seat at the Table, Security, and Resources	• Apply resources to personal and professional passions

7.1.1   Family Brand

The brand, or distinctive meaning of a company's public identity, has especial importance for leaders of family businesses, due to its association with the family name. Whether the clan name is on the masthead or simply known among the clients, customers, and employees, it gives an impression, sets standards, and opens doors within its community. This creates both opportunities and some pressure, inside and outside of the organization (Table 7.1).

John Darby is CEO of The Beach Company, a large real estate development company based in South Carolina. He believes that brand is the most valuable asset of a business. He describes how he leverages his family name to help his business, and how clients use it as well.

We have a large family and they are all ambassadors of the company. The benefit is while they're in their own careers and their own social networks, we share the same name. Clearly that gives you an edge over a non-family member. I leverage that every day. It also goes both ways – they leverage their association with The Beach Company as well …. Very often I walk into a meeting and they say, "you know, I remember your grandpa."

A family brand is more personal than nonfamily variety and can work for (or against, as we'll reference later) both the business and the individual. For The Beach Company, this brand includes a mission of creating enduring value, evaluating each development opportunity for its potential to improve the quality of life and contribute to long-term economic vitality, across generations of clients and behind the four-generation family business. Family members are, to some degree, assumed to embody the known family traits and to be loyal to the family enterprise. In his quote above, **Darby** speaks of promoting his family brand across not only the company's existing stakeholders, but also counting on family members who work outside of the business to extend the reach of the family brand. This creates goodwill and opportunity for the individual family member for their own careers and networks as they operate outside the family business, as well as creating further prospects for the company.

The power of the family brand exists in some part due to its advantage for the client as well as for the family business. The client and other stakeholders get to deal with a known quantity, a personal business, and a person who they can trust. As **Darby** put it, they say *"Your grandfather really helped out my father, so we can work together."*

Of course, the family brand does not do the work for the leader, nor even necessarily define the leader's path. Several family business leaders who we spoke with decided to shift the focus of their family business, whether through modernizing (**Todd Schurz** of Schurz Communications), founding an allied business (**Wade Murphy** of Murphy Oil, Marmik, and Source-Rock), or leveraging into another field entirely (**Vernon Holleman**). As **Russ Carnahan**, US Congress member and a third-generation political scion, put it, the family brand *was best described as, opening a door or having a good introduction. But it was really up to you to really build on that and then make it your own.*

The family brand can therefore provide a family business leader with access to stakeholders and supporters beyond those typically earned through their own efforts. However, being born into the family brand is no guarantee of leader effectiveness; indeed, some of our early interviewees objected to our original conceptualization of this path as "inherited" because that could imply a much easier trek to success. Investing time and energy to develop personal bonds with prior generations and extended family members operating in other businesses helps to create a network of contacts and harness the power of the family brand for the family business leader. Leveraging the brand then requires alignment with the mission, values, and passions of the family, as discussed below.

7.1.2   Culture of Family Values and Founder DNA

The culture of a family business fulfills the typical role of representing organizational values and practices, but goes further for the family leader. Family business leaders are more directly influenced by the organization's values from an early age, provided with relevant role models and decision scenarios from childhood. As the family members step into leadership roles, they often have greater ability to align the organization with their espoused culture to help shape decisions. This enables the leaders not only to be a good fit with the culture of the organization, but to make sure that the organization continues to fit their idea of what the culture should be.

The early introduction into the family business culture can put leaders a step ahead of their nonfamily competitors, as family business consultant **Aronoff** describes:

There is a culture in that family, what the family talks about around the dinner table. That gives family leaders a much longer runway as it relates to their ultimate careers than non-family members do in general. So you're being trained from birth, instead of being trained after getting your MBA.

This culture helps to define both limits and possibilities for the current and future family generations. As **Murphy**, a member of Murphy Oil's fourth generation (G4, in the lexicon of many family businesses), puts it, "*The meta family history is kind of defined by Murphy Oil.*" Thus, a strong family culture creates its own story and enables family business leaders to draw on the strengths of their predecessors to build their workforce and clientele. **Darby** calls this the effect of the "Founder DNA" in the company, which also enables family business leaders to make the difficult decisions which govern their business.

We teach and discuss the history of the company. We believe in that Founder DNA. It's part of our culture so if we need a controversial project approved, we talk about our legacy.

This may be especially viable when multiple family members are involved in the business as shareholders and managers. **Darby**'s Beach Company is owned entirely by family, with 80 members across 5 generations, and the Founder DNA has been essential in tough times:

Probably the best example I can give you is the great recession. There we were, a healthy company. We had projects in different phases and were distributing money to the family and everyone is happy. Then the recession hits and we basically notified the shareholders, "We're stopping distributions. All perks are off the table. And we don't know how long it's gonna last." Basically we were in survival mode, like everybody else. But the amazing thing, looking back at it, is that we got the exact opposite from the family. They said, "We get it. We're behind you and the company." That Founder DNA kicked in.

7.1.3   Passion and Shared Commitment Across Generations

A family business leader's passion to succeed may come from a different place than non-family leadership, and it may have a different scope. **Todd Schurz** of Schurz Communications, a fourth-generation media and investment company, relates it as concern for the upcoming generations of the family.

For my father's generation, their father said, "You'll never successfully pass the company along." So in effect, they had the challenge to deal with the estate planning issue, valuation and all those things, and they came up with a solution. .... And now our generations' BHAG [Big Hairy Audacious Goal[2]] became "better and stronger". We want to pass along an organization and a family that is better and stronger than the one we received.

---

[2]From *Collins & Porras famous 1994 book, Built to Last (HarperCollins).*

Schurz illustrated how he and his family operate, with an apocryphal story about a family business whose ancestors are buried in a cemetery on a hill outside of town:

> *So in their family meetings they talk a lot about the "voices on the hill" – "what would the voices on the Hill have to say about this discussion?" I think this was where my brother came up with our BHAG: "If we have to make a choice between the voices on the Hill and the next generation. What do you do?"*
>
> *We had a good conversation and I weighed in very, very late. I'm the oldest of my generation, and I remember that I said "This is an easy answer for me. I love and appreciate my parents' generation and everything they did and they gave to us" I said, "but if the choice is doing what I think is right between these two groups. I'm going to do it for my children's generation every single time." My two uncles in the room said, "If you'd answered any other way we would have been ashamed of you."*

Like founders discussed in the preceding chapter, family business leaders tend to have a strong affinity for the core product or service of the company. Since the business did not originate with them, however, it may be more than simply personal; because it represents a bond of kinship, it may be even more dear to them. As **Schurz** alludes to above, the leader becomes responsible for legacy not just of the business, but also for the future of the family, the relationships within, and sometimes even maintaining peace on family holidays! The passion that fuels the leader thus has a greater scope than is typical at non-family businesses, due to the combination of professional and personal stakes.

Dr. **Jody Olsen**, director of the Peace Corps for the US federal government, also discusses the passion shaped by her family legacy path in the context of public service. **Olsen** spoke of learning from her grandfather (Senator William King) and father (Ambassador and Representative David King), who both represented Utah as members of US Congress, among other service roles.

> *My father grew up here in DC when my grandfather was in the Senate, so politics were always a part of the conversation. Politics is about reaching out, pleasing people, making policy decisions, public good, service – politics is always about public service. You go out there and you might get beat up, but your goal is to serve that public.*
>
> *So I grew up with that and also with my father's campaign. Part of it was seeing how you structure a campaign, so I had, I think, an example of aggressiveness in him. His political background was very important for me to have the courage to seek out the [Peace Corps] Regional Director. It was him guiding me through the*

political process in terms of how to get the position. And I learned! So when you fast forward eight years later, and I saw who the next Peace Corps director is going to be, I decided I really want to go back. So I put my name in.

7.1.4   Seat at the Table, Security, and Resources

One often-presumed hallmark of a family business is the implicit or explicit guarantee of a seat at the table for family members. While family members may argue, often correctly, that they must actually perform to keep their leadership positions, it also should be acknowledged that family members generally have a better chance at leading than those coming from outside. Overall, most family business members will admit that a seat at the table can be, at least, an advantage. As a family business coach and former family business leader, **Cathy Carroll** admits that "*the competitive set is small*" for the chance of making it to the top of the business organization.

If a close family member joins the organization, they are often given a chance, or more than one, to contribute and to succeed. **Kathy McDevitt**, an executive with her family's National Fulfillment Services company, puts it like this:

> *You always have job security because you know that Dad is not going to fire you – or if he fires you, he is going to rehire you because he was probably just mad.*

She goes on to explain that this security can create an advantage that may be more difficult for non-family businesses to achieve, in terms of giving feedback and broaching difficult conversations that may not typically be directed to top executives.

> *It is a blessing that you know that the owner is your Dad so you can really be honest, say "this is what's going on, this isn't what I think is right." You can have honest conversations without any worry that you would lose your job.*

Family resources. This seat at the family business table may also be realized not exclusively by an executive position, but more in terms of either direct ownership or right of access to the resources and fruits of the family enterprise. These multigenerational family business resources provide opportunities for leaders and other family members in a variety of ways. These include the job security and pre-established business relationships described above. Some family businesses, especially those that have been financially successful, provide additional benefits in terms of resources that can be used to support a desirable lifestyle for individual family members, for the company to engage in management practices in line with its values, and even for the family business to grow in new directions.

Privately held companies are often given greater liberty to make long-term investments and/or decisions that promote values beyond the bottom line, relative to their publicly traded counterparts. In the case of a family business, these benefits are amplified because the "investors" are interested in the family interests beyond financial. This may result in generous benefits for all employees, for instance. Understandably, when the financial stress that often influences decisions is removed, leaders of family businesses can act based more on relationships, core values, and family brand.

In some cases, family leaders leverage these resources to change the direction of the family enterprise. Family business consultant **Aronoff** identifies this shift as a trend in established family businesses from business owning to asset owning—"*over the past 30 years, family owners have become increasingly sophisticated with regard to expecting a rate of return.*" This refers to families who may diversify their investment, moving their focus from the original family business to a more general investment strategy, spreading their finances across a portfolio of holdings.

Schurz, CEO of Schurz Communications, has exemplified this movement. He has led his company to translate decades of media business, including newspapers, radio stations, and more, into a more generalized investment management firm. As he explains,

> We grew, we did all these things. So I think "what will be my hallmark on the company?" I'm 58 now. Will it be that I've effectively sold my father's generations business to prepare the business for the next generation? And so we exited.
>
> …Since then we have been growing, developing. I think the last time I checked, had little over $80 million under management. And we have also been able to include big distributions to family shareholders.

This shift allows the family business to extend its reach, while simultaneously being protected from the vagaries of the market—in the case of **Schurz**, from the changes in the media industry. His family can now influence and manage a broader swath of companies to continue their legacy.

Capitalizing on the family resources to afford an exit from the family business can also be used as a strategy for managing the challenges of the inherited leadership path. We will visit an example of this, later in the chapter.

Strategies to Leverage Opportunities

<u>Record the family narrative</u>. A consistent message from our interviewees was that to succeed in a multi-generational enterprise, a family business leader must develop a "family narrative" that serves as a bridge from past to future. More than merely a family history, the narrative provides guidance for family business purpose, direction, investments, and roles of the family members as, for instance, the organization grows or changes. It can undergird and guide a strategic plan for the family as well as the business (for more on this, see the use of the narrative in addressing family leader challenges, later in this chapter). Family narratives leverage the opportunities described above, extending the family brand and culture as well as providing a basis for commitment across generations, prescribing roles for family members, and planning resource use.

Family narratives vary widely in their format, but they have consistencies in their functional utility, describing both successes and failures of the past, paired with a plan for the future. A good narrative establishes the value proposition for the family business:

- Why does the business exist? What product, service, or function does it provide? To whom, and for what need? How does this develop or fit the family brand, distinguishing it from others?
- Family narratives also often provide a succession plan, or at least a commitment to the values to guide how decisions about future leaders and company direction will be made.
- This succession is not merely at the top of the organization; good narratives differentiate roles for other family members in the organization, while limiting their influence as needed. They often prescribe holding regular family meetings, often with their own traditions intact, and outline processes for resolving family conflict.

As **Cathy Merrill**, second-generation President and Publisher of Washington Magazine, Inc (a company that includes the popular magazine Washingtonian, among other media ventures), relates:

My whole life, even now, we have a family meeting on Thanksgiving every year. This is not in a conference room, it's in the living room after dinner. The first point of it, ever since I was a little kid, was that we meet on Thanksgiving to do our philanthropic giving. It's a day of giving thanks… That also became a format for discussing family business, and what would work and what wouldn't work. Communication was key.

While some narratives are developed more exclusively by founders or long-time family leaders, our interviewees recommend that family narratives should be developed through an inclusive process which accounts for the interests relevant to the business. This means involving not only the emerging next-generation leaders and family shareholders, but also at times non-owning family members and other stakeholders such as senior employees. This approach allows a family narrative to interpret the past, make sense of the current climate, and provide a strategic guide for the benefit of future generations. It also ensures buy-in from these strategic stakeholders, who by contributing to the narrative are more likely to support its continuance.

Generally, the process of developing a narrative should include all those who are core to the family business, with emphasis on founders or longtime family leaders coupled with emerging leaders from the next generation.

Having a coherent family narrative can help externally as well, such as leveraging the family name to connect with strategic partners, aligning with appropriate philanthropic endeavors, and building its own workforce. **John Darby** describes how he relates his family narrative to make his company more attractive to prospective employees:

> *We're recruiting someone to come to the company now. We talk about our history and the legacy; the tough times we've been through and the successful times we've had. It's a huge advantage over companies that really don't even have a story.*

(The tool 7.1 **Family Narrative** in the Appendix offers suggestions on ways to articulate and operationalize a story of the family, in order to lead culture and engagement in their organization.)

Clarify & instill family values into all parts of the company. To gain full advantage of the opportunities provided through the family's culture, practices, and passion for the organization, family business leaders must instill their family values throughout their organization. This can be done by modeling particular values and practices, but not necessarily by constantly talking about the family, as **Darby** explains,

> *You've got to be careful that you don't say, 'it's just all about family.' Because that at the end of the day, an employee might think, 'well, it's all about THEIR family.' So we just treat employees as though we would treat our own. This allows us to recruit good people. We have employees that have been here 20, 30, 40 years - we have two guys that are having 50-year anniversaries next year.*

One key may be to speak personally with non-family employees when feasible, listening to their ideas, imparting family norms, and assuring them of the continuity of the enterprise. **Merrill** shares her family's frequent and open transparency with her employees, communicating both personally and symbolically.

> *When I took over Washingtonian, I had small lunches with every single person on staff. I had five people come to lunch every few days, making sure they were all from different departments.... In May when my brother and sister and our accountants come, we meet to go over the family foundation. Every year, there's a rumor 'she's selling the company.' But I intentionally keep my door open. Then, I went out for drinks with the younger people after work to get to know them better.*

Provide and support early-life mentoring. Family legacy leaders often have opportunity for mentoring relationships with company executives—members of their own family—early in their career, long before other employees typically can connect with the top of a company's hierarchy. Not only do family members typically have more mentoring opportunities through simply spending time together, but this relationship can also expand the breadth of the lessons offered. Family leaders have often lived and breathed the business throughout their lives. Thoughtful mentoring and advice-seeking can clarify and strengthen the organizational brand and culture, as well as helping to develop family bonds that may otherwise be precarious in the midst of running a business.

As **Murphy** recalls,

> *I worked for my grandfather in summer jobs; I roughnecked* [hard manual labor on a drilling rig]. *I remember him saying once, "If you're interested in this business at all, there's no point in sitting in an office if you don't know what they are doing in the field. And if you don't have their respect, then it doesn't matter what you do." These guys in the field, they all knew my grandfather and they said, "Oh, Mr. Charlie, he comes out and he'll always ask you if your lives were good, kids, whatever." It was kind of this interesting dynamic that he was teaching me life lessons through his company.*

Darby also mentions how his grandfather, representing the founding generation of his family business, started inculcating the opportunities and responsibilities early on.

When I turned 16, my grandfather did this with everybody. We would go to his house. It was "Happy birthday", and he gave you a birthday card and your shares of the company were in there. He gives you a little slip and you're now part of The Beach Company. It was just always in the conversation because it was all around, like the things that the company has done for the community.

The early and deep mentoring relationships among family members of a multigenerational business leverage the family brand and culture, influence the family business leader, extending the reach of their values and work.

<u>Apply resources to personal and professional passions.</u> Perhaps a less obvious way of leveraging family resources, at least in terms of typical assumptions of focusing on the core business, is instead translating the family assets into a related business or way of life. **Murphy** comments on the ability of his extended family members to pursue their career interests beyond the five-generation energy business.

We've got people who do sustainable farming, who work with grants, work with investment, work for Goldman Sachs, teach. The gamut in my generation goes from grant writing for nonprofits to Teach for America to wealth management. So we see the total spectrum of what you would expect. … My generation had the asset base that allowed us to have a base salary; not huge, but not insignificant. So it was much easier for many in my generation to say "I can be a teacher because I have some supplemental income. I don't really have to worry about much."

The Legacy path holds unique opportunities that leaders can leverage to achieve success for themselves personally, for their families, and for the family business itself. Each family leader embodies, in whole or in given aspects, the family brand, a culture infused with the founder DNA, passion and commitment beyond themselves, and some security through their status as a family member. Next, we will discuss the challenges that the Legacy leader may encounter along the Family path.

7.2   Legacy: Challenges and Strategies of the Family Path

Table 7.2   Family path: Legacy challenges and strategies

Family path challenges	Strategies for managing
1. Managing Family Relationships	• Build a transparent governance structure (roles, succession plan, board representation) • Apply the family narrative to strategic plans • Gain experience outside the family business • Develop limits and accountability for family members
2. Beliefs about Entitlement and Positions in the Family Business	• Import outside perspectives
3. Limited Perspective: Family Culture and Family Insularity	• Provide options to leave the family business
4. Resource Pressures	• Structure effective family communication

7.2.1   Managing Family Relationships

A family business leader must deal with much of the good and bad that may come with any family—pressures borne by intimate relationships, sibling rivalry, more traditional practices of founding generations (sometimes including diminished capacity of family members advanced in age), and expectations of fair treatment and equitable outcomes. Other challenges relate more to the roles that such family might fill in the legacy business, including those members who desire more authority and responsibility, often regardless of whether they are the best fit, and those who would rather reduce their involvement in the family business. Still others may want to be involved, but are intent on differentiating themselves or their work products from what has previously been successful for the family. In any of these roles, some persons may demand or feel compelled to hold a leadership position, and may even consider themselves untouchable in terms of their place in the organization (Table 7.2).

Note that role security was previously characterized as an opportunity for the family leader. Indeed, other opportunities discussed previously—brand, culture, shared commitment, and resources—may often also have a challenging aspect as well, sometimes in the same instance. For instance, the family brand and culture may create strong expectations for how the family business will be run, regardless of the wishes or strengths of the legacy generation.

Cathy Carroll, former third-generation COO of her family's Pro Equine Group, believes that much of this pressure is because family businesses are "*the crossroads of love and money.*" These roads intersect, and interests collide:

> *if you make a decision with a business mindset, get the right answer; make a decision with a family mindset, you get the right answer – but they are different answers!*

Family pressure. Family pressure on the legacy leader can be brought by other family members, and sometimes also by the leader from the expectations they attribute to the family and their desire to prove worthy of that legacy. This pressure therefore influences decisions and performance of both the leader and the organization. As **Merrill** puts it,

> *My father used a Latin phrase* "**like hand from the grave**". *If I put things through a lens of what my father would've done, I'd be sure to fail. You have to do things the way you want to do them and what you think is right; you have to trust your instincts.*

Even considering this, **Merrill** does believe that she can use some of the family expectation to help guide her leadership, especially if she thinks of it as advice, rather than directives.

> *My father had successful careers in business, in politics, in philanthropy, as a diplomat. He would give out nuggets of wisdom, and one of his aides wrote them down. We teased him relentlessly for that! But it turns out when my dad died, it was so nice to have a piece of paper that had all his wisdom on it. I still think of it and refer to it a lot.*

The legacy leader often feels pressure from his desire to fill the expectations of family over all others. **Jeff Nally**, a family business consultant, shares a story of a client who inherited the leadership positions of his family's large tile company.

> *The father has moved into the chair of the board role and the son is now the president and CEO. His biggest challenges in the son's inherited role now are, "I don't lead like my dad did. How do I find my leadership?" If he's led operations solely, but now has to lead finance and marketing, external relationships, etc., he must take his blinders off and see the whole organization. The other thing I'm*

noticing is that as a leader who's inheriting a role, he's very tentative, still too careful. He's worried about what the rest of his family members will think about his decisions, their lack of trust; just no reinforcement or acknowledgement of what he can do. ... He's not afraid of his investors, and they're not too worried at this point either. It's just that the family and parent approval is much more weighted than anything else.

So, the pressure from parents and siblings is often a driving force, even in circumstances where the judgment is largely in the mind of the legacy leader. Of course, in some situations, or at least some families, the judgment can be very real, as discussed below.

Sibling rivalry. The dual roles of family and business complicate the relationships among brothers and sisters. As **Kathy McDevitt** of National Fulfillment Services points out,

When you run a family business, roles, workload and compensation are not necessarily aligned. Think about how that can affect your relationship with your siblings. Further, if one sibling gets chosen over another to lead the business, that can have lasting impact on the family dynamic.

Even in cases where there are agreed-upon roles and financial policies, decisions made by one sibling can change plans for the others. This can be seen when siblings, or other family members, share equity in the business. Those who hold equity may have more influence than their objective percentage, as when one sibling or family group has controlling interest but still must take the rest of the family's opinion into account. **John Darby** gives the example of a large development opportunity, Kiawah Island, championed by his brother and a cousin. The family was divided over the investment,

There were some in the family that thought it should stay within The Beach Company. And there's some who didn't want to do it, didn't want anything to do with it.

The family ultimately decided to let the venture split from the company, with some resources and the backing of JP Morgan bank. Although many family members were upset over the split, **Darby** notes that:

It did make more solidarity within our company; we know now what we are by what we're not, because we didn't want to keep that investment. Looking back, it is probably the best thing that could have happened.

Some family dynamics intrude on the business, for reasons that have nothing to do with the business. **Jeff Nally** offers an example from another client company,

> *One brother was promoted, inheriting the position of President and CEO. The other brother is not responsible, has had a history of drug abuse, is not being consistent working with the company.… His brother actually has called for a sale, whether he wants to be bought out or put the whole company up for sale. So the inherited leader now is focused on trying to find enough resources to buy out the brother, which could put the firm out of business if he did it all in cash at once. The brother leading could lose the whole thing if he doesn't get this relationship right and figure out how to resolve that.*

As can be seen in this case, rivalry can not only stem from a non-business issue, but also can manifest through ownership distribution as well as management decisions.

There's also what is sometimes called the "Fredo effect" after the older son who was bypassed for family leadership in the Godfather movies. More of the instances we heard from our interviewees was actually the opposite of this, with the oldest child being gifted with the spoils of the family business. In cases like these, decisions about leadership and even ownership are not made on the basis of merit or suitability, but rather on a system that seems more like primogeniture—the oldest child, sometimes oldest son, gets the responsibility for carrying the mantle of leadership for the family business. Where this dynamic existed among our interviewees, none were eager to go on record, which is understandable—most families would like to stay intact in some form—but also is perhaps telling a bit about the difficulty of addressing the issue. The consequences for the business and the family are potentially severe. As **Vernon Holleman**, now a consultant who previously was part of his family's three-generation insurance business as well as voicing his insights through a popular family succession podcast, phrases it, "*Probably the biggest mistake people make is putting somebody on a path that seems destined when they ultimately can't handle it.*"

7.2.2 Beliefs About Entitlement and Positions in Family Business

As we discussed above, the "seat at the table" expected for family members can serve as an opportunity, but clearly can be a challenge in many ways. The sometimes seemingly untouchable aspect of those in leadership positions is often earned by ownership or sway of the majority board representatives.

Some leaders in that position take both the responsibility and the privilege. One board member of a $40 billion family-controlled business described the family leader as, "*He'll remind everybody that his name is on the door, 'so if I don't want to do that, we are not going to do that'.*" This includes finding a place in the business for the children of the leader, who may progress to top executive roles one day.

Leaders may not always have joined their family business on their own volition. There is a "*profound gravitational pull of the family business*" for family members, according to family business consultant **Stephanie Brun de Pontet**, including

> *enormous pressure from the broader ecosystem. For example, all of your friends are saying "of course you should join your family business, you'd be crazy to pass up the opportunity."*

Some of those placed in positions of family business leadership, perhaps especially those convinced by the pressure of others to take the reins, may experience the "imposter syndrome," notes **Brun de Pontet**. Defined as "feelings of inadequacy that persist despite evident success[3]" especially with regard to achievement of highly sought positions or honors, this phenomenon may occur more frequently for family business leaders due to their seemingly privileged path up the corporate ladder.

External complications. Even among those who want to be involved and have the talent or insight to succeed, there may be complications. **Cathy Carroll** describes her time as COO of Equine Pro Group, a $20 million business centering on rodeo equipment manufacturing—saddles, ropes, and such—after decades of building her career in unrelated organizations. She did not necessarily relish the change; in addition to the professional shift, there is often the potential challenge of dealing with any family dysfunction—"*all of your childhood drama is right there in the office*"—but noted that in many cases, there is little choice.

> *Some of my clients express that they never really had an option, such as the clothing industry executive who said, "my dad told when I was three years old that I would be running this company." In my own case, I envisioned myself the hero of the family, but at the cost of my personal and professional independence.*

---

[3]Corkindale, G. (2008). Overcoming imposter syndrome. *Harvard Business Review*.

Carroll found the most difficult part of the job to be outside of the company. She was a Chicago-bred and MBA-educated airline professional thrust into a macho Texas rodeo culture. It was an uphill battle just to gain credibility with her supply chain and her market—"*credibility with the cowboys*," as she terms it—and ultimately she left the family business to her brother's stewardship.

Equity complications. The place of family businesses and its equity in supporting aspirations can also go beyond the core family members. Those in the extended family are often expected, as with the earlier "brand" discussion, to back the business in principle and hold its goals above their own. Those who marry into, or who are not in the company executive cadre, might find themselves "house poor" while most of their potential liquidity is held in the business for further investment. **Cathy Carroll** articulates that the spouses in these situations, often wives, consider themselves to be "sailors' widows" waiting for their ships to come in.

Also, as alluded to above, the equity assumptions and distributions vary in family business, and may or may not correlate with role. Some families accept salary or dividend distribution differences commensurate with position in the company but often, as in **McDevitt**'s statement about fueling rivalry above, this is not the case. **Cathy Carroll** has seen this dynamic in her current family coaching business, Legacy Onward. She gives the example of a large Chicago-based family business, where every family member was compensated identically, regardless of their position or their efforts in running the business. The CEO was the youngest son, which added more pressure to keep things equal—they were letting him lead, from their perspective. In spite of this, the CEO realized that this was not the best plan for supporting himself or the company, so hired consultants and passed a new compensation policy through the governing board, which gave everyone a fair base but included incentives for roles and performance.

Prior generation failing to step back. Despite what seemed to be a good approach to addressing the family equity issue, this story did not have a happy ending, highlighting one more aspect of family pressure—the parent who will not step and let the next generation run the business. In this case, the father, who had influence as much through psychology as through company shares, vetoed the new compensation package, directing them to go back to equal pay within the family generation. He wanted, and insisted that, all family members be compensated equally. As **Carroll** points out, this can come from a good place—"*the parent's mindset is 'I love everyone equally, so I can't pay one person more than the other'.*"

7.2.3   Limited Perspective: Family Culture and Family Insularity

Many strengths of a family business—training from birth, a strong dose of "founder DNA" in the culture, strong commitment, and resources – may also present challenges for a family business leader. Organizations generally need diverse perspectives to meet their markets, attract a talented workforce, and drive innovation. Family leaders also may suffer if they are not challenged by those who do not share their background and possibly their perspective, opening the door to the possibility that no one will speak up as the leader sashays down the runway wearing an invisible set of clothes.

The culture that works so strongly to build the organization can also limit its ability to adapt and change. Some family businesses also become risk-averse or complacent, protecting the resources which are so precious to the livelihoods and lifestyles of their relatives. Other leaders, as we've discussed, are reluctant to shake the reins of expectations from prior generations or current family members.

Some families are resistant to, or sometimes not aware of, what **Cathy Carroll** calls "breaking the cultural bubble" by allowing outsiders to invade and settle on their organizational turf. Aside from the direct effect on the leaders and their kin, this family insularity can tell a dangerous tale to those not part of the family, but within the organization. Many or perhaps most family businesses employ beyond the family members. This makes the practice of emphasizing family values and relationships into what may be a fairly obvious disadvantage—those who are not kin may feel less important in the organization, regardless of their role.

7.2.4   Resource Pressures

Similarly to other challenges, the resources of a family business can be a sword that cuts in multiple directions; sharply valuable when they can be drawn on to support work and lifestyle, but also a stockpile too precious to risk, when the consequences would threaten a leader's entire family circle. The ready availability of such resources early in a leader's career may also constitute a set of handcuffs—not golden, but perhaps tin—that make it difficult to consider career options outside of the family.

Further, as **John Darby** points out, one of the major challenges to successive generations is that "*the family grows faster than the company.*" The resources in a family business are not infinite and in fact are cut into ever smaller pieces with each subsequent generation. Family enterprises like The Beach Company take pride in ownership, with a plan for keeping it "*in the* *bloodline*"—sharing the ownership in a structured manner among a limited definition of family members, which does not include even the spouses, much less in-laws or others, even if they are brought into work for the company. This, of course, engenders personal challenges including the potential for family discord, even as the plan works to stave off the eventual dilution of a like-minded contingent of close family members.

As the potential individual share of family business resources shrinks, the company may also lose ability to attract and retain younger generations. **Craig Aronoff** suggests that when the family assets are distributed across proliferating generations, there are at least two predictable, challenging results. One manifestation could be in "*lots of competition among brothers and sisters for the top jobs, with low levels of trust,*" a struggle that could prove unhealthy especially in an organization that might already be starting to fragment as its earlier generation exits the business. The other result is more basic; when the resources offered by the family business shrink, the enterprise itself may not be as attractive to the next generation of potential leaders, and younger generations may simply choose not to join the family business in the first place.

Performance complexity. Together these issues demonstrate that family enterprises may define performance differently than non-family businesses. As we saw earlier, some decisions may be right for the business but wrong for the family, and vice versa. A family business leader may not really have free rein to lead the company in directions that may be profitable, but not in line with the family narrative and plan. Instead, such leaders may be tasked not just with making decisions good for bolstering profit, products, and services, but that also consider what is best for family relationships. As **Darby** warns, no matter how fair and business-minded the company was,

> *while being a family member didn't matter inside the office; outside the office it definitely matters – and outside is where you have to live your life.*

7.3 Successful Strategies for Managing Challenges

7.3.1 Build a Transparent Governance Structure

A family governance structure refers to the policies and processes that guide collective decision-making and operation of a multigenerational company operation. Family governance documents and agreements are often used to clarify family roles, processes, and relationships. Many families have established norms and processes for dealing with these issues in documents such as family constitutions, estate plans, strategic plans, and sometimes in a less formal manner. Clearly outlined policies can help to navigate tricky family roles and relationships, including sibling dynamics. For instance, **Holleman** discusses the complexity of sharing resources across generations and dissimilar opportunities for leading a family business, in the context of his family business consultancy:

> *Sibling rivalry and then of course equalization of inheritance can play a role. If one child is going into the family business, we often use life insurance for the other siblings who are not going to be in the business, to allow a relatively equal amount of inheritance. That, of course, it gets tricky. The business may have been worth X, but the sibling in the business grew it to multiples of X. You've got to have a plan.*

As these points hint, a family narrative is not necessarily meant to equalize all family members, or even to give each member a feeling of fairness or happiness with the outcomes they received. The message in **Cathy Merrill**'s family was that when it came to family resources and inheritance, fair did not necessarily mean equal:

> *My father would always explain that there's a difference between equal and fair, and you need to understand the difference. Equal is "I paid for your kid to get medical treatment and it cost $5,422, therefore your sister gets $5,422." That's equal. Fair is "your kid got hurt and I'm the grandparent, I pay the medical bill. It means if your sister gets hurt, I pay the medical bill." That's fair, but it's not equal. So this relates to the larger concept that you can't equally divide a family business. What's fair is I do this, while my brother and sister do something different. It's fair, but it will never be equal.*

(See tool 7.2 **Family Business Governance** for assistance with developing governance documents that clearly outline the rules of the road for the family business to support family legacy leaders.)

Succession planning for family members. The succession plan, an outline of the qualifications and process for filling future roles that are specific to the executive direction of the company, is critical for families seeking to clarify their governance and relationships. It is sometimes part of the strategic plan, as a private codicil, or is at least consonant with strategy. For family businesses, the succession plan takes on additional importance as a tool to clarify how each family member fits into the company plan, or just as important, how he or she does not fit. A good succession plan outlines transparency in roles and how decisions involve or are made among family members. In many cases, the succession plan, or another portion of the strategic plan, should include guidelines for transitions in ownership, as well as specific management roles and broader leadership influence, including governance authority.

For instance, the succession plan should differentiate between shareholder rights versus compensation packages for executives who are also family members. In other words, the salary and benefits of an executive position should ideally be separated from dividends, distributions, or benefits of ownership shares. More than one legacy CEO we interviewed expressed the sentiment that the family ownership group, collectively, might be able to kick them out of the C-suite, but not out of the family or the ownership rights.

The succession plan should also cover, when applicable, the designation of an appropriate role for former family leaders. These may explain or expand on governance policies or strategic plans to clarify the rights and limitations of members of previous generations who move on from executive roles or relinquish their controlling interest in the company. Some family firms create non-voting advisory roles for those who have served in such capacities. It should also be remembered that changes at the helm of a family firm influence, and generally must be accepted by other members of the business—family and non-family, at least to some extent. **Merrill** tells us,

> The questions include, 'how do we move the father on into another role? Where is he going now and how do I manage that?' And at the same time, the new family CEO has to re-engage all the people who worked for the company – because they worked for dad, and now they work for me. It's not like they're just going to have to stick around. It is like starting over, because what engaged an employee while Dad was here may not be the same things that engage an employee now that the daughter is in charge of the business.

It should be emphasized that succession planning is a process, not merely a document with directives and policies. Family members must work over time to develop, implement, and adjust the plan when necessary to reflect the preferred direction of the firm and the talent available for its workforce.

Family representative to the board. The Beach Company also adopted a useful approach to communicating about the business to the family, in form of a memo written to the family by a designated family member who serves as liaison to the company's board of directors. For The Beach Company, this procedure is a result of an in-depth plan to revamp their family and business governance as the business grew and increased in generations. **Darby**'s family hired outside consultants to plan the future of the business, which resulted in radical restructure of the organizational departments, bylaws, and the board of directors. The board evolved from a body of representatives from each family to a composition of experts from outside the family. With this new structure, the family chose a single representative to attend board meetings. This person then writes a long memo detailing the board actions; a recent yield was a 15-page document. This is distributed to everyone in the family 25 years and older. The memo is designed to speak to the family, addressing direction, questions, and needs across the four family generations. They follow with a family stockholder business meeting discussed above, where family members can deliberate and ask questions. **Darby** credits this process with increased clarity, curbing misinformation in the family.

7.3.2   Apply the Family Narrative to the Strategic Plan

Under "opportunities" for the Legacy leader, we discussed the power of the family narrative as a tool to build brand and culture to align the organization with its values and guide decision-making. Strategic plans extend the reach of the narrative, building on the family business' past, present, and future, filling gaps, and reining in where needed. Failure to strategically develop and adapt the family narrative could hold back a leader from maintaining effectiveness for both the business and the family relationships.

Like the narrative itself, the strategic plan should be a product of an inclusive process, but likely an even broader set of stakeholders. All family members affected by the provisions of the plan, while not necessarily substantially involved in the development, should at least be made to feel like their input and disposition are important. Ideally, the consensus of those family members involved—whether as owners or simply as influencers—will be to support both the general strategic direction and the leader chosen to oversee the business. The strategic plan takes the first broad steps in operationalizing the vision born in the family narrative. It sets a course by identifying overall goals, key functional objectives, performance targets, timelines, and resources. Generally, a strategic plan may outline roles and responsibilities, at least in terms of executive management and overall organizational structure.

John Darby emphasizes that family businesses, whatever their form, should not run without a strategic plan. Even plans requiring continual development and revision can be helpful in identifying company strengths, limitations, and potential directions. **Darby** reports that it took The Beach

Company three successive strategic plans to get it right, but that the effort has been worth the investment. Keys for connecting the strategy to the family include establishing clear roles and guidelines for fulfilling them, while in **Darby**'s words, "*don't underestimate someone's relevance; but don't overestimate it either*." He also cautions that family organizations must show through their plan that they are willing and able to change and grow with the market and the times. For instance, The Beach Company includes provisions for working remotely, as long as family members are seen as part of the team at key times, largely to capture the millennials in the emerging generation.

In keeping with the idea of avoiding exclusion of non-family employees, in perception or in fact, the strategic plan should be clear in how it concerns the entire workforce. For some leadership, this means getting into the details of issues that are of particular importance to their employees, such as job security and healthcare insurance benefits. As **Merrill** explains,

> *The responsibility weighs hard. I never forget that the livelihood of the people who work here is dependent on me. It's a little easier when there's 3.5% unemployment, but lots of news organizations have laid off people this year. It's not just a question of the employee's job; it's that person's family, that person's kids. If we don't have a good year, it affects everyone. If we have to let people go, it affects everyone. That is a burden that my 'owner' friends feel uniquely. I spend a lot of time with our health insurance. It's not for me, per se, but I want to make sure we have really good medical and mental health insurance. In a giant company, they may say 'here's the budget, get the best healthcare we can.' For us, I'm in the details of our 401k because it's on me.*

Many leaders reported that confiding in a small set of non-family employees helps them to formulate and implement strategy. This inclusion helps non-family staff to see their roles as important, even potentially demonstrating a path to the top for non-family members. It also is a useful general strategy for the leaders, sharing recognition of their own limitations and leveraging all the talent around them to fill the gap. **Todd Schurz** discusses how he relied on non-family employees when he came back to run the family business after an outside career stint.

> *My family owned newspapers, real estate, magazines. I took over the magazine. We went from being a larger company to standing on its own. I knew we had to grow and expand, and I needed a time to do that. I will say I shored up my team before I came over here. I had lunch with the key people here. I mean, we were small office, at the time between 55 and 60 employees. But the three or four people who I knew most of my life, I took them to lunch and I told them I need your help, I*

need your support, I need to learn. I never tried to pretend to know something that I didn't know. People find that out.

This also serves as a nice preview of the use of importing outsider perspectives to help run the family business, discussed further below.

Modifying family history to fit current goals. Some of our legacy leaders revealed that their family narrative was modified to better fit the direction desired by the current family leaders. This was not framed as a nefarious or dishonest act, but more along the lines of revisiting the core values and thinking about how they may apply to the modern world in a manner different than what the founders expected. This includes opportunity to forswear (if not necessarily prevent) future changes, such as when a farming family publishes their intention to keep their land together for future generations. It also allows the family leaders to be clear about what the company is not, as well as what it is. **Wade Murphy** of Murphy Oil and Sourcerock explains,

> *It allows us to also redefine our family history. History can be written and rewritten, and this especially applies to the corporate world – almost with every new board, if not every new CEO – but the core remains. I know what my grandfather did, I know what my dad did, I know what we've done together. I also know what we didn't do.*

Such an approach did not always gain support from the entire family ownership group, and sometimes the consensus of the group helped to determine who would ascend as the legacy leader.

7.3.3 Gaining Experience Outside the Family Business

Many of our interviewees discussed having future leaders work for companies outside their family business, a strategy that addresses challenges of the family legacy path while building on the base opportunities provided by their family brand and resources. We heard how gaining this outside experience helped to diversify their perspective and professional network, important for understanding and extending the reach of the family business. They also spoke of earning their stripes—finding success—from what at least appears to be less biased sources than their own family. This can be a critical steppingstone for managing any perception of the leader having undue entitlement due to his or her family connections. As **Todd Schurz** explains,

I worked for a couple years out of Brown University, then worked in media outside my family business for a couple of years in the Washington DC suburbs. I did that for a couple reasons. Number one, I wanted to see if I liked the industry. And second, "was I any good at it?" Because it's hard to get an honest evaluation in your own company.

After rejoining the family business in 1989, **Schurz** went on to hold positions in nearly every area of the business, including running a publication in California, being editor and publisher of the Tribune, and heading their flagship TV station. Ultimately, in 2007, he became CEO of the entire company.

The strategy of procuring outside positions can arise from opportunities created by the family business, leveraging the reach of its members either through direct network contacts or by virtue of the future leader's allied experience early on in the family business. It can also be a strategy, as Schurz intones above, to combat the otherwise limited perspective available within the insular culture of a leader's own family business. Family business consultant **Stephanie Brun de Pontet** also recommends that her clients require family members to work elsewhere, ideally for a significant number of years and, importantly, to have been promoted before coming back to the family business.

What that allows is for a future leader to have true self-confidence, from a situation where their capabilities have been tested in a context where their last name is irrelevant.

Being honest about the limitations of family leaders, and how outside experience might allow a leader to leverage the strengths of their family business, is important for **Schurz**, who acknowledges "*I probably would have fallen flat on my face if I had no prior leadership experience.*"

7.3.4 Develop Limits and Accountability for Family Members

It can be seen that in addition to providing direction, strategic and succession plans also often serve to place limits on family members and their roles, responsibilities, ownership rights, including positions beyond just the executive suite. Family firms often find it helpful to further delineate policies, rules, and expectations for how family members participate in family governance, how they join or leave the family firm, and more. Most of the family business leaders and experts who we interviewed spoke to the importance of this and even established some consistent patterns in their recommendations.

Company needs first. For instance, most suggested the basic strategy of establishing role and job descriptions based on the company's strategic needs, rather than creating specific positions to be awarded to particular family members. While this is sometimes difficult to accomplish in practice, it can be augmented by another frequent suggestion to design plans for family members (and others) to gain skills that will be valuable to the family business, such as through training and programs of study through universities. A related strategy was a policy of requiring significant outside professional experience before joining the family firm, especially for a management or executive position. This experience might be within the industry, even at a competitor of the family business, or outside the industry to maximize potential for creating a distinctive mindset from the family business. These outside experiences typically will vary according to the needs of the business and the interests of the family member, although some who have been in the position of being expected to return to the family business report a certain amount of pressure to pursue a particular set of experiences.

Higher standards. Several of our interviewees suggested that the criteria for evaluating family should be different non-family, but not in the perhaps expected direction of leniency. Instead, for instance, **Darby** suggested that the standards must be higher for a family member to join the business, vetting them more thoroughly, so as to be clear to the non-family staff that "*being a family member doesn't matter inside the office.*" Others (**Wade Murphy**, **Craig Aronoff**, **Todd Schurz**) emphasized that family members must have experiences and skills gained outside the family business, a requirement that does not stand for non-family members. They noted that it was best in most cases for family members to start at lower hierarchical positions, ideally rotated across organizational divisions, in order to learn the business from the ground up. **Cathy Carroll** suggested that family business should be very specific about their criteria, especially for appointing family members to high-level executive positions. She gives the example of a client who believes that he is ready to ascend to an executive position in the large family business, but lacks the prescribed international experience. While he initially expected the family to relax the requirement, considering that he had been raising a young family, he was surprised at their insistence. In that situation, the family was right to withhold the promotion, **Carroll** told us, because "*if the family decided it was* *strategically advantageous to have an executive with international experience, they should stick to their guns."*

Family members who are not in named managerial or leadership roles should be cautious about weighing in on operational issues, or even on strategic governance issues when outside their family ownership meetings. In keeping with expert recommendations on governance policy, **Murphy** suggests that managers must be given purview to make decisions in their scope of work, so that other family members should *"create a space and leave authority to the manager."*

Accountability through performance measures. Family businesses should also emphasize the development and use of objective performance metrics to track and limit members operating in their roles. Without clear goals, performance targets, and viable ways of measuring performance, it can sometimes be tempting to allow family members to operate without consequence. However, as **Craig Aronoff** advises, *"being a family business is no excuse"* for not holding leaders accountable. Establishing clear measures that are in line with the strategic plan has value for both the leader and other family members with an interest in the company. These measures may include traditional areas (e.g., profitability, market share, long-term return on investment, liquidity, workforce productivity) or more specialized markers for the family business (benchmarks for developing the next generation of family leaders, increasing the security of family investment and passive income, etc.). Family leaders gain the benefit of knowing how they will be evaluated, while the others can get a clear window into the effect of leaders on the performance of their valued asset. This has the additional important benefit of reducing the risk of relationship conflict within the family, because the clarity provided by the measures helps set expectations for all relevant parties.

Stephanie Brun de Pontet adds that *"future family leaders must be given roles where they could fail"* in terms of objective, measurable, performance goals.

> *Success should not be guaranteed; prospective leaders must prove themselves with skills and effort. Too often families put a next-generation prospective leader in a role that 'protects' them from any real accountability out of a sense that they cannot be allowed to fail. This is shortsighted as it is important that leaders experience failure so they can learn and grow from this experience.*

This risk, coupled with the relatively obvious success or failure that is afforded by visible objective measure, allows leaders to grow.

7.3.5 Import Outside Perspectives

Our interviewees almost universally recommend that family business should seek, develop, and utilize outside perspectives to guard against family insularity, to generate new ideas, and to reach markets beyond their family limits. The external view can be realized through consultants and coaches, executives hired from the outside, employees operating at the production levels, and even through supply chain relationships.

Work and education outside the family. Probably the most common strategy for gaining outside perspective, as discussed above, is simply to encourage family members to work outside the family business. Family members are sent off to college, sometimes with a directive to study an area compatible with the family business and sometimes given freer reign, but nearly always with the goal of eventually bringing back new ideas. Some of our interviewees stressed that, in line with strategic family succession planning, it should not be assumed that family members would come back to the family business. Instead, they can be given a privileged opportunity to get a foot back in the door, but for any position offered must meet the rigorous qualifications like any other job candidate.

Independent board as external lens. **Todd Schurz** describes how he structured his board of directors to maximize the potential for understanding the broadcasting industry and other fields relating to his family business. The process took time, negotiating with the family board members, selling the idea to the extended family ownership group, and determining the profile of potential outside board members.

> We added independent directors to our board in 2009 for the first time. We had nine directors, two independent and seven owners. The next year we went to three independent and six owners. Now we are five owners and four independents; this past July we made the decision to go to a majority independent board next year.

Schurz finds that the more externally-focused board gives him opportunity to learn industry trends and get feedback on the direction of Schurz Communications. For example, he reports that it helped in thinking through the diversification strategy, reducing investment in broadcasting to become a more general investment family firm. At the same time, he balances their input with careful consideration of the will of the family owners. He also brings in third-party consultants to gain additional insights and reactions to the idea.

So for example, when we decided to exit the broadcasting industry, the board said, Okay, let's hear what the owners think because I made the recommendation. I brought in a third party as well. We had conference calls among the family members, and were able to reach consensus on what to communicate back to the board. We seek guidance, while we're very careful about what are owner decisions and what are board decisions.

Family business associations and fora. There are a growing number of family business associations that focus on the specialized needs of families, providing information, sponsoring fora, conferences, and other opportunities for networking. **Cathy Merrill** discusses the external support she gets from YPO, an organization founded (as "Young Presidents' Organization") for family-legacy business leaders.

YPO works through a forum of eight to ten person groups that are highly confidential and they're seen as your personal board of directors. They're there to help you; think of it like group therapy. My forum's been together 12 years. What was very helpful to me, when I joined YPO the year after I took over here, was having people who I could talk to. One of the biggest issues is dealing with people you've known your whole life. Often people have problems dealing with their siblings and their parents. Often people take over while their parents are still alive, so they still have a hand involved.

We'll note as well that many of our interviewees lauded their own siblings and extended family members for their support, good relationships, and sometimes even for stepping away to give the designated sibling room to lead. **Merrill** states,

I do know from other people in my [family leader group] *forum that one of the biggest issues is dealing with people you've known your whole life, such as problems with your siblings and parents. Often people take over while their parents are still alive, so they still have a hand involved. I did not have those challenges. I had very supportive siblings, my mother was alive, she was super supportive. If anything, we had a challenge the other way. I felt she wasn't giving me enough advice; saying "You're so wonderful, you will figure it out," and I would be thinking "I need your wisdom." But when I had to let someone go, she also was not there saying "Hey, he's responsible for a lot of my family." She was very much like "You have to do what's best for the business, what's best for the company".... It's not that I have a better way, it's that I have a different way and maybe my path is different because I'm trying to get to something else.*

Coach or consultant to give non-family view. Executive coaches are a growing category of professionals who can be particularly useful to family business leaders. They are ideal for family leaders in some ways; they are outside experts who generally have experience with leaders from many other organizations; they do not have fealty to the family or to the leader him/herself; and they can share feedback with the leader without much fear of reprisal. A challenge for coaching family leaders is to understand what distinguishes them from leaders in non-family firms, and what is similar across the firms. For example, leadership coach **Jeff Nally** notes that family business leaders often compare themselves to prior family leaders, even if that is the best referent for their business, "*because that's their only contrast, as opposed to other organizations where they could work for many different leaders.*"

One tool **Nally** and other coaches use is a multi-rater performance feedback process such as 360 performance appraisal. Coaches typically ask a variety of stakeholders—family members, non-family employees, sometimes business partners and customers—to rate the family leader in areas such as strengths, weaknesses, opportunities, styles, behaviors, and outcomes. This can be especially useful when a new family leader takes over a company and has doubts as to whether their leadership is being well-received, as **Nally** describes:

> *In those situations, the 360 feedback usually shows that there is some percentage of employees who are ready to move forward; they're okay with the new inherited leader. The other surprise usually is around what other people see this inherited leader doing really well, plus new things they want them to do, or to stop doing, or to start doing differently. Once they have that list, it becomes relatively focused because now we know what to coach. For every leader, including inherited, there's always some big surprise, so they'd say "I had no idea these people saw that strength in me; I never saw it through their lens before. And yes, I've got to stop doing these other things. I'm aware of it. I just didn't know what had that big of an impact on how I lead and how they do their work."*

The process for the coached family leader then becomes to move toward capitalizing on their own strengths in relation to the intended direction of their family business. This helps to orient them to the current point in time, rather than modeling behavior that may have been effective to reach goals in the past. This allows reduction of comparison to the leaders of prior generations, especially within the relatively safe space of the coaching interaction. Ultimately, they must come up with a way to communicate and enact their own strengths, as **Nally** puts it,

they need to claim their strengths, then be proactive about it and not just live it in
the confidential private coaching space.

Sometimes this involves criticizing, directly or indirectly, prior family leaders, and the coaching process helps support the optimal path to success.

7.3.6   Provide Options for Leaving the Family Business

Any leader of a family business ought to ensure there are good options and support for leaving the family business, so that those who stay not only have the skills but also have committed to leading the business. While some family members enjoy being involved in the family business, others would prefer to pursue their own interests. An example of this was Wade Murphy's description above of how extended family members leveraged company resources to fuel their passions and launch other careers. Some family members may find niches in related businesses, and even can be of mutual benefit with those who remain in the family business, as when **Darby** tells of his network of family contacts across the industry. Some family members leave to keep the peace in the family, or to allow remaining members to consolidate ownership and management of the company by divesting their interest in the family business. There are also times, not surprisingly, where those who would like to gain positions of leadership are not seen to be the best fit.

In some cases, family members leverage the resources of the organization to create or support their own independent businesses. **Wade Murphy** and his father divested their share of the family business, Murphy Oil, using the proceeds to gain control of the family company's original holding company, Marmik Oil.[4] **Murphy** further founded a new company, Source-Rock Partners,[5] which invests in allied energy projects and other sectors (the company website states that it is "a private asset management and thought leadership firm with a focus in the energy, geopolitical, finance, retail and real estate sectors and their respective penumbra"). **Murphy** explains,

My family story is one where some of us took the position that Murphy Oil was
more of an asset base that we own. But the world has changed, and we can build
on that. So my father and I made a choice after my grandfather passed away in
2002. Over the intervening years, we made the decision to divest our holdings of
Murphy Oil.... We said, 'We have to make a choice to do what's right for these
assets.'

---

[4]http://marmikoil.com/service/our-history/.

[5]www.sourcerockpartners.com.

Murphy and his father chose to cash out at some great cost. Not only did they have to carefully manage the communication about their choice to the family, to minimize damaging relationships where possible, but also took a large financial hit. Because the family business had been founded in the mid-1900s, the capital gains were substantial, consuming up to 80% of the value. While this may be viewed merely as a planned sacrifice for future earnings, it also represents a considered strategy for leveraging family assets into the career desired by a family leader.

7.3.7   Structure Effective Family Communication

The most basic and perhaps most ultimately effective strategy for leaders dealing with the challenges of family business is to plan, create, and maintain effective communication practices. As family business member and consultant **Vernon Holleman** puts it,

> *Communication is critical. Honest, regular communication about where the business is, how it's doing, how it's sort of being run and operated. Because it's in a family dynamic, you may not be publicly traded, but you basically have kind of an ownership responsibility to the other owners. So I've seen the ones who have the most success are very heavy on communication.*

Good communication is not just a matter of transmitting information among interested parties. It starts with a clear understanding of family business goals, associated strategies, and roles, shared through channels that will be most acceptable and effective in communicating the intended message, and following up to ensure understanding.

Several of the strategies that we have discussed so far relate to, are products of, or require good communication to be successful. The family narrative, for example, is an important communication instrument, of a relatively formal nature, which combines family history, culture, goals, and strategy. In this section, we'll give examples of a few more ideas related to communication process and structure, according to our family business leader interviewees: family consensus, family meetings, and personal communication.

Family consensus to the world. **Todd Schurz** believes that one strength of the family behind the business is the varied perspectives and collective will that they can exert. For the family to buy in and support the direction of the business, there must be an opportunity for members to share their ideas, including their differences in opinion, then reconcile as a family collective. He believes that the family should strive for consensus—not necessarily everyone agreeing completely with every step of the company direction, but after honest dialogue the family should come up with one direction that everyone can support, reconciling through compromise, voting, or other decision rules. Once this consensus is reached, each member of the family should support it to the rest of the company, particularly the board and employees, as well as present a united front to the rest of the world. As **Schurz** describes,

> *We can have lots of discussion, debate, and disagreement within the ownership group. But when the board hears from the ownership group, it's with one voice. We put that in writing, so there is a written record over the years about what the owners think about different issues. For example, when I recommended exiting the broadcasting industry, the board said, 'Okay, let's hear what the owners think.' In April, we brought in a third party to help with conference calls, through which we were able to reach consensus. We communicated this back to the board, saying 'this is what the owners think about this decision.' This gives the board the guidance they need. We're very careful in planning what our owners decide, and what our board decides.*

Family business consultant **Stephanie Brun de Pontet** emphasizes that it is important for family businesses to achieve this consensus even when the family no longer necessarily has ownership control of the company. Family members remain part of the company brand, even when they no longer own or directly work for the business. **Brun de Pontet** gives an example of a Chicago-based company whose board was empowered to make a difficult and important decision about selling a portion of the business, yet took the time to engage with the family first. Although the board was entitled to make the decision, they asked the family to meet, deliberate, and weigh in, because

> *the family had 100 years of history with this legacy asset of the company, and their comfort and buy-in for this decision was considered essential.*

Family business meetings. **Darby** discusses how good family business communication can be supported by agreement and efforts of particular generations within the family. He relates that The Beach Company had very little formal processes or organization in 1990 when it came to strategic and succession issues, although the company was 45 years old at that point. The annual business meeting at that time was on Christmas morning with the family gathered for the holiday. The founding generation of grandparents would let the family finish their breakfast and then pass around a two-page letter, sometimes with cash in it. There was no real shareholder discussion, just the letter. While this worked when the company—and the successive generations—were younger, it became apparent that the leaders must develop another approach. Equally problematic, but in another manner, **Murphy** describes how the growing Murphy Oil family business meeting essentially replaced the holiday celebration among members of his extended family, contributing to an evolution from a family that might have been close, to being more of a business entity.

The Beach Company relied on its second generation of family leaders—the G2s—to create a plan for family communication through business meetings.

There are almost 80 of us now, including between the family members in each generation and their spouses. We looked at the G2s. They have really worked hard to teach us and to bring the families together, to celebrate what we have. We are all business now at the shareholders meetings. The G2s have been instrumental in guiding us through the traps; they worked hard to manage expectations and create full transparency. We don't want family to hear company business on the street or in the newspaper.

The inclusiveness, organization, and transparency of family meetings can have other positive effects. As **Darby** mentions,

It would have been easy for us to go our own way – we're all over the United States – and they have kept the family very close.

Personal communication. It is clear that family business leaders should plan for and enact clear communication procedures within their family, and within their business. Ultimately, family business leaders should strive for shared understanding of the business purpose and direction. There are many communication tools and processes that can support this aim, such as those detailed in this chapter. However, none of these should be considered to take the place of the simple desire to communicate in a family whose members share a sense of what they see in the business. As **Darby** notes, "*if you have good rapport with family, you'll just get on the phone.*"

While direct communication is likely to be effective in many families, the best practice of this should include sensitivity to the manner of speaking and the continuing relationships beyond the workplace. As **Kathy McDevitt** concludes,

The challenge is that because you are family members you talk to your family members like they are in your kitchen, and not in your office. You can sometimes, I don't know if disrespect is the right word, but you are far more informal because you are talking to your siblings. But you have to be careful because you need to live with these people for the rest of your life and have family events. So you have to resolve any issues so you can have peace in your life.

7.4   Navigating the Family Legacy Path

In this chapter, we have described many opportunities and challenges associated with the family legacy path, as well as strategies for leveraging them. Being a leader in the second or successive generation of the family conveys certain advantages, such as the value of the *Family Brand*, the *Culture of Family Values & Founder DNA*, the *Passion & Shared Commitment across Generations*, and the security and resources that come with a *Seat at the Table*. To leverage these advantages, family leaders should develop a *Family Narrative* (including a strategic plan), *Clarify Family Values for the Company*, and utilize the *Early-life Mentors*.

Family leaders also face challenges that are often unique to multigenerational businesses. They must manage *Relationships in the Family Business*, *Beliefs about Entitlement and Positions*, *Limited Perspective*, and *Resources and Performance Complexity*. To manage and mitigate these challenges, family leaders can support the development of the *Family Narrative, Strategic Plan, Succession Planning* (not only for leaders, but also for family owners and managers), *Gaining Outside Experience, Limits and accountability, Importing outside perspectives, Leaving the family business*, and *Family Communication*.

As we have seen, family businesses are nearly as unique as the variety of families who found, own, manage, and lead them. The lessons in this chapter, as with the other paths discussed in this book, hold value for those walking any of the six paths to leadership.

Reflection Questions
- Where are the lines between your family and your family business? How do you balance and manage the division?
- What does it mean to be a legacy leader? Does this entail continuing the family traditions, or extending the family reach?
- What is your personal readiness to lead your family business? Where do you want to target your development?
- What is the family's story around your selection to lead the family business? How will that support and/or hinder your leadership?

- Will your relationships both in the family and in the organization need to change as a result of your new position? How do you intend to manage these challenges?
- For non-family members who lead family businesses, what unique perspectives are brought that may be most valuable to family owners and other members? What sensitivities should the non-family leader develop?

8

Leading on Your Own Paths

Understanding the Paths

We hope that the preceding chapters have established both a structure for understanding how leaders are influenced by the context of their entry into their positions and an appreciation for the opportunities and challenges encountered as they walk the six distinct paths to leadership. Because our goals in writing this book include providing guidelines for navigating the paths, we also outlined strategies for leaders to add to their repertoire. Learning these strategies may be beneficial for leaders who wish to enhance their own skillset, as well as for organizations that seek to increase the effectiveness of their executives and to better align their leaders with the workforce. Below we outline some summary thoughts on each path and the overall strategic approach across paths and then offer a set of integrative thoughts on how leaders can apply these lessons to orient themselves on the paths they choose.

Brief Distinctions of the Six Paths to Leadership

In Table 8.1, we compile the opportunities and challenges of all paths, from the more comprehensive descriptions with strategies provided in each chapter. We also draw these brief summary distinctions:

© The Author(s), under exclusive license to Springer Nature
Switzerland AG 2021
M. A. Clark and M. Persily Lamel, *Six Paths to Leadership*,
https://doi.org/10.1007/978-3-030-69017-5_8

- **Insiders**, on the Promoted path, fill a leadership position as a result of a change in responsibilities within an organization of which they are already a member. They may have the most success when capitalizing on their existing knowledge of the organization, of the work, and of their relationships, while carefully constructing new tactics to lead from their changed position.
- **Outsiders**, on the Hired path, are acquired from the external market, often from competitors or having specialized backgrounds that have value to the hiring organization. Their specialized knowledge, relatively novel perspective, and external network should be leveraged to overcome unfamiliarity with local culture and work practices.
- **Representatives** reach the Elected path through votes from their constituents. These leaders personally embody the full power and clear authority of their position, allowing them to extend their vision through many connections, but often suffer from restrictions of time and as targets of public attention.
- **Proxy** leaders, on the Appointed path, are assigned their position by a political principal, board of directors, owner, or other authority. They benefit from a clear focus of task and the authority to carry it out, but may have difficulty being fully accepted by the non-appointed workforce, who they need to accomplish their goals.
- **Creators** start ventures on the Founder path, rising into leadership positions as the organizations grow. They are buoyed by their unique vision, bringing a unique idea or process to reality, and can use the credibility this grants to achieve their goals through early challenges when resources are tight and decisions are difficult.
- **Legacy** leaders, those on the Family path who take up the mantle of their family organization, can often rely on the brand, culture, and relationships created through their "founder DNA" to carry them through the challenges of potentially insular perspectives.

8.1   Six Paths to Leadership

Table 8.1 Comparing opportunities and challenges of six paths to leadership

	Opportunities	Challenges
Promoted (Insider)	• Cultural awareness • Relationship network within the organization • Proven track record and commitment • Organizational succession planning and leadership development programs	• Manage former peers • Shift perception to become a change agent • Adapt habits and metrics to new role • Be a "First"
Hired (Outsider)	• New perspective • Expertise from outside • External networks • Perception of earned hire • Been there, done that • Willingness to take risks and introduce changes	• Cultural assimilation • Not Knowing: Who and What • Organization onboarding deficiency • Identification with former organization brand • Lack of support from rivals • In the fishbowl (visibility)
Elected (Representative)	• Leader as the entity • Clearly delineated authority based on position • Power to convene; A seat at the table • Responsiveness of stakeholders • Ability to help people maneuver the government bureaucracy • Exceptional talent availability	• Term limits/fixed terms • Constituent expectations and public exposure • Associations with your party leadership • Tenure weighs heavily for many leadership positions • Schedule, travel, family toll
Appointed (Proxy)	• Reputation, power, and agenda from principal • Outside perspective • Access to the principal and their network • Short timeframe, low expectations	• Perception of qualifications and basis of power without merit • Perceived as managing up rather than leading • Short time-frame to make an impact

(continued)

Table 8.1 (continued)

	Opportunities	Challenges
Founder (Creator)	• Personal vision and values • Founder passion • Credibility: Commitment, Knowledge, and Authority	Resource scarcity Founder personal limitations Sharing and giving up power Engagement of non-founding employees Professional vs personal relationships Celebrity status and approachability
Family (Legacy)	• Family brand • Culture of family values and founder DNA • Passion & shared commitment across generations • Seat at the table, security, and resources	• Managing family relationships • Beliefs about entitlement and positions in the family business • Limited perspective: family culture and family insularity • Resource pressures

© 2021 Six Paths to Leadership

8.1.1   Path Strategies and Connections to Leadership

While the opportunities and challenges of each path may vary dramatically, the strategies associated with them harbor underlying similarities. Therefore, the process for a leader to develop strategies for any path could be guided through a set of basic questions.

1. What do I need to learn?
2. What do I bring to this job? What do I lack?
3. How will my relationships support and/or prevent my success?
4. What assumptions do my stakeholders have about me and my role?
5. What organizational support will I have for my onboarding and continuous development?
6. Where should I focus my energy?
7. Given the path possibilities and constraints, how will I measure my success?

The strategies that leaders employ in response to opportunities and challenges, as well as the increased awareness of path contexts, will support effectiveness in their efforts. It should be remembered that such strategies are also dependent on other non-contextual attributes of leaders, briefly referred to in our introductory chapter, such as traits, competencies, and characteristics. While we do not detail these in this book, we should point out that simply being in a leadership role does not make a person into a leader. An important measure of leaders is their influence on others. In 2014, Representative Tom Cole shared a truism from then-Speaker of the House John Boehner that illustrates this:

> I said to the speaker, 'Why in the world are we letting the guys who didn't vote for you drive the conference?' And you get that typical Boehner: 'Well, I learned a long time ago if you're a leader and nobody's following you, you're just a guy out for a walk.'[1]

On its own, recognition of a particular path does not guarantee an effective level of leadership. A leader's success on any path, or failure on a particular path, depends on what is done with the position rather than just being in the right place for leadership.

8.2 Leaders in the Context of Paths: How Do You Fit?

Some of our readers may have traveled multiple leadership paths in their career; others may have chosen one path; some may now be preparing for a new path as a first-time leader or as a career switch. Regardless of where you fall, there are some key insights you now have about the six leadership paths. Let's take each of these one by one.

8.2.1 Not Everyone Is Best Suited for Every Leadership Path

When it comes to your leadership approach, both the attributes of the person and the particulars of the context matter. While we might like to think that anyone can intentionally manage a career across any of the paths, there are certainly factors that may better position you for success on one path over

---

[1] "Boehner Uses New Mandate to Muffle Talk of a Shutdown," *New York Times*, Nov 30, 2014.

another. In strategic planning, organizations commonly use SWOT analysis (internal Strengths and Weaknesses, external Opportunities, and Threats) to align strengths with market opportunities to better position themselves vis a vis their competitors. Similarly, at a personal level, leaders can use a SWOC (Strengths, Weaknesses, Opportunities, and Challenges) to align personal strengths with the opportunities that a particular path may include.

For leaders who are considering multiple paths, we suggest completing a personal SWOC analysis (described below in the Appendix). To do this, leaders should capture the opportunities and challenges for each path they are considering, and then reflect on their core strengths and weaknesses. What comes more naturally, and what is more difficult? As the SWOC analysis develops, especially when considering two different options, leaders should consider which path better leverages their strengths, in relation to opportunities and ways to manage challenges. Which path will require additional development in leader skills or attributes?

In order to better demonstrate this process, below we present a sample **SWOC Analysis** for the promoted path.

Sample SWOC Analysis: Sonia on the Promoted Path.

Goal: Align your strengths with the path opportunities, be ultra-mindful when paths reinforce your weaknesses (Fig. 8.1).

In this example, Sonia's reputation for results orientation and her ability to build strong relationships will serve her well in the promoted path. However, her discomfort networking may get in the way of her ability to successfully adapt to a new role that requires developing new relationships quickly. Additionally, the promoted path, more than any other, challenges leaders to leave their previous identity in order to embrace the responsibilities of the new

	Individual Traits		
	Strengths	**Weaknesses**	
Positive	• Possesses strong, trusting relationships • Reputation for results orientation • Strategic thinker	• Discomfort networking • Difficulty delegating • Managing conflict	**Negative**
	Opportunities	**Challenges**	
	• Cultural know-how • Track Record • Organizational development plans • Proven Commitment to the organization	• Managing former peers • Difficulty setting new direction • Adapting to a new role in the same organization • Letting go of former responsibilities	
	Path Traits		

Fig. 8.1 Sample SWOC analysis: Sonia on the promoted path

role. As a result, given that she already has difficulty delegating, that need to let go of former responsibilities will be absolutely critical.

While there are certainly no steadfast rules about who should or should not pursue any of the paths, potential leaders should familiarize themselves with the core attributes of each path and how they align with one's own preferences and strengths.

Jody Olsen, Director of the Peace Corps, shares that the first question someone should ask before pursuing a political appointee position is "*Why do I want this position?*" Is it because I want to serve in a presidential administration? Do I want this position because I support the political philosophy of this President? For Director **Olsen**, who previously had worked for the Peace Corps, the reasons were clear: "*I feel I have this gift to protect the legacy of Peace Corps as long as I'm there.*" Dr. **Olsen**'s prior service demonstrated the loyalty that, in an appointed leadership position, would help her to manage the common challenge associated with those who resist political appointees because they consider them to be short-timers.

8.2.2 Actively Manage Transitions Across Paths Through Factors Associated with the New Path, While Challenging Past Success Strategies

Over their careers, leaders may develop particular habits; when success follows, they may reinforce those habits, believing in their efficacy regardless of fit to the next position. However, it would be a mistake to assume that strategies in one path automatically transfer effectively to another path. For example, the dynamic between leaders appointed in a federal government position and their direct reports is likely to differ dramatically from that of outside hires and their subordinates. As discussed with regard to the Appointed path in Chapter 5, a key strategy for success is to pick a small number of important projects that can be accomplished in a short period of time. These projects ought to last across administrations, given that federally appointed leaders rarely hold a position for more than four years, and quite often just 18 months. Additionally, appointed leaders ought to include input from career professionals in order to learn quickly and decrease the likelihood of resistance among their direct reports. However, the circumstances of an outside hire are usually drastically different. They are often brought in from the outside because their expertise does not exist internally, or they want someone to disrupt the status quo. As this demonstrates, it would not be effective to approach both paths in the same manner.

8.2.3 To Better Support Leaders as an HR Partner, Coach, or Colleague, Consider the Key Distinctions of the Paths

For both HR partners and coaches, the six paths provide valuable context for onboarding and development plans. For instance, a basic question for most leaders could be about how they are thinking about their current path, and how it might differ from previous paths.

Transitions across paths. In Washington DC, we often work with professionals around the challenge of transitioning from the public to the private sector, or vice versa. While traditionally these may be considered no differently than industry transitions, the path context provides additional insights. For example, some Capitol Hill staffers who have worked only for elected leaders will find themselves transitioning to industry. They are on the external hire path, yet working for a new boss who likely traveled the promoted path within the organization. In these cases, there are many intersecting assumptions of the diverse leadership paths. We may arrange these assumptions as data maps that can be reconciled as the leaders work with new colleagues, needing to align assumptions and expectations (likely driven by previous experiences). Both coaches and HR partners can help leaders uncover such assumptions and explore new ones related to the six paths.

Extending founder passion. Creators, those leaders on the founder path, often have a remarkable level of passion and commitment that drives their success. A challenge for their HR partners is how to ensure that this passion cascades throughout the entire organization. Executive coaches play a role as well as they help onboard leaders. Can they fully incorporate the founding leader's path into their coaching engagement goals? Coaches who use the six paths framework can introduce ideas from paths other than the one walked by their client, to offer a new perspective on challenges. For example, consider the case of a client, promoted from within, who is struggling with how to introduce a major change initiative due to concern about how it will be received. The coach can ask,

How would your approach be different if you were hired into this role from a competitor? How would you introduce this change if you did not know the history and baggage associated with the proposed change?

Likewise, in the case of a founder who is struggling with making a decision about the composition of his team, a coach can ask how they would approach the decision as if they were appointed as interim CEO by investors. The lens of a different path can help to evoke new awareness and thinking that can lead to more confident leadership.

Colleagues. Understanding the six paths can also be useful for colleagues, particularly the direct reports of a leader, who play a critical role in the overall success of their organizational leaders. The best followership likely includes both challenging incoming leaders—it may be natural, for instance, for subordinates to assess whether the leader is serving their needs—and also supporting leaders to be their best. Simply appreciating the opportunities and challenges of the respective paths of the leader can enhance understanding and benefit the working relationship. Ideally, colleagues can use their knowledge of the paths to support their leaders' development. For example, at times elected leaders may be challenged by the demands of their diverse constituencies. Rather than judging leaders on their potential blind spots, their staff can ensure that the leader is well prepared for interactions with those constituencies who they might know intimately.

8.2.4 There Is More to Leadership Effectiveness Than Simply Managing Your Path

We wrote this book because despite the many great leadership books on the market, the field lacks recognition and understanding of leadership contexts as accounted for in the six paths framework. As discussed previously, however, it would be a mistake to ignore the wide-ranging research that exists around competencies, actions, and other aspects of effective leadership. For example, most leadership competency models include the essential behaviors for leading people, projects, and change in organizations. These leadership traits and competencies often include at a minimum the following:

- Developing and sharing a compelling vision;
- Collaborating and leading teams toward performance goals;
- Thinking strategically;
- Communicating effectively;
- Developing others to reach their potential;
- Exemplifying honesty and integrity.

This list of competencies is likely to support effective leadership regardless of context. Adding the six paths framework will enhance the understanding of how context works for and against leader efforts. We encourage leaders to solicit feedback regularly and continuously invest in their own development, regardless of path. These development journeys should include these common leadership competencies, in addition to those that are critical in their own organizations. Therefore, the onboarding checklist of leaders or those supporting them should include not only the factors appropriate to their path that are found in this book, but also those related to the many key findings around effective leadership.

8.2.5   Leadership Literature and Conversations Will Gain Insight and Relevance When Including Consideration of Leadership Paths

Related to the insight above, we encourage both scholars and practitioners to begin incorporating career path distinctions into their research and systems. At minimum, this means ensuring that leadership conclusions are assessed against the different paths and other contextual variables. For example, what does excellent execution look like for the elected leader, as opposed to the founder? When leading change, how might a promoted leader approach a change initiative differently than an outside hire? We believe that the approach will differ based on leadership path, especially as they face distinct challenges and hold unique path-related benefits. By ensuring that research samples reflect a variety of leadership paths, we may gain understanding of important differentiating factors that make leaders on one path more successful than they would on another.

Diversity, equity, and inclusion. While we interviewed leaders of diverse gender, sexual orientation, racial, and ethnic backgrounds, we believe that it is critical to further extend leadership paths research to diverse and inclusive organizations. For example, when you consider an additional layer of the difference of the hired path, how does that affect the onboarding strategy and likelihood of success? The Outsider leader, already managing the challenge of having to lead those who did not receive the promotion, may further confront bias and assumptions about the reason for their hire. In another case, what happens when the organizational practice is to promote from within, which may conflict with goals to have more diverse representation in senior ranks? Rather than promoting the "next in line" for that C-suite position, the organization may open the search to a more diverse set of candidates. There is opportunity to explore how the six paths to leadership support or prevent attracting a diverse set of candidates, how perceptions may play out differently, and which strategies further support inclusive organizations.

Continue on your Path

We hope you will continue on your leadership journey, whether as a partner or as a leader yourself, with a new level of appreciation for distinctions of the six paths to leadership. Based on these, we offer summary questions for reflection:

For the experienced leader:

– What path(s) have I traveled? Are there paths I still want to travel?
– When presented with a leadership opportunity along a different path, how will my approach differ from what made me successful in the past? What are my potential blind spots?
– When I have struggled in my career, is there a path explanation for that struggle?
– Reflecting on the paths I have traveled, how do these distinctions give me new insight into how I could have approached my challenges differently? How do I apply those learnings going forward?
– How can I use my experience along my path(s) to support other leaders who have less experience in my path?

For the new leader:

– Which path is most appealing to me based on my differentiating characteristics?
– Which path ought I avoid? Or what development areas should I target in order to better prepare for that less desirable path?
– How can I better support my leaders through a path lens? What blind spots can I help uncover and/or support?
– What can I do now to better support my readiness across the different paths?

We invite you to continue the conversation with us at www.sixpathstoleadership.com. On our website, you will find additional tools to support your leadership journey. Further, given that we appreciate the newness of this framework, we also invite you to share your experience with our tools and make suggestions for how to enhance research and practice in this area. Finally, recognizing that as a society we all want to support great leaders, if you know leaders who have applied some of these strategies or who have traveled certain paths exceptionally well, we welcome the opportunity to hear their stories.

Appendix: Tools for Navigating the Six Paths to Leadership

Our six paths framework makes a strong case that leadership is not "one size fits all" for either the person or the mode of entry into the role. There are important distinctions across the six leadership paths, and understanding them may provide value for both emerging and experienced leaders. Indeed, failure to understand the advantages and disadvantages inherent in each path can confound new leaders who otherwise may follow the footsteps of leaders on incompatible paths. By identifying the consistent factors within each path, leaders can focus attention on what is working for and against them and learn from those who have walked ahead on their path. We also believe that leaders will be more effectively walk their own paths if they also consider the experiences of those making tracks in other directions. Overall, we hope this work will be helpful to those who seek to understand and support leader emergence and operation across multiple paths.

In this chapter, we provide a set of tools to support the strategies we suggest in the book. While generally most relevant for the particular path where they fall, some of the tools may serve well in multiple paths with slight modifications. Our research also demonstrates that "trying on" a new path could help bring a new perspective to a leader's path, especially when stuck. For example, when traveling the promoted path, leaders may be so entrenched in the organization's culture and the way of doing things that it is difficult to consider a more disruptive, outsider perspective. How might it help for these leaders to "try on" the outsider path while navigating the promoted path? What benefits could that bring?

This appendix includes a sampling of tools. For additional tools, please visit www.sixpathstoleadership.com.

M. A. Clark and M. Persily Lamel, *Six Paths to Leadership*, https://doi.org/10.1007/978-3-030-69017-5

Chapter 2: The Insider Path

The tools for the promoted path are focused on leveraging the tremendous benefits of being that insider while also ensuring that leaders arrive at their new position with the same intentionality as one would when an outsider. While insiders will likely know many of the key players, they often fear implementation of change due to past experiences. We often hear, "for this position, we need to go outside in order to change how we are doing things." You can utilize these tools to leverage the knowledge you have while also managing the challenges of an insider mentality.

© 2021 Six Paths to Leadership
2.1 Personal Network Analysis and Action Plan

Purpose: Your internal network of relationships is a significant advantage of the promoted path. However, these relationships have traditionally served you well in previous positions. Now it's time to reflect on these relationships in the context of your new role.

Instructions: Answer the following questions about your internal network. Identify the top three actions you could take to adapt your relationships to support your success in your new role. How will you hold yourself accountable for these actions?

- What is my current network of relationships?
- In what areas do I need to diversify my network of relationships? Sample areas include information, political support, personal support, skills development, mentorship, influencers.
- Which relationships should I prioritize either by improving existing relationships or by investing in new relationships?
- What relationships, if any, do I need to de-prioritize in order to create space for new relationships?
- Top three actions to improve my relationship network

2.2 Listening Tour Action Plan (Applies to All Paths)

Purpose: During the first few months in a new role, leaders must prioritize learning from their new colleagues through 1:1 conversations, often referred to as a listening tour. Depending on the path, however, some questions may vary. See www.pathstoleadership.com for listening tour questions for each path.

Instructions: Document the answers to these questions as part of your listening tour. This tour should include key stakeholders up, across, and down in the organization.

---

1. What are this stakeholder's expectations for my role?
2. What did the stakeholder most appreciate about my predecessor?
3. Where does the stakeholder see an opportunity for greater impact of this role?
4. How does the stakeholder view (strengths, development areas) my team/department? How does the stakeholder and/or his/her team interact with my team/department?
5. Where does stakeholder suggest I focus my efforts over the next 90 days, 6 months, 1 year?

After completing the listening tour, what actions will you take to incorporate what you learned into your priorities, behaviors, and actions?

2.3 My Personal Onboarding Plan

Purpose: Onboarding plans more commonly support the outside hire, as outlined on the left side of this tool. Along the promoted path, leaders may need to take ownership of their own onboarding even though many of the same challenges exist as for the outside hire.

Instructions: This tool will support your ownership of your own onboarding into a more senior role in your organization. Take the steps in the right-hand column to build out your onboarding plan. Capture your top insights and actions as you go through the steps. Ideally you will review your plan with your manager, HR partner, or executive coach.

Outside Hire		Promoted
Learn corporate policies and procedures		Identify norms and practices of new forums (meetings, decision-making processes, etc.)
Interview previous position holder		Interview previous position holder (even if former boss)
Job description included in hiring process		Write job description if not provided and confirm assumptions with stakeholders
Listening tour for expectations, early wins*, and retention conversations	➡️	Listening tour for expectations, early/short-term wins*, and retention conversations
Identify key deliverables and performance metrics		Identify key deliverables and performance metrics, delegate former deliverables and assign metrics
Focus on first impressions		Identify where to focus reputational shift
Receive primer on the culture		Promote desired team culture early and often
Receive schedule of lunches and meetings for first month		Develop a schedule of meetings on topic of onboarding. Host a team lunch.
At senior levels, recruiting firm may provide feedback to support a development plan for first year.		Adapt your development plan to the new role.

*"early wins" is a key concept in Michael Watkins, First 90 Days and "short-term wins" is in John Kotter's Eight Step *Leading Change* model.

© 2021 Six Paths to Leadership

Key Takeaways:

1.
2.
3.

Action Steps:

1.
2.
3.

Chapter 3: The Outsider Path
3.1 Talent Assessment Action Tree

Purpose: When coming in from the outside, there will be many opinions about how to manage the team you inherit. Too often, leaders postpone making hard decisions that may result in losing precious time and/or losing key talent that is essential to their success. Upon coming into a new role and organization you will want to immediately conduct a talent assessment and identify the goals and expectations of your team. For those team members you want to retain, especially those who may have also applied for your job, you want to immediately identify key steps for retaining the critical talent. This includes reinforcing their value and supporting their career growth and development. Likewise, for those whom you want to depart, move to a strategy for departure, assuming your organizational policies allow. The sooner you have your ideal team in place, you will be able to focus on realizing the potential of your role and organization.

Directions: A talent assessment can be done in many ways. While a 2x2 matrix on performance and potential is a common approach, we suggest working with your HR department to access all performance history and talent development on your team. Additionally, part of your listening tour will include questions about others' perceptions of your team members' value. You will also assess your team's commitment to your leadership and vision. For the Outsider Leader, engaging in development conversations early with the talent you wish to retain and investing the time into team member career growth and development are absolutely critical. While it may feel like a secondary priority for you, it is at the forefront of the minds of your team members. Early indications of whether you are someone who will support their career growth will be judged and acted upon. Once you determine the conversations you need to have, schedule them to hold yourself accountable.

Talent Assessment Action Tree

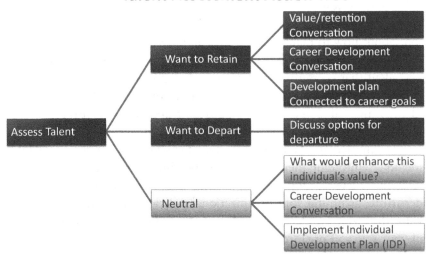

© 2021 Six Paths to Leadership

3.2 Competitor Profile

Purpose: When coming from a competitor of your new organization, your new colleagues may be resistant to trusting you, even if the core reason for your hire was your experience and impact at the competition. Part of the process for earning that trust includes what and how you reference your former employer and how you introduce new ideas. While it's essential to be generous with the experience and networks you bring, if overdone, promoting ideas can be perceived as being critical of your new organization, that nothing they do is good enough or that your loyalty is still elsewhere. In other words, if they do everything better there, why did you leave and come here? This reflection tool will help you to consider how to prioritize what to bring from your past experiences to enhance your new relationships and your overall effectiveness.

Directions: When coming from a competitor, reflect on these questions to better manage your perception. Develop your core messages. Once you develop your core messages, identify opportunities to share and reinforce them with your new organization.

Compare your former company/organization against your new company/organization along the following dimensions:

- Market position
- Areas of admiration
- Areas of critique
- Cultural differences

What do you want to bring from the competition?
What do you want to leave from the competition?
Identify your **core messages** that support the following:

- Promote what you admire/respect about the company you joined
- Serve to build trust between you and your former "competitors"
- Reinforce the reasons the company hired you (skills, knowledge, experience)
- Highlight your top focus areas of influence

DO NOT:

- Constantly reference the competition "When I was at X, we....."
- Hoard relationships from your past experiences
- Assume they want to replicate your past successes

Core Messages (related to previous employer)	Opportunities to Reinforce

© **2021 Six Paths to Leadership**

Chapter 4: The Representative Path

The tools for the Elected Path reinforce the unique opportunity of the leader being the entity. Early and deep personal reflection for elected leaders will help to center them on their personal purpose for running for office and how their organization can best be an extension of their brand and priorities. Starting with their personal strategic plan and stakeholder analysis, the upfront awareness and prioritization will help set both the representative and the staff up for success. Later, intentionally managing conflict around party affiliation and the stresses for the family of a public official will support stronger relationships and networks of build for the elected leader.

4.1 Elected Leader Strategic Plan

Purpose: The strategic plan for an elected leader varies significantly from a department, functional or organizational plan. Again, one of the great advantages of the elected path is that the leader is the entity/product. By doing your personal strategic plan, this can serve as your north star as you are bombarded with the many requests for your time and energy and as you set a culture for your staff.

Directions: Within the first three months of holding an elected position, develop a personal strategic plan, ideally with a core team who knows you well and is rooting for your success. Below are the questions to answer as you build out the plan. Revisit your plan every quarter as the environment changes and you learn more about how you are most effective in role.

Personal Mission Statement: Why did I run for office?

SWOT Analysis: What are my personal strengths and weaknesses. What are the opportunities and threats to my success in my role?

Personal Values: What values do I want reflected in how our office works with our constituents and other stakeholders?

Expected Behaviors: How do I expect my staff to treat me, each other, and our stakeholders? What behavior will I role model?

Strategic Priorities: Where will I focus my efforts? In what areas do I most want to make a difference? How can I leverage by comparative advantages (committee assignments, caucuses, region, background)?

Action Plan: What do I want to achieve, by when? Who will do what?

© **2021 Six Paths to Leadership**

4.2 Stakeholder Analysis

Purpose: An opportunity and challenge of the elected path are that stakeholders will come to you, ask for your time, and make requests. However, staying solely reactive and not prioritizing your time and efforts will eventually get in the way of measurable success. For the elected leader, engaging in a stakeholder analysis exercise will better align your outreach activities with your desired impact. This exercise, to be conducted with your team, will enable you to more objectively prioritize your stakeholders and ensure that you are leading your stakeholder engagement. Ultimately, you should identify those stakeholders with whom you want a proactive strategy so that their needs are met.

Directions: List out your constituencies and stakeholders. Assign your stakeholders according to the following categories:

Category A: Key partner and influencer. Strive to meet all needs.
Category B: Consistent stakeholder reactively meet needs when asked as long as does not conflict with category A or C.
Category C: Target stakeholder. Seeks to enhance relationship. Aligns with strategic priorities.
Category D: Do not engage. Cannot meet stakeholders' needs and can undermine stakeholders A-C.

Given the outcomes of this exercise, what are your top priorities to better align your stakeholder efforts with your strategic priorities? How will you operationalize your stakeholder management?

1.
2.
3.

© **2021 Six Paths to Leadership**

4.3 Party Affiliation Venn Diagram

Purpose: As an elected leader, your party affiliation serves as both an opportunity and a challenge. As a result, it's critical to be more intentional about that association. There ought to be a significant amount of overlap, where you and your party agree on issues and approaches. However, your constituencies may differ in certain areas and those differences can be challenging to maneuver. This exercise will help you, with support of your team, to identify where and in what ways you and your party are similar and where you differ. This then sets the path to engage in these conversations and develop a collaborative strategy. If you recall from the chapter, elected leaders suggest that giving party leaders the heads up will be essential in your ability to diverge when needed.

Directions:

- Identify the top areas where you differ from your party leadership;
- Explore the impact of your position with various stakeholders;
- Begin educating party leadership about your positions and your reasoning behind it;
- Collaborate with party leadership about how to message your differences;
- Explore ways to influence party leadership toward your position, if appropriate.

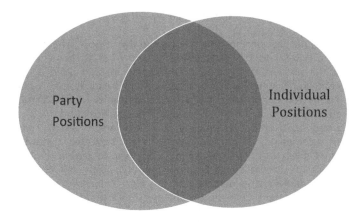

© 2021 Six Paths to Leadership

4.4 Managing the Family of the Elected Leader

Purpose: Work-Life balance is one of the most overwhelming challenges for elected leaders as they not only lose control of their schedule, but they are constantly under public scrutiny. These challenges move beyond the leader to the entire family. Staff members who support elected leaders can support the leaders and their families by engaging with the leader's partner or other family members around the following questions to develop a relationship that benefits the leader's office and also supports the family.

Directions: Either the Chief of Staff or Executive Assistant/Scheduler should engage in conversation with the elected leader on the following four questions early into the elected leader's term. Aligning these expectations early will prevent many misunderstandings and tensions in the future. After these conversations, the Chief of Staff can put together a set of norms agreed to and share them with the parties affected.

Four Critical Questions for Elected Leader/Family Relationship

1. How should the Member balance time between personal and professional demands? After they reach an agreement, it is essential that the elected leader, and not the partner, communicates and reinforces the understanding to the staff. Elected leaders with small children at home are especially torn between their official and family duties. When the official duties interfere with family responsibilities, the chief of staff should step in and ask the boss to re-negotiate this balance with the partner (rather than putting the onus on the staff).

2. What role should the partner/family play in the office? Many partners want to be helpful to the elected leader and to staff. Immediately discover what the partner is good at, or interested in, and build a role for them in that arena: whether it's making visits to senior homes, being a sounding board for Congressional scheduling decisions in the district, managing campaign details in the off-season, or participating in local community groups to be the eyes and ears for the elected leader. If you are coming off a campaign, ask the campaign workers how they benefited from the partner. Even those partners who only want to play a minimal role in the public life of the elected leader will most likely still want to have significant involvement in determining the elected leader's schedule. Early in the term, explore their expectations and those of the family and take advantage of the wealth of knowledge they have about their partner so they can benefit from it before conflicts arise.

3. What is a legitimate request for partners to make of staff? Because there is no broad consensus on this question, it is again essential that the elected leader and his/her partner reach an understanding among themselves before the staff becomes resentful or even feels they must refuse a request from the partner. Hold a meeting with the partner, elected leader, scheduler, chief of staff, and district or state director where the agreement is presented, staff can ask clarifying questions, and everyone can make mutual commitments.

4. What information should partners receive and what is the staff's responsibility to provide? A regular communication system should be worked out between partners and staff. Key staff members who regularly interact with partners should meet with them and determine what information a partner would like to receive. Usually the scheduler is the main point of contact.

Source Adapted from Meredith Persily Lamel's column in *Roll Call*, March 25, 2009

© **2021 Six Paths to Leadership**

Chapter 5: The Proxy Leader

For the appointed leaders who likely bring essential trust and enforcement from the principal, they will strongly benefit from reflecting not only on what they bring to their role but also where and how they must learn what they lack. Appointed leaders ought to develop a learning plan from day one to set their learning objectives and methods to address them as well as to assess the talent they will need to draw upon to supplement their skills. Additionally, in order to not get stuck in the reactive nature of most of these roles, they will benefit from setting their priorities early on that both support the principal's agenda and are achievable in the likely timeframe of the position.

5.1 Learning Plan

Purpose: The appointed leaders must overcome the perception of often being less qualified that the career professionals serving under them. At the same time, they are not expected to (nor should they) become subject matter experts. In fact, the more successful appointed leaders will likely know when to defer to the experts. That said, as part of appointed leaders' onboarding, they would benefit from identifying a few core learning goals that can enhance their leadership and hold themselves accountable through a learning plan

Directions: Appointed leaders are likely to need to expedite their learning curves. At the time of taking a position, identify top learning goals and how to meet them. Solicit input from the team about what they think would be most useful to learn about their area and organizations.

What are my learning goals?	How will I learn? (people, resources, experiences)	Metrics for Success

5.2 Project Prioritization

Purpose: As appointed leaders are leveraging a clear agenda from the principal, they are also managing the challenge of their short timeframe to have an impact. Given the many priorities, especially in a new administration or leadership, this tool serves to help appointed leaders to prioritize the list of possible projects.

Directions: As you determine which projects to prioritize, consider the timeframe for necessary completion by mapping against this 2x2 of impact on principal's agenda and time to implement. While each administration may take on some long-term projects, your ability to focus on those high impact/low time to implement will likely bring you greater job satisfaction and sense of accomplishment. After completing the exercise, the low-time, high-impact projects are the clear ones to pursue. Then, it's about picking a couple of the high-impact, longer-time projects and determine what is feasible.

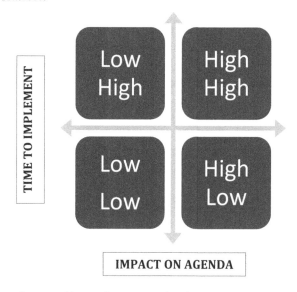

©2021 Six Paths to Leadership

Chapter 6: The Creator

To capture the full benefit of leading the organization that they initiate, founder leaders can create the culture that best reflects what they care about by intentionally identifying their core values and the behaviors they will both role model and reinforce in their organization. Additionally, like other paths, founders must fully reflect on their own strengths and shortcomings to build the team that will take the organization forward. More than other paths, founders are often considered the leaders who have the most difficult time "letting go" or delegating power to others. To shift that feeling from a loss to an opportunity, they can methodically assess their own value to build a more complete team.

6.1 Establishing a Value-Based Culture

Purpose: As the founder, you have the opportunity to intentionally create a culture that reflects your personal values. This tool will help founders get clarity about how they want their values to show up in their organization through policies and norms that reinforce the values.

Directions: Early in your tenure, identify your core values and document how you want to reinforce those values through your corporate policies and behaviors. Communicate these connections with your employees. Then develop an accountability structure to reinforce these values.

Personal Value	Policies/Norms that Reflect the Value

© **2021 Six Paths to Leadership**

6.2 Founder Self-Assessment and Action Plan

Purpose: Rarely do founders begin with all the necessary skills and knowledge to lead their organization from day one. As the organization grows, additional requirements for the job emerge. This tool forces founders to reflect on where they are strongest and weakest. Once identified, they are then able to determine the best way to supplement their leadership. While leaders on all paths benefit from this exercise, in the case of founder-leaders, they are likely to build their core team as the organization grows and need to more intentionally break the mental habit of trying to do it all.

Directions: Use this table to identify your strengths and deficiencies as you and your organization grow. Ensure you place yourself in roles where you can best leverage your assets. Develop a strategy for addressing what you lack. Determine which resources you will build (develop), buy (hire), borrow (consultants).

	Skills	Knowledge	Experiences	Relationships
What do I offer?				
How will I best leverage my strengths?				
What am I missing?				
How will I build, buy, borrow?				

© **2021 Six Paths to Leadership**

Chapter 7: Family Legacy

While a strong family business and history likely include constant story-telling and family references, these tools support the formalization of this process to ensure that the story is told in a way that supports legacy leaders into the future. Additionally, while we suggest that family leaders access the many resources prescribed for family businesses, ensuring that the governance is clear and supported by the family will help not only set up the leader for greater success, but more importantly, will help to lessen some of the potential threats to the family relationships.

7.1 Family Narrative

Purpose: The family narrative can serve as a top advantage for family leaders to lead culture and engagement in their organization.

Directions: Document the family stories that all family members as well as all employees should hear in order to appreciate the family brand, values, triumphs, and challenges. They can be documented over video, voice, or written. Below are some key insights to capture from each story.

What was the challenge or opportunity?
Which family members were involved?
How did they overcome or address the challenge?
What family values were reflected in the approach?
What should future generations take away from this story?

© **2021 Six Paths to Leadership**

7.2 Family Business Governance

Purpose: Each family business should have governance documents that clearly outline the rules of the road for the family business to support family-legacy leaders. The process of building these documents objectively helps to manage the challenge of navigating family relationships and the desire to maintain family harmony.

Directions: Most family businesses will work with a consultant to build out a governance document. That said, below are the key topics that family business leaders ought to clarify before taking the reins. The documents should serve as the guiding principles and processes for the family.

    I. Family Mission Statement;
   II. Family Values;
  III. Family Business Governance Practices;
  IV. Family Employment Policies;
   V. Succession Planning;
  VI. Company Ownership and Financial Planning;
VII. Board of Directors and Family Representation.

© **2021 Six Paths to Leadership**

Chapter 8: Managing Your Path

After reviewing the many paths available to leaders, the final step is assessing one's own position relative to the different paths. This final tool will help bring new perspective for leaders and emerging leaders as they consider how best to manage their own leadership journey.

SWOC Analysis

Purpose: Similar to SWOT analysis for an organization, your SWOC analysis can help you to reflect on which path(s) best align your strengths with the path advantages and how to avoid paths that might reinforce your weaknesses.

Directions: Start your SWOC analysis by identifying your core strengths and weaknesses. If these are unclear to you, consider reflecting on past performance reviews, talk with former colleagues, or administer a skills assessment. Then list out the key advantages and challenges of the path(s) you are considering. Refer to the respective chapter for the path to identify them. What insights have you gained? What path might set you up for success and where might you be unnecessarily challenged? Consider these insights and challenges as you pursue your leadership journey.

	Individual Traits		
	Strengths	**Weaknesses**	
Positive			**Negative**
	Opportunities	**Challenges**	
	Path Traits		

© **2021 Six Paths to Leadership**

Bibliography

Banister, B. (n.d.). *How Black Lives Matter In Corporations—This Time Can Be Different*. Corporate Board Member. Retrieved from https://boardmember.com/how-black-lives-matter-in-corporations-this-time-can-be-different/.

Bridges, W. (2009). *Managing Transitions: Making the Most of Change*. Da Capo Press.

Cappelli, P. (2019, May–June). Your Approach to Hiring Is All Wrong. *Harvard Business Review*.

Corkindale, G. (2008). Overcoming Imposter Syndrome. *Harvard Business Review*.

Lewis, M. (2019). *The Fifth Risk*. Norton & Company.

Peter, L. J., & Hull, R. (1969). *The Peter Principle: Why Things Always Go Wrong*. William Morrow & Co., Inc.

Raz, G. (2017, January 23). *How I Built This* [Audio podcast]. Zappos: Tony Hsieh. https://radiopublic.com/HowIBuiltThis/s1!574ab.

Raz, G. (2019, May 6). *How I Built This* [Audio podcast]. Framebridge: Susan Tynan. www.npr.org/2019/04/26/717496919/framebridge-susan-tynan.

© The Editor(s) (if applicable) and The Author(s), under exclusive license to Springer Nature Switzerland AG 2021
M. A. Clark and M. Persily Lamel, *Six Paths to Leadership*,
https://doi.org/10.1007/978-3-030-69017-5